World Aircraft

ORIGINS–WORLD WAR I

World Aircraft
ORIGINS–WORLD WAR I

BY
ENZO ANGELUCCI
PAOLO MATRICARDI

FULL-COLOR ILLUSTRATIONS
Vincenzo Cosentino

BLACK-AND-WHITE ILLUSTRATIONS
Claudio Tatangelo

RAND McNALLY & COMPANY
CHICAGO
NEW YORK
SAN FRANCISCO

Printed in Italy
by Officine Grafiche di Arnoldo Mondadori Editore, Verona

Published in U.S.A., 1979
by Rand McNally & Company, Chicago, Ill.

Library of Congress Catalog Card No. 78-72304
ISBN: 0-528-88165-5

Contents

Introduction

The idea of flying has always fascinated man and continues to do so even today, when the aeroplane holds few mysteries and anyone can fly, at any moment. But our fascination with flight is almost instinctive, and one is always amazed at how an aircraft rises from the ground, takes to the air, and flies over great distances. How did man first take to flight? What dreams, what sacrifices, what failures and achievements were involved. Although the history of aviation is really fairly short, barely a century old, it may well be the most complex of all mankind's adventures. After germinating for centuries, the flying machine blossomed within the space of a few years. A look at the history of aviation gives one an indirect view of man's progress in science and technology in general. And since the history of the aeroplane is also the history of air warfare, many planes have contributed to the destiny of modern nations.

This first volume presents the history of aviation up to the end of World War 1. All the important early aeroplanes are examined in this book which contains a representative selection of civil and military aircraft. Some are present because they have become landmarks of aviation history or exhibit a particular technical development, others because of the immortal feats they performed.

Each machine is carefully described and is supported by detailed illustrations. The latter consist of a three-dimensional colour drawing to show the markings and bring out any salient design and structural features, while two or three line diagram views give an idea of the dimensions, and comparative proportions of each aeroplane. The main textual matter for an entry is composed of the history of the aircraft and its relative importance in the context of aviation development. Technical specifications are in tabular form, where such items as engines, dimensions and performances are given. Military particulars are included when appropriate. The figures quoted in the specifications have been culled from a number of authoritative works and where data has been found to vary, the authors have chosen the figures quoted in at least two different sources. Some specifications reflect the fact that modifications and changes were made to the basic models and many of these variants have also been illustrated with line drawings.

The manner in which the material is set out enables the reader to trace aviation progress country by country. The aeroplanes are displayed by nationality, and chronologically arranged within each group. As the result of every one being presented in a similar way, one machine can readily be compared with another.

The first two chapters of this volume cover the experimental years of aviation. The historic attempts at flight of the nineteenth and early twentieth centuries are described, including those of 1903 when it is generally agreed that real flight was first achieved with the initial efforts of the Wright Flyer. It is logical, however, that the opening discussions deal with the earliest pioneers in the theory of flight. The first of these was Leonardo da Vinci who approached the problem of flight scientifically. It was at the time of the Italian Renaissance, therefore, that the concept of modern aviation was really first conceived.

A firm foundation is thus laid for the ensuing chapters which examine the years when the development of the aeroplane advanced at a considerable pace, due to the advent of a world war. As in so many other industries, the war greatly increased the speed of technological development. The research carried out benefited other fields and the true value of the aeroplane was at last realized. It is ironic that confidence in the aeroplane was so slow to establish itself when today, not only is the aircraft industry of world wide importance, but the whole concept of man and flight has surpassed the confines of our planet.

It is probably the speed with which aviation expands and extends that makes its history so fascinating. Few other industries have made such an immediate and substantial contribution to the wealth of nations. Untouched areas of the earth could be reached and now there is virtually no corner unexplored. This book presents all the relevant facts and gives a full account of the tremendous and uncertain first steps, to the days when the aeroplane came to play a vital role in the destiny of nations. The wealth of information provided in this book will prove invaluable to both enthusiast and student of the subject and, together with the second volume, forms an important reference work.

Leonardo da Vinci (1496)

From da Vinci to the Wright Brothers

In 5,000 manuscript pages, 35,000 words, and 150 plans, Leonardo da Vinci anticipated many of the principles, theories, and experiments that were to make one of the man's oldest dreams a reality. He studied the flight of birds and speculated on mechanisms that could help man imitate them. He analyzed the basic principles of aerodynamics and physics, and designed machines to apply them. And he anticipated the parachute, the helicopter, and the propeller. Paradoxically enough, however, Leonardo da Vinci's major contribution to the birth of aviation was lost for almost three centuries. Leonardo's codices did not come to light until 1797, 278 years after he died.

Leonardo's was the first scientific approach to the problem of flight. He began his bird studies in 1486, while he was in Milan in the service of the Sforzas. His first plans for a flying machine appeared ten years later. The ideas Leonardo developed were the result of direct observations, and the mechanisms illustrated in hundreds of sketches and drawings (for ornithopters) were designed to operate movable wing structures similar to the wings of birds.

Leonardo's investigations remained theoretical because of two mistaken premises: that the wings of birds beat back and forth, rather than up and down, and that human musculature can generate sufficient power to lift a man's body and a machine as well. Leonardo eventually realized that this line of research was impractical, and he turned his thoughts to the fixed

Miscellaneous Ideas (1670-1808)

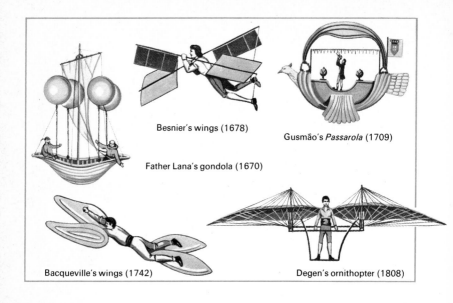

Besnier's wings (1678)

Gusmão's *Passarola* (1709)

Father Lana's gondola (1670)

Bacqueville's wings (1742)

Degen's ornithopter (1808)

wing and then to gliding flight. But the first gliders were built three centuries later.

Leonardo may have realized that muscular energy was an inadequate means of propulsion. This is suggested by some drawings in which an ornithopter and a helicopter are propelled by a spring.

The next centuries were marked by timid, imaginative, and empirical experiments in flight. Francesco de Lana (1631–87), a Jesuit from Brescia who taught literature and science in a Roman monastery, fairly accurately determined the pressure of the atmosphere at sea level. He showed that the air is 'lighter' at higher altitudes and tried to apply his theories to the creation of a flying machine. He described this airship in a book entitled

Prodomo, overo, saggio di alcune invenzioni nuove ('Prodome, or an Essay on Some New Inventions') in 1670: a gondola held aloft by four copper vacuum spheres, each about 19.5 feet (6 m) in diameter. Climbing speed could be regulated by small sacks of sand for ballast. The aircraft could be lowered by letting air into the spheres.

In 1678, at Sablé in France, a locksmith named Besnier tried to fly with two pairs of wings driven by his arms and legs. In 1709, in Lisbon, the Brazilian Jesuit Laurenço de Gusmão (1686–1724) tried to launch his 'Passarola', a kind of bird-shaped glider. In Paris, Jean-François Boyvin de Bonnetot, Marquis de Bacqueville, fastened four wings to his arms and legs and jumped off the roof of an

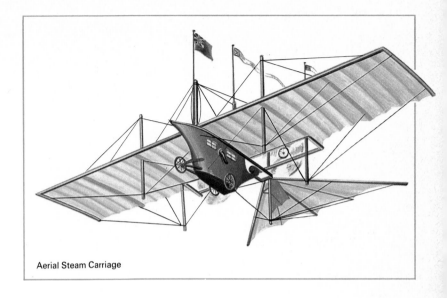

Aerial Steam Carriage

hotel on the Seine. That was in 1742, and such attempts at flight continued for many decades. In 1809, the Swiss Jacob Degen tried out his ornithopter in Vienna and, unlike many others, managed not to die in the attempt.

Sir George Cayley and the Development of the True Aeroplane

The first half of the nineteenth century saw the beginning of a new phase in the history of heavier-than-air machines. A fundamental contribution, which many have compared to that of Leonardo da Vinci, was made by an Englishman, Sir George Cayley (1773–1857). He resolved most of the

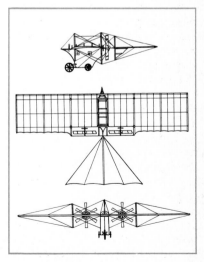

13

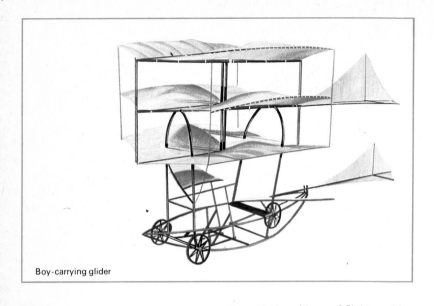

Boy-carrying glider

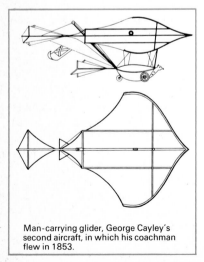

Man-carrying glider, George Cayley's second aircraft, in which his coachman flew in 1853.

theoretical problems of flight, and he is considered 'the true inventor of the aeroplane and one of the most powerful geniuses in the history of aviation'. After defining the principles of mechanical flight ('to make a surface support a given weight by the application of power to the resistance of air'), he indicated ways of maintaining the stability and control of an aircraft. He studied aerodynamics and was the first man to make widespread use of models in his flight studies. And most important, he indicated the basic importance of a propulsion system for aeroplanes. Sir George Cayley applied his theories to what can be considered the first 'real' plane in history: a glider model about five feet (1.524 m) long, built in 1804. This model anticipated Cayley's own first full-size manned triplane gliders, which ap-

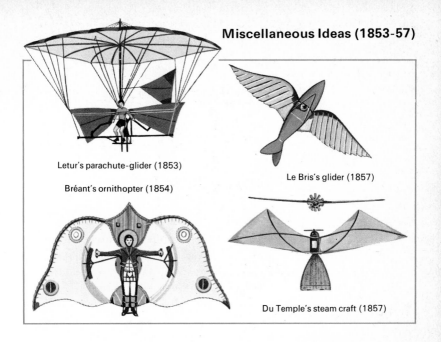

Letur's parachute-glider (1853)

Bréant's ornithopter (1854)

Le Bris's glider (1857)

Du Temple's steam craft (1857)

peared about the middle of the nineteenth century. The first full-size model, built in 1849, just bore the weight of a boy. The second, built in 1853, was successfully launched in a valley with Sir George's terrified coachman aboard as 'human ballast'.

Cayley's work was immediately influential. In 1842, the Englishman William Samuel Henson (1805–68) designed and patented an impressive flying machine that was never built: the Aerial Steam Carriage. This aircraft, based on Cayley's doctrines, was to have a wingspan of 150 feet (45.72m), a wing area of 4,500 square feet (418 sq m), and a 25 to 30-hp steam engine installed in the fuselage to drive two pusher propellers. This was the first design in history for a propeller-driven plane with fixed

wings. Henson, who had gone into partnership with his friend John Stringfellow, had ambitious plans for developing his flying machine, and hoped to set up an air transport company, the Aerial Transit Company. A twenty-foot (6.1-m) wingspan model was built. It was tested from 1845 to 1847 but never managed to get off the ground.

The great publicity given to the Henson Aerial Steam Carriage, and the spread of Cayley's theories of flight, had repercussions in France. In the years 1853–54, Louis Charles Letur built and tested a parachute-glider, the first pilot-controlled, heavier-than-air machine to be tested in flight. Tests were carried out in France and Great Britain. After several successful descents, Letur had a serious accident near London on June

Michel Loup (1853)

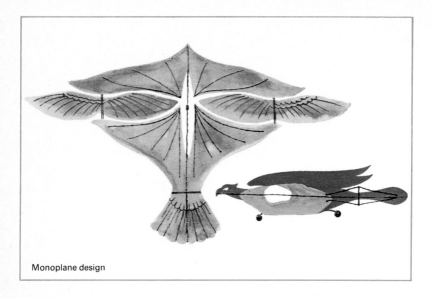

Monoplane design

27, 1854, and died of his injuries.

In 1853, a mechanic named Michel Loup designed a large winged 'bird' with a three-wheeled undercarriage and two enormous propellers. A year later, Bréant designed an ornithopter in which the pilot pulled the wings down with his arms, the wings then being raised by elastic. A sea captain, Jean-Marie Le Bris, revived the glider. Between 1856 and 1868 he tested an aircraft based on the lines of the albatross, a bird he had studied on his sea voyages. His attempts at flight were fairly successful, but the glider finally crashed.

Another naval officer, Félix Du Temple (1823–90) displayed his talent and considerable understanding of aerodynamics in his 1857 design for a tractor monoplane with swept-forward wings set at a slight dihedral angle and a retractable three-wheeled undercarriage. Du Temple built an ingenious model that was first propelled by clockwork and then by a steam engine. The model managed to fly and to land. For some years attempts to achieve the same results with a full-scale plane had no success, because of the lack of an adequate propulsion system. In 1874, the plane was tested with a steam engine and managed to rise a few feet from the ground with a sailor on board.

The 1860s saw the return of the ornithopter and a wave of enthusiasm for another type of flying machine, the helicopter. In 1860 Smythies introduced a complex mechanism with wings that were partly fixed and partly beating. Propulsion was provided by a steam engine, and the pilot sat on a movable seat so that he could shift the

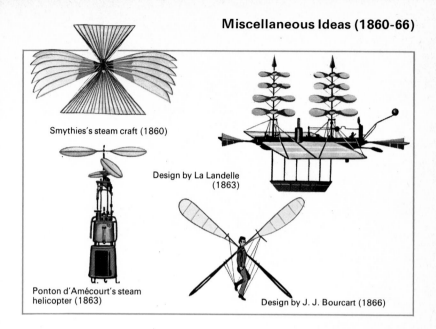

Smythies's steam craft (1860)

Design by La Landelle (1863)

Ponton d'Amécourt's steam helicopter (1863)

Design by J. J. Bourcart (1866)

centre of gravity. In 1864 Struvé and Telescheff planned an even more fantastic ornithopter: it was equipped with five pairs of wings for greater stability. This machine was to be powered by the pilot's muscles. In 1866 J. J. Bourcart built an ornithopter with two pairs of beating wings worked by an ingenious system of wires connected to the pilot's legs. Eight years later, in 1874, another ornithopter caused the death of a Belgian shoemaker, Vincent de Groof, who launched his aircraft from a balloon and plunged to his death in a London park.

The helicopter aroused great excitement in France. An association was even set up to assemble the many models and designs that had proliferated during the previous decade. One of the most imaginative was de-signed by the Vicomte Ponton d'Amécourt. In 1863 he built a model helicopter with counter-rotating propellers and steam engine propulsion. This machine was a failure, but a second model using spring propulsion had more luck. The project developed by Gabriel de La Landelle the same year was wholly impractical.

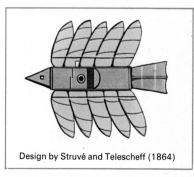

Design by Struvé and Telescheff (1864)

Miscellaneous Ideas (1871-75)

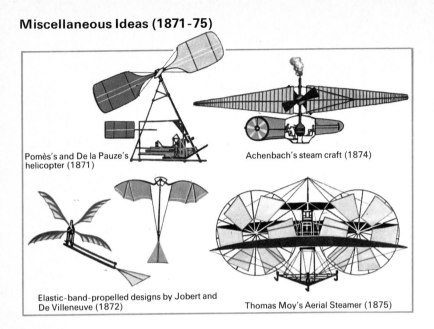

Pomès's and De la Pauze's helicopter (1871)

Achenbach's steam craft (1874)

Elastic-band-propelled designs by Jobert and De Villeneuve (1872)

Thomas Moy's Aerial Steamer (1875)

The year 1866 was one of the most important in the history of aviation. The Aeronautical Society of Great Britain was founded to bring together students of mechanical flight. The publication of technical journals began, and new theories and experiments were widely discussed. An aero-

De Groof's ornithopter (1864)

nautical exhibition, the first in history, was held in 1868 at the Crystal Palace in London. It was a strange collection of the products of ingenuity and naïveté. John Stringfellow's triplane model was one of the most interesting designs in this show. The British engineer had developed a plan for a highly original aircraft, which, though it failed to rise from the ground, had a great influence on later work. What was most interesting was the superimposed form of the wing surfaces. Stringfellow, incidentally, won a prize of £100 for his steam engine, which was found to have the best power-to-weight ratio of those tested.

The 1870s and 1880s saw many new designs and many new theories. In June 1875 a steam-engined model made its first take-off. It was designed and built by the Englishman Thomas

Triplane design

Moy, who called it the Aerial Steamer. This aircraft was a tandem-wing monoplane (with two wings on the same longitudinal level). The front wing had an area of 50 square feet (4.6 sq m), the rear one 64 square feet (5.9 sq m). There were two large fan-shaped propellers powered by a 3-hp steam engine. These propellers were six feet (1.83 m) in diameter and were installed between the two wing surfaces. They provided sufficient thrust to lift the 120-pound (54.4-kg) aeroplane six inches (2.4 cm) off the ground.

One of the most important figures of the period was the Frenchman Alphonse Pénaud (1850–80), who made a fundamental contribution to the world of aviation. He developed theories about wing contours and aerodynamic principles and applied them successfully to model aero-

planes, helicopters, and ornithopters. Pénaud brilliantly promoted an already existing propulsion system, by using twisted rubber strips. Perhaps the Frenchman's best-known model was his 1871 'planophore', one of the forerunners of the modern aeroplane. It was a monoplane with an 18-in (45-cm) wingspan, and the wingtips were bent up to provide lateral stability. This machine had a two-blade pusher propeller, eight inches (20 cm) in diameter, which was powered by a twisted elastic band. This model was the first really stable aeroplane in history. It was tested in the Tuileries Gardens in Paris on August 18, 1871, and flew 131 feet (40 m) in 11 seconds. But Alphonse Pénaud's finest design was a two-passenger amphibian monoplane, which he projected before committing suicide at the age of 30.

Miscellaneous Ideas (1876-77)

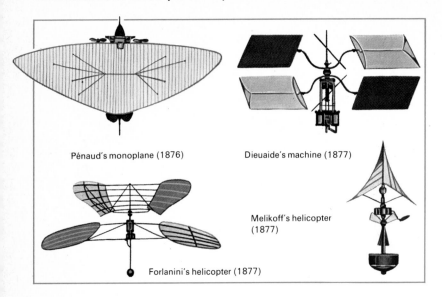

Pénaud's monoplane (1876)

Dieuaide's machine (1877)

Melikoff's helicopter (1877)

Forlanini's helicopter (1877)

The patent was applied for in 1876, even though the model was never built. This machine anticipated many ideas of the aeroplane of the future: two counter-rotating propellers, double elevators, a rudder connected to a fixed vertical fin, a glassed-in cockpit, retractable landing gear, and piloting instruments. The estimated weight was to have been 2,635 pounds

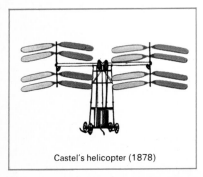

Castel's helicopter (1878)

(1,195 kg), the speed 60 mph (96.5 kph).

Another Frenchman, Victor Tatin (1843–1913), became one of early aviation's most authoritative theorists. He built a remarkable model in 1879. The fuselage acted as a tank for the compressed air that drove a small engine linked to two tractor propellers. The model had a 75-inch (1.9-m) wingspan. It was attached to a pole, and flew circles for about 49 feet (15 m).

Vertical take-off still intrigued aviation enthusiasts and helicopter models continued to be built. In 1871, Pomés and De la Pauze designed one that had a rotor powered by gunpowder. In 1874 Achenbach designed a gigantic helicopter with a steam engine. Three years later, in 1877, Emmanuel Dieuaide designed one with contra-

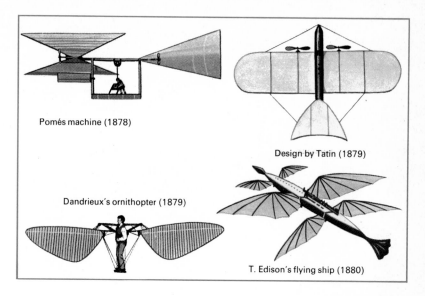

Pomés machine (1878)

Design by Tatin (1879)

Dandrieux's ornithopter (1879)

T. Edison's flying ship (1880)

rotating rotors. The engine boiler was on the ground and connected to the machine by a flexible tube. Melikoff designed a helicopter with a conical-shaped rotor that doubled as a parachute for descent. That same year, an Italian engineer named Enrico Forlanini produced a team model that managed to climb to a height of 39 feet (12 m) and remain in the air for 20 seconds. In 1878 Castel, a Frenchman, brought the formula to its highest peak. He designed and built a helicopter with eight rotors on two counter-rotating shafts, driven by compressed air. This model did not work, but a smaller one built by Dandrieux between 1878 and 1879 and driven by elastic bands did.

An interesting experiment was made in Russia by Alexander F. Mozhaiski, a captain in the Imperial Navy. He designed an aeroplane in 1881 and finished building it in 1883. It was a monoplane with a large tractor propeller, and two small pusher propellers, driven by a steam engine. It was successfully tried out at Krasnoye Selo, near St Petersburg, in 1884. The model was launched from a ramp and shakily 'flew' about 98 feet (30 m). After Du Temple's achievement in 1874, it was the second powered take-off in history.

Lighter Than Air

Heavier than air, lighter than air: these were the two poles of early aviation experiments. Attempts to

Alexander F. Mozhaiski (1884)

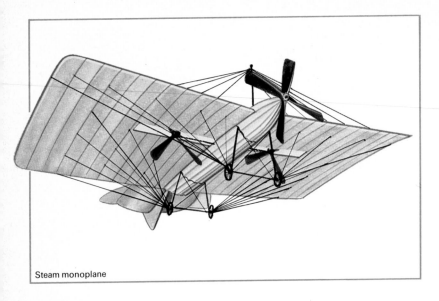

Steam monoplane

harness dynamic action to the wings of heavier-than-air machines were crowned with success only after the turn of the century. But the first man to fly a lighter-than-air machine got off the ground 120 years before the Wright brothers.

The date was November 21, 1783, and the place was Paris. The men were chemistry professor Jean François Pilâtre de Rozier (1756–85) and an army major, the Marquis François d'Arlandes. Pilâtre de Rozier designed and built a two-man gondola attached to a hot-air balloon. The flight lasted for 25 minutes and covered a distance of about 1.86 miles (3 km).

This achievement had been made possible by the brilliant work of two Frenchmen, Joseph Michael (1740–1810) and Jacques Etienne Montgolfier (1745–99), two brothers who owned a paper-mill in Annonay, near Lyons. They observed the ascending force of smoke and saw that paper bags placed over a fire also tended to rise. They concluded that if they managed to enclose what they thought was gas inside a fairly large and very light envelope, the envelope would rise from the ground. After experiments with larger and larger models, they finally built a large cloth-and-paper balloon (32.8 feet, 10 m, in diameter) and tested it on June 4, 1783, in the market-place of Annonay, where a wool and straw fire had been prepared to fill the balloon with hot air. The balloon – called a *Montgolfière* from that day on – left the ground and rose to a height of about 6,560 feet (2,000 m).

The Montgolfier brothers went to Paris and built a second balloon. On

Pilâtre de Rozier (1783)

Charles (1783)

The first Montgolfier to leave the ground

Jacques Charles's hydrogen balloon

Montgolfier (1783)

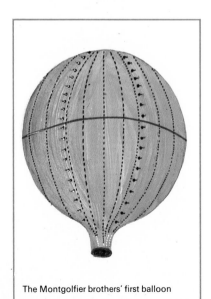

The Montgolfier brothers' first balloon

September 19, this balloon lifted a sheep, a goose, and a rooster. The third balloon was manned by Pilâtre de Rozier and Major d'Arlandes. With Louis XVI and Marie Antoinette as spectators, they became the first men in history to fly.

Another advance was made just nine days later. Jacques Alexandre César Charles (1746–1823), a member of the French Academy of Science, successfully tested a new type of balloon, in which hot air was replaced by hydrogen, the 'inflammable air' that English scientist Henry Cavendish had discovered 17 years before. Charles had already tested an unmanned hydrogen balloon. After a long flight it came down near Paris, where it was destroyed by some frightened farmers. On December 1, 1783, the new balloon, called *Charlière*,

23

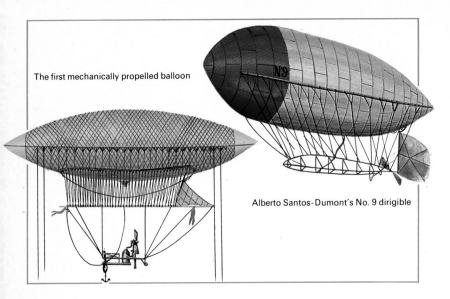

The first mechanically propelled balloon

Alberto Santos-Dumont's No. 9 dirigible

after its inventor's name – successfully rose into the air, carrying Charles
and a passenger, M. N. Robert. The
Charlière flew 27 miles (43 km) before
touching down safely.

Jacques Charles's discovery cost Pilâtre de Rozier his life. On June 15,
1785, the French chemist and a friend,
Pierre Romain, left Boulogne for
Great Britain, on board a balloon
Rozier had built. The balloon con-
tained both hot air and hydrogen. At
an altitude of about 2,950 feet (900 m)
the hydrogen, expanded by the hot air,
suddenly exploded and the two men
fell to earth. They were the first fat-
alities of real manned flight.

The new flight fever spread like an
epidemic. *Montgolfières, Charlières,*
and many other kinds of balloons
filled the skies. On January 7, 1785, the
Frenchman Jean-Pierre Blanchard

and the American John Jeffries carried
out the flight that had proved fatal to
Pilâtre de Rozier, the first English
Channel balloon crossing. Blanchard
again, on January 9, delivered a letter
from President George Washington in
Philadelphia, and air mail was born.
On November 7–8, 1836, the huge
'Vauxhall' balloon flew from London
to Weilburg, Germany, covering a
distance of 480 miles (772 km) in 18
hours. On board were Charles Green,
Robert Hollond, and Monck Mason.
Frenchman François Arban was the
first man to fly over the Alps – from
Marseilles to Turin on September 2–3,
1849. On July 2, 1859, American John
Wise flew from St Louis to New York,
covering 812 miles (1,305 km) in 19
hours 50 minutes.

Seven years earlier a new phase in
the evolution of lighter-than-air

Zeppelin LZ-1 (1900)

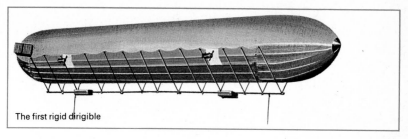

The first rigid dirigible

Zeppelin 1 (1909)

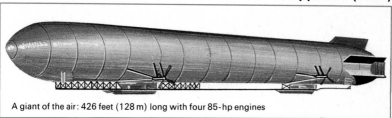

A giant of the air: 426 feet (128 m) long with four 85-hp engines

machines had begun. Thanks to the studies of a French engineer, Henri Giffard (1825–82), the balloon had ceased to be a uncontrollable machine, and subject to the caprices of winds and air currents. Horizontal balloon flight could be controlled: the dirigible was born. Giffard equipped a balloon with a 3-hp steam engine driving a propeller, and installed a rudimentary vertical rudder. The first flight took place on September 24, 1852, and covered 16.78 miles (27 km) from the Paris race-course to Trappes at a speed of 5.6 mph (9 kph).

This new type of machine evolved quite quickly and continued its development even after the birth of the aeroplane. Dirigibles were built until 1936, and construction techniques became more and more refined and complex. The first machines, such as

those built in Paris between 1898 and 1905 by the Brazilian Alberto Santos-Dumont, a future pioneer of the aeroplane in Europe, were crude. The last dirigibles were veritable giants of the air, with rigid or semi-rigid structure, streamlined in shape, powerful engines, and large cargo and passenger capacity.

One of the major figures in the development and testing of these new techniques was a German, Count Ferdinand von Zeppelin (1838–1917), who literally revolutionized the world of lighter-than-air craft. His interest in flying machines began in 1874, and his first designs appeared about 20 years later. Only in 1898 and 1899, though, did von Zeppelin design and build what was to be considered the prototype of all future rigid dirigibles, the LZ. This machine was built in a float-

Otto Lilienthal (1896)

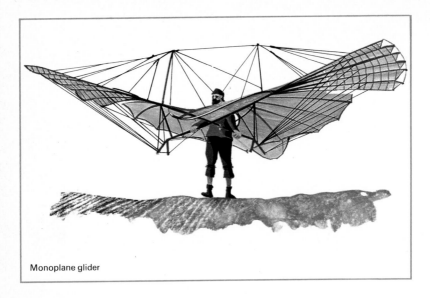

Monoplane glider

ing hangar at Manzell on Lake Constance. It took 30 workmen one year to assemble the cylindrical aluminium structure, which was subsequently covered with cloth. The dirigible had 17 hydrogen cells, and it was driven by propellers connected to two 15-hp Daimler engines. The LZ made its first flight on July 2, 1900, with the inventor at the controls and a crew of five. This dirigible was not particularly successful. It was slow, hard to control, and structurally weak. After further tests carried out three months later, it was finally scrapped.

But Ferdinand von Zeppelin did not give up. Over the next 14 years, he built many other airships, forerunners of the giants of the First World War and the 1920s and 1930s. His greatest success was the L.56, which flew 4,180 miles (6,725 km) in 98 hours.

The 10 Years Before the Wright Brothers: The Prelude to Mechanical Flight

The final advance before the conquest of flight was made in the last decade of the nineteenth century. Theories and

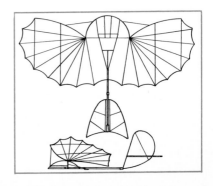

Ader's first design

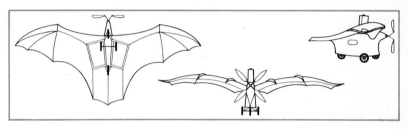

experiments culminated in a host of efforts that were the direct prelude to the achievements of Orville and Wilbur Wright. The most important contribution to the success of the two American pioneers was undoubtedly the solution of the problems of glider flight. These problems were solved once and for all by a German engineer, Otto Lilienthal, and an American named Octave Chanute. Chanute, too, was an engineer. He was the first historian of aviation and a great friend and backer of the Wright brothers, who followed Chanute's lead and made sure they had mastered gliding flight before attempting powered flight.

Otto Lilienthal (1848–96) is considered to be one of the giants in the history of aviation. He was the first man to launch himself into the air and

fly. If he had not been killed during one of his experiments (on August 9, 1896, near Stölln), he might have won the laurels that went to the Wright brothers. Lilienthal entered the world of aviation as a young man. In 1889 he published a book on the flight of birds, which outlined his theories. Between 1891 and 1896, he built several monoplane, biplane, and triplane gliders and applied and tested the results of his studies. Success was almost immediate. After the first hesitant launchings, Lilienthal began covering quite long distances. He made almost 2,500 glider flights and applied his unique experience to designing and building motor-powered gliders. He never managed to test these machines, but they might possibly have been as successful as the glider on which he lost his life.

27

Among the last attempts at engine-powered flight of this period, mention should be made of an engineer from Toulouse, Clément Ader (1841–1925). He built two planes, the *Eole* (1890) and the *Avion* III (1897). After research on bird and bat flight and experiments with small models, Ader began building a monoplane powered by a steam engine of his own design. This aircraft was extraordinary in appearance. It was bat-shaped and had heavily cambered wings of 45.9-feet (14-m) span. The *Eole* was tested by Ader himself near Gretz on October 9, 1890. Apparently it rose a few inches off the ground and made an uncontrolled 'hop' of about 165 feet (50 m). The French War Ministry heard about the experiment and commissioned Ader to build a new plane. That was in 1892, and the designer took five years to build the *Avion* III. The aircraft had the same general design as its predecessor: bat-shaped wings 52.5 feet (16 m) in span, two steam engines, instead of one, driving two tractor propellers. This machine weighed about 882 pounds (400 kg). But Clément Ader ignored the lessons of his contemporaries. The *Avion* III was tested on October 12 and 14 at the Sartory military base near Versailles. On the first day, the machine simply rolled along the circular track laid out for it. Two days later it rolled for a short way, shot off the track, and ended up in a field. The experiments were abandoned, and the *Avion* III never got its wheels off the ground.

Nevertheless there were people who maintained that he was the first European to fly. In 1906, Ader himself, irritated by all the talk about Santos-Dumont's flights, declared that on October 14, 1897 (the day of the *Avion* III's final test), he had flown about 1,000 feet (300 m). This was untrue, but his claim was credited until 1910, when the French War Ministry published the official report of the unsuccessful *Avion* III tests, a report that had been drawn up on October 14, 1897, by General Mensier.

The last unsuccessful attempt at powered flight was made six years later in the United States, just nine days before the successful effort of Orville and Wilbur Wright. The aircraft – a tandem wing monoplane powered by a 55-hp petrol engine – was built by Samuel Pierpont Langley

Clément Ader's *Avion* III (1897)

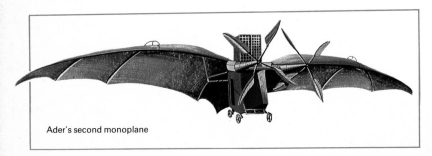

Ader's second monoplane

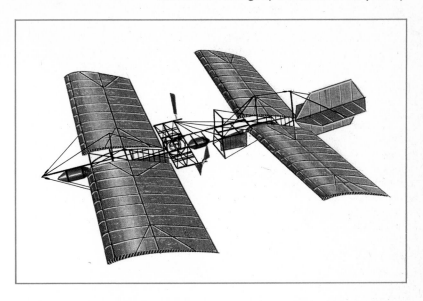

(1834–1906), mathematician, astronomer and secretary of the Smithsonian Institution in Washington, United States. After studies begun in 1890 and completed in 1896 with the successful testing of various small models, Langley tried out a new model in 1901, the first in history to be powered by a gasoline engine. Encouraged by the results, he then built a full-size plane, which he called the Aerodrome. He installed a new gasoline engine developed by his assistant, Charles Manly. The Aerodrome had a 48-foot (14.63-m) wingspan and a wing area of 1,040 square feet (96.62 sq m). It weighed 730 pounds (331 kg). The designer intended to take off from a houseboat with a catapult complementing the engine's take-off thrust. Tests took place on October 7 and December 8, 1903, on the Potomac River. Both tests ended in failure. The Aerodrome fell into the water both times. Samuel Pierpont Langley was embittered by the violent attacks of the press and Congress (which had financed his project) and abandoned his work.

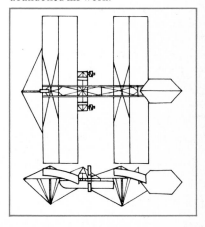

From the Wright Brothers to World War 1

The realization of man's most ambitious dream met with total indifference. Because of American press attacks on Samuel Pierpont Langley and his Aerodrome, the historic Wright event of December 17, 1903, went all but unremarked. The press was shy of anything to do with flight, and the achievement of Orville and Wilbur Wright was considered another crackpot claim. The Wright brothers fared no better four months later, when they invited reporters and photographers to be present at the first take-off of their improved Flyer II. On that occasion (at the Huffman Prairie in May 1904) engine trouble prevented the aircraft from leaving the launching track, the same thing happening on another occasion.

Although Europe was not to see manned and powered flight for three more years, it took America several years to realize the immense importance of the conquest of flight. Even in October 1905, after the Flyer III had flown 24.2 miles (38.95 km) in just

over 38 minutes, the War Department turned down the plane. This action was symptomatic of the prevailing scepticism. Orville and Wilbur stopped flying, concentrating instead on improving their machine and solving their last problems. They had to wait until 1908 before their achievement was fully appreciated.

The development of European aviation came to a halt after Lilienthal's death in 1896. Only in 1901 were the theories of the German pioneer revived by a French army captain, Ferdinand Ferber. After testing gliders very much like Lilienthal's, he turned to the gliders the Wright brothers had developed. In 1904 Ferber developed an original glider design that was to have widespread repercussions on pioneer European planes. Ferber built a biplane glider with a fixed tail, an inherently stable aircraft. Ferber's new machine was tested with some success, and most of the problems of glider flight were considered solved. That same year, the French pioneer made the first heavier-than-air flight with a passenger. He took Burdin, his mechanic, with him on a short flight at Chalais Meudon. Ferber himself was the first to acknowledge his great debt to the work of the Wright brothers. 'I'd never have got anywhere without that man,' he said in 1908, in reference to Wilbur Wright. 'My experiments would never have taken place without him.'

New enthusiasm was kindled. The work of people like Louis Blériot, Gabriel Voisin, Robert Esnault-Pelterie, and Ernest Archdeacon – who were to become world-famous in the next few years – became almost frenzied as a result. To stimulate the growth of aviation in Europe, the *Aéro Club de France* offered many prizes, including the Ernest Archdeacon Cup for the first plane to fly more than 25 metres; a prize of 1,500 francs for the first man to fly more than 100 metres; and the Deutsch-Archdeacon Grand Prix of 50,000 francs to the first pilot who managed to fly a one-kilometre circle.

Two years went by before the first two prizes were awarded. They were won by Alberto Santos-Dumont on October 23 and November 12, 1906. The Brazilian pioneer's short flights could not compare with those made by the Wrights with their Flyer III one year earlier, but Santos-Dumont's 'hops' did show that Europe had entered the aviation age.

The great year was 1908. And the event that thrilled the aviation world was the Wright brothers' decision to make demonstration flights. Orville stayed in the United States to carry out evaluation flights that were to

32

culminate with the sale of the Wright A to the Army, while Wilbur went to France. And here his demonstration flights at a racecourse near Le Mans thrilled European flight enthusiasts. They were most impressed by Wilbur's obvious mastery of the machine and his exceptional flying technique, qualities almost unknown to the French pioneers.

The Wrights were unquestionably the best flyers, and they were proving the fact to the world at large, but were no longer alone. Equally important landmarks were soon to be set by the record flights of Farman, Delagrange, and Blériot. And Great Britain entered the field with men like Samuel Franklin Cody and Alliott Verdon Roe. In the United States, the Aerial Experiment Association began building successful planes such as Glenn Curtiss' June Bug and J. A. D. McCurdy's Silver Dart. In Italy Léon Delagrange's demonstration flights in Rome, Turin, and Milan aroused great enthusiasm.

The year 1909 marked the beginning of aviation's early maturity. The aeroplane was no longer a curio. It was a new and practical means of travel and transportation. Two important events helped to establish this new attitude: Louis Blériot's crossing of the English Channel and the Reims Aviation Week (August 22–29). Blériot demonstrated the level of performance aviation had already reached; the Reims air show was the forerunner of the racing competitions that were to have such great effect on the later development of planes and engines. The *Grande Semaine d'Aviation de la Champagne*, organized by the Champagne Wine Growers' Association under the patronage of the President of the French Republic, offered 200,000 francs of prize money, and several records were set. Some of the records: distance, 112 miles (180 km) set by the Henri Farman III; speed, with 47.75 mph (76.95 kph) set by the Blériot XII; and altitude, with 508.5 feet (155 m) set by Hubert Latham's Antoinette VII. Furthermore, 23 of the 38 planes taking part in the meeting got into the air; and 87 flights of more than 3 miles (5 km) were registered at Reims, which also crowned the success of two new aviation products: the propellers built by Lucien Chauvière, the first rational and efficient ones made in Europe; and the revolutionary Gnome rotary engine designed by Laurent and Louis Séguin.

After the Antoinette engine of Léon Levavasseur (an 8-cylinder inline V water-cooled engine weighing 110 pounds, or 50 kg, giving 50 hp, with direct fuel injection and evaporation cooling), which had made possible the successes of the first European pioneers, the rotary engine designed by Laurent and Louis Séguin initiated a type of engine that characterized a whole era of aviation history. The principle of the rotary engine – discovered by Australian Lawrence Hargrave before the turn of the century – was developed in a most ingenious and reliable way by the two Frenchmen. They found a particularly brilliant solution to the problem of getting fuel into the rotating cylinders by eliminating mechanical inlet valves, and effecting induction direct from the crankcase. The engines in the Mono-

soupape series were landmarks in aeronautical technology. The first models had five cylinders, and later models had seven, nine and finally fourteen cylinders. The last, a double-row model, was in use until the end of the First World War.

But Reims was most important because it laid the trail for the great racing events of later years: the Circuit of Britain races, the Circuit of Europe race of 1911, the Gordon Bennett Aviation Trophy (won for the first time in Reims by the Curtiss Golden Flyer), and the Michelin Trophy for endurance. There were a great many aviation meetings, including the famous Schneider Trophy seaplane races. The French industrialist Jacques Schneider established the competition on December 5, 1912, and the first race was flown in 1913. It continued until 1931, and impressive records were set. There were individual sporting ventures as well, including the Brazilian Geo Chavez's fatal Alpine crossing. The Blériot monoplane he flew over the Alps crashed on landing on September 23, 1910, and Chavez was killed. In 1911 Calbraith Rodgers made a flight across the United States in a small Wright Baby (4,000 miles or 6,440 km, from September 17 to November 5, 1911).

By that time, the significance of aviation had at last been thoroughly grasped all over the world. Italy came on the aviation scene later. After the unsuccessful flight of the first Italian-built plane, Aristide Faccioli's triplane, the *Club Aviatori* was founded in Rome on February 9, 1909. The club brought Wilbur Wright to Italy. The American pioneer stayed in Rome from April 1 to 26, and on April 15 he began demonstration flights at the Centocelle military base. Before leaving Rome, Wilbur Wright trained the naval officer who was to become Italy's first pilot. This was an engineering corps officer, Lt. Mario Calderara. A year later, the first Italian military flying school was set up at Centocelle. The year 1909 also saw the first important Italian aviation rally, the International Air Circuit at Brescia (September 9–20), and the appearance of the first really efficient aircraft designs, by Franz Miller, the Asteria company, and Giovanni (Gianni) Caproni. And aviation boomed in Italy during the next few years. The first serious theoretical consideration about the use of the heavier-than-air machine for military purposes was due to an Italian, General Giulio Douhet. In 1909 he was already considering the strategic possibilities of the aeroplane for war-time use as a dominant combat weapon.

When the Turko–Italian War broke out in 1911, the aeroplane went to war. (There is a certain amount of controversy about this first use of aircraft in war, for it is fairly certain that an American pilot, Hector Worden, flew for the Mexican government in operations against rebels earlier in 1911. The Italian air effort against the Turks in Libya, therefore, was more properly the first use of organized, formal aviation forces in war.) The Italian Aviation Battalion and its aircraft were immediately mobilized and quickly dispatched on three steamships to Tripoli. The planes were two Blériot XIs, three Nieuport monoplanes, two Farman biplanes, and two Etrich *Taube* monoplanes. The unit's commander was Captain Carlo Piazza, a well-known racing pilot. War operations began on October 22 with some test flights. The next day, Piazza himself made history's first reconnaissance flight. On November 1, 2nd Lieutenant Giulio Gavotti carried out the first aerial bombardment mission, dropping four bombs on two Turkish-held oases. And in March 1912 Captain Piazza made the first photographic reconnaissance flight in history.

Soon all of Europe was to go to war, and speed and range would no longer be the only standards of performance for heavier-than-air machines. The new planes were planned above all for payload capacity, for easy handling, and for manoeuvrability to avoid the enemy. Although Italy had been the first nation to use the aeroplane in combat, other European countries had been developing military aviation as well. The French army bought its first planes in 1910 and trained 60 pilots, and began to install armourment in its reconnaissance craft in 1911. In the United States Glenn Curtiss experimented with the plane as a means of bombardment in June 1910. A year later, a Curtiss biplane made the first take-offs and landings on the deck of a warship. And in Russia, Igor Sikorsky built the first 'air giant', the forerunner of the multi-engined strategic bombers of the First World War. The Royal Flying Corps was formed in Great Britain on April 13, 1912, and in June 1914 the Naval Wing of this formation was removed to constitute the basis of the Royal Naval Air Service.

Wright Flyer I

Modern aviation was born at Kill Devil Hills, North Carolina, four miles south of Kitty Hawk, between 10.30 am and noon on Thursday, December 17, 1903. Five local residents were present. Orville and Wilbur Wright took turns piloting their Flyer I in four sustained flights, the first time in history that a powered machine under human control rose from the ground, was sustained in flight, and then landed in a place no lower than that of the take-off. Orville took off first, at 10.35, against a 20-mph (32-kph) wind. The Flyer flew for 12 seconds, covering a distance of 120 feet (36.6 m). The second and third flights covered 175 and 200 feet (53.3 and 61 m) respectively. In the fourth and last flight, Wilbur remained aloft for 59 seconds and flew 852 feet (259.7 m).

Orville and Wilbur Wright had been interested in aviation ever since childhood, when their father gave them a model helicopter. As adults, they studied the mechanics of bird flight and the hang-glider experiments of Otto Lilienthal, the German pioneer of aeronautics. Their studies led them to reject Lilienthal's system of controlling flight by the shifting of the pilot's body to alter the plane's centres of gravity. The Wright brothers developed a new system in which lateral control was obtained by warping the wing-tips.

In 1899, they built a kite to experiment with actual flight. They were on the right path, and in September 1900 the brothers built a glider which they flew successfully at Kitty Hawk. The following year, they made piloted flights with a larger glider, this time at Kill Devil Hills. This aircraft was not satisfactory, however, and it was only

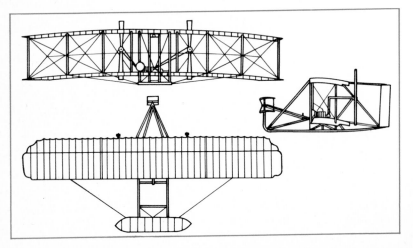

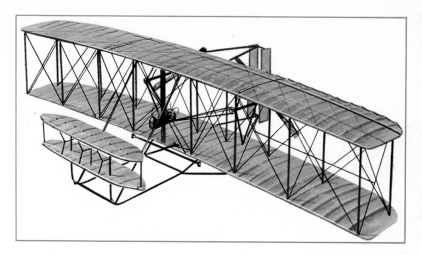

after the building and testing of a third glider – which flew in September and October 1902 – that Orville and Wilbur Wright thought they had solved their major problems and were ready to face powered flight. The basic innovation of this third glider was the adoption of a movable rudder to replace the double fixed fin used on the first two gliders.

The Wrights built their Flyer I during the summer of 1903, but two enormous obstacles had to be overcome before it could take to the air. The engines of the time were too heavy, and really efficient propellers were not available. So the Wright brothers built their own engine (4-cylinder, 12 hp) and succeeded in devising satisfactory propellers.

The first Flyer, as the Wrights called their planes, was a biplane with a skid undercarriage. The elevator was installed forward of the wings and had a biplane configuration, and the double

Aircraft: **Wright Flyer I**
Manufacturer: **Wilbur and Orville Wright**
Year: **1903**
Engine: **Wright 4-cylinder water-cooled inline, 12 hp**
Wingspan: **40 ft 4 in (12.29 m)**
Length: **21 ft 1 in (6.43 m)**
Height: **8 ft (2.44 m)**
Wing area: **510 sq ft (47.38 sq m)**
Weight: **750 lbs (340 kg)**
Speed: **30 mph (48 kph)**
Frame: **spruce, ash**
Covering: **muslin**

rudder was to the rear. The engine drove two pusher propellers by means of two transmission chains, one of them crossed to counter-rotate its propeller. For take-off the plane sat on a wheeled dolly, which was in turn placed so as to face into wind at the end of a wooden rail about 60 feet (18.3 m) long. The aircraft was held back until the engine reached full power and then released, whereupon it took off under its own power after moving forward, accelerating the whole while, on the dolly.

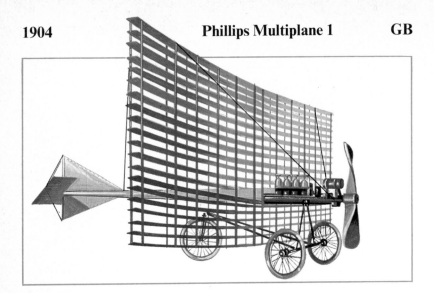

Phillips Multiplane I

The 1904 Multiplane was Horatio F. Phillips' practical application of the theory of lifting surfaces he worked out between 1884 and 1891 and tested with a steam-powered model in 1893. In Phillips' projects, aerodynamic lift was generated by a row of superimposed 'winglets', very much like the slats of a Venetian blind. There were 20 lifting elements of this kind on the Multiplane. The aircraft had a cruciform tail unit and was supported on a three-wheeled undercarriage. The engine, built by Phillips himself, powered a wooden tractor propeller. The Multiplane was tried out at Streatham, but the test results were disappointing. Although the plane had adequate lift, it was unstable and could not be controlled in flight. Three years later Phillips flew some 500 feet (152.4 m) in another multiplane.

Aircraft: **Phillips Multiplane 1**
Manufacturer: **Horatio Phillips**
Year: **1904**
Engine: **Phillips 4-cylinder water-cooled inline, 22 hp**
Wingspan: **17 ft 9 in (5.41 m)**
Length: **13 ft 9 in (4.19 m)**
Height: **10 ft (3.05 m)**
Weight: **600 lbs (272 kg)**
Speed: **34 mph (55 kph)**
Frame: **spruce, ash, steel tube**
Covering: **calico**

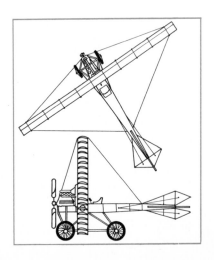

Wright Flyer III

The Wright brothers' third Flyer was the first practical aeroplane in history. It was fully controllable and could remain aloft for more than 30 minutes.

The Flyer III had the same overall layout as its predecessors, but there were important differences, such as the longer booms to support the forward elevators and the rear rudder. The plane was thoroughly tested at the Huffman Prairie, a field eight miles (12.9 km) east of Dayton. Flights were continued from June 23 to October 16, 1905, about 40 in all being made. An endurance record was established on October 5, when the aircraft remained aloft for 38 minutes and 3 seconds. When the test flights were completed, the Wright brothers offered their plane to the United States War Department for study and development, but the offer was turned down.

Aircraft: **Wright Flyer III**
Manufacturer: **Wilbur and Orville Wright**
Year: **1905**
Engine: **Wright 4-cylinder water-cooled inline, 20 hp**
Wingspan: **40 ft 6 in (12.34 m)**
Length: **28 ft (8.53 m)**
Height: **8 ft (2.44 m)**
Wing area: **503 sq ft (46.73 sq m)**
Weight: **855 lbs (388 kg)**
Speed: **approx. 35 mph (56 kph)**
Frame: **spruce, ash**
Covering: **cotton**

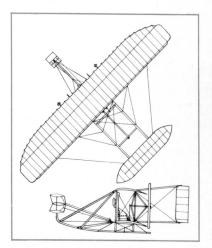

Santos-Dumont 14-bis

The first officially recognised aeroplane flight in Europe took place almost three years after that historic morning at Kill Devil Hills, and one year after the Wright brothers' Flyer III set its endurance record of 38 minutes 3 seconds. The Santos-Dumont 14-*bis*, an aeroplane designed and built by the Brazilian Alberto Santos-Dumont, made its first 'hop' of 23 feet (7 m) on September 13, 1906, at Bagatelle, near Paris. On October 23 the plane flew a distance of 197 feet (60 m), and on November 12 it remained aloft for 21.2 seconds, landing 722 feet (220 m) away after reaching an 'altitude' of just under 20 feet (6 m).

Alberto Santos-Dumont had arrived in Paris in 1898, where he devoted all his energies to building and flying airships. He designed a dozen dirigibles in a few years. He became famous in October 1901, when he flew his airship No. 6 around the Eiffel Tower and won a prize of 150,000 francs. Later he also built a glider and a model helicopter but was unable to find adequate engines to power them. Only after the Wright brothers' flight did Santos-Dumont design and build his first powered aeroplane, the 14-*bis*.

The plane was constructed at Neuilly-St James, on the outskirts of Paris. It was a canard-type biplane: that is, with the fuselage and 'tail' forward of the main lifting wings. The box-kite 'tail' unit was connected to the fuselage in such a way that it could be moved up and down to act as an elevator, and from side to side to act as a rudder. The original engine, a 24-hp Antoinette, was later replaced by a 50-hp model, and drove a metal pusher propeller 8.2 feet (2.5 m) in diameter.

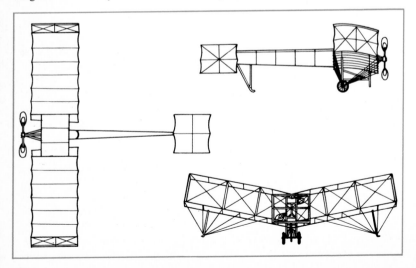

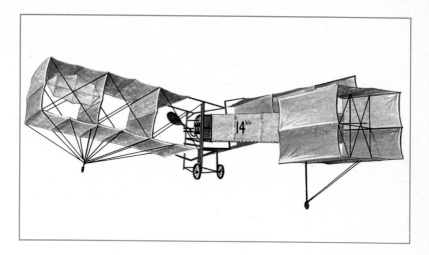

The pilot sat in a kind of basket in front of the engine, and the main landing gear consisted of two wheels with rubber shock-absorbers. A skid supported the front part of the aircraft. To improve lateral control of the plane, Santos-Dumont later added two octagonal ailerons at the wingtips. The controls were operated in a remarkable way: the control cables were attached to a harness worn by the pilot. To right the plane he merely shifted his body away from the tilt.

The 14-*bis* was tested extensively without power. Static tests were performed, and then the aircraft was hung on a pulley moving along a cable. A harnessed donkey pulled the plane along the cable! The final tests were made in July 1906, with the 14-*bis* slung underneath the Santos-Dumont dirigible No. 14.

A first attempt at flight was made on September 13, but the plane was damaged. On October 23 the plane flew

Aircraft: **Santos-Dumont 14-bis**
Manufacturer: **Alberto Santos-Dumont**
Year: **1906**
Engine: **Antoinette 8-cylinder water-cooled inline V, 50 hp**
Wingspan: **36 ft 9 in (11.2 m)**
Length: **31 ft 10 in (9.7 m)**
Height: **11 ft 2 in (3.4 m)**
Wing area: **560 sq ft (52.00 sq m)**
Weight: **661 lbs (300 kg)**
Speed: **25 mph (40 kph)**
Frame: **bamboo, pine**
Covering: **cotton**

197 feet (60 m), winning Santos-Dumont the Archdeacon Prize of 3,000 francs, for the first plane in Europe to fly more than 25 metres (about 80 ft). On November 12, with a 'hop' of 722 feet (220 m), the Brazilian won another prize, this one 1,500 francs, offered by the Aéro-Club de France to the first plane to fly more than 100 metres.

Although the plane and its performance were not technically outstanding, Santos-Dumont's flights did much to stimulate interest throughout Europe in heavier-than-air machines.

Vuia I

Although this unusual plane was a failure, it was notable for being the first monoplane with a tractor propeller. And the tractor monoplane formula was to have an illustrious future in the hands of men like Blériot and Levavasseur. The Vuia was designed and built by a Romanian lawyer named Trajan Vuia, who lived in Paris. The aircraft had a rudder but no elevators. A device that changed the wings' angle of attack in flight took over the function of elevators. The plane had a bat-wing structure mounted on top of a frame housing the engine, the pilot, the directional rudder and the landing gear. The landing gear consisted of four pneumatic-tyred wheels, the front two of which could be turned together with the rudder. The Vuia I's best flight was 79 feet (24 m).

Aircraft: **Vuia I**
Manufacturer: **Trajan Vuia**
Year: **1906**
Engine: **Serpollet carbonic acid gas engine, 25 hp**
Wingspan: **28 ft 6.5 in (8.7 m)**
Length: **9 ft 10 in (3 m)**
Height: **10 ft 9 in (3.28 m)**
Wing area: **215.3 sq ft (20 sq m)**
Weight: **531 lbs (241 kg)**
Frame: **steel tube**
Covering: **cotton**

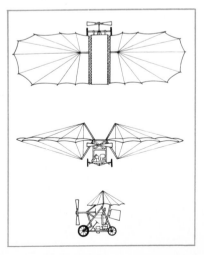

Blériot VII

Vuia's attempt to build a tractor monoplane stimulated Louis Blériot, who had been designing and building less original aircraft. Blériot's first tractor monoplane, the model VII, which appeared in 1907, was a milestone achievement for flight performance and aerodynamics. The plane had low, cantilever wings, covered fuselage, a rudder and a large, all-moving tailplane. The two parts of the tailplane could be moved in concert to act as elevators, or differentially to act as ailerons (the modern term for such control surfaces is 'elevons'). The enclosed Antoinette engine drove a four-blade metal propeller. The plane was tested in November and December at Issy, and made a total of six flights. In two flights the plane covered more than 1,640 feet (500 m) at a speed of about 50 mph (80 kph).

Aircraft: **Blériot VII**
Manufacturer: **Louis Blériot**
Year: **1907**
Engine: **Antoinette 8-cylinder water-cooled inline V, 50 hp**
Wingspan: **36 ft 1 in (11 m)**
Length: **26 ft 3 in (8 m)**
Height: **9 ft (2.75 m)**
Wing area: **269.1 sq ft (25.00 sq m)**
Weight: **937 lbs (425 kg)**
Speed: **50 mph (80 kph)**
Frame: **ash, spruce, steel tube**
Covering: **aluminium, plywood, cotton**

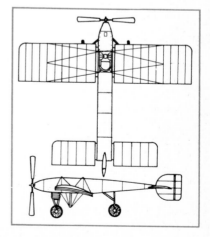

Voisin-Farman I

The Voisin brothers, Gabriel and Charles, were the first men in Europe to build powered aircraft on a commercial basis, but the success of their planes was due to the innovations made by another great aviation pioneer, Henri Farman. The best example is the biplane that Farman ordered, on June 1, 1907, from the Voisin workshop in Billancourt. The plane was almost identical with the one built earlier that year for Léon Delagrange, a plane that had not been a success. After Henri Farman modified his Voisin, it became the second flying machine (after the Wright brothers' 1904 Flyer II) to remain in the air for more than one minute and fly a complete circle. On November 9, 1907, at Issy, the Voisin-Farman biplane flew 3,379 feet (1,030 m) in 74 seconds.

The Voisin brothers' second plane, the one ordered by Léon Delagrange, was a great improvement. It is now called the Voisin-Delagrange I. (It was standard Voisin practice to inscribe on the aircraft as a designation only the name of the client who had ordered the machine. The Voisin-Delagrange I, therefore, was known at the time as the Delagrange No. I.) The Voisin-Delagrange had a box-kite tail, a double forward elevator, and a 50-hp Antoinette engine that drove a metal pusher propeller. The machine was tested at Bagatelle from March 16 to April 13 and made six 'hops'. The best covered 197 feet (60 m) in six seconds, with Charles Voisin as pilot. An unsuccessful attempt was then made to transform it into a floatplane. After being restored to its original shape, the Voisin-Delagrange made another flight in November. It covered 1,640 feet (500 m) in 40 seconds and crashed on landing. The plane was completely destroyed.

But the third biplane, the Voisin-Farman I, was a resounding success. When the Voisins delivered this plane, all that distinguished it from the Voisin Delagrange were the empennage (with a single central rudder), a wingspan 7.9 inches (20 cm) greater, and about 150 lbs (70 kg) more in weight. After the initial tests, Farman made extensive modifications. The biplane elevator was replaced by a monoplane one, the wings were rigged to give a small angle of dihedral, for greater stability, and the broad empennage was reduced in span from almost 20 to 6.9 feet (6 m to 2.1 m).

This plane made some twenty take-offs at Issy, between September 30 and November 23, 1907, and proved itself enormously superior to its predecessors. On October 26, it covered 2,530 feet (771 m) in 52.6 seconds; on

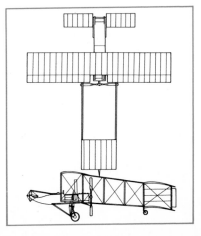

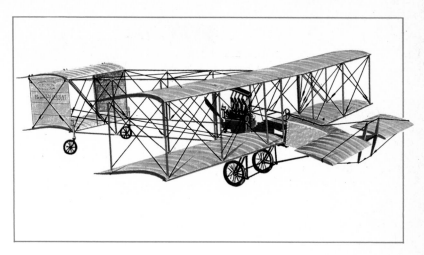

November 8, it flew its first turn; and on November 9, it won the Archdeacon Cup for the first official flight of more than 150 metres (492 feet), covering 3,379 feet (1,030 m) in 1 minute 14 seconds.

After the success of the Voisin-Farman I, the Voisin brothers built a second biplane for Léon Delagrange, incorporating all of Farman's modifications. The plane was shown in various European countries in 1908 and gave excellent performances everywhere. After a crash in May two side-curtains were fitted at the inner ends of the wings, leading to the designation Voisin-Delagrange III. These curtains were later replaced by four, enclosing the outer bay of each wing. On June 23, 1908, in Milan, the Voisin-Delagrange III flew 8.87 miles (14.27 km), its best performance.

Henri Farman, who was an excellent pilot and potentially a designer of great talent, made further improvements on his plane. He completely recovered his plane to compete for the 50,000-franc Deutsch-Archdeacon prize for the first plane to fly a complete circle of one kilometre diameter. He won the prize at Issy on January 13, 1908. In May he added two side curtains between the wings to increase stability, and in October he installed ailerons on all four wings. In this modified form, the plane made the first proper 'cross-country flight' in Europe, flying 17 miles (27 km) from Bouy to Reims, on October 30, 1908.

Aircraft: **Voisin-Farman I**
Manufacturer: **Voisin Frères**
Year: **1907**
Engine: **Antoinette 8-cylinder water-cooled inline V, 50 hp**
Wingspan: **33 ft 5.5 in (10.2 m)**
Length: **34 ft 5 in (10.5 m)**
Height: **11 ft (3.35 m)**
Weight: **1,150 lbs (522 kg)**
Speed: **34 mph (55 kph)**
Frame: **ash, steel tube**
Covering: **cotton**

Esnault-Pelterie REP. 1

Aircraft: **Esnault-Pelterie REP. 1**
Manufacturer: **Robert Esnault-Pelterie**
Year: **1907**
Engine: **REP 7-cylinder air-cooled radial, 30 hp**
Wingspan: **31 ft 6 in (6.9 m)**
Wing area: **193.75 sq ft (16 sq m)**
Frame: **wood, steel tube**
Covering: **fabric**

The REP. 1 was Robert Esnault-Pelterie's first experience with powered aircraft. It was not a success, nor were the next two models, the 1908 REP. 2 and the 1909 REP. 2-*bis*. Even though these planes demonstrated the designer's technical abilities, they also betrayed his initial inability to overcome mistaken judgements and premises. Thus this French pioneer's name was at first connected mainly with subsidiary aviation problems: safety belts, load testing and strength of materials, engines, and hydraulic brakes for landing gears. In 1907 he designed and built an excellent 7-cylinder, 30-hp radial engine and decided to install it in a tractor propeller monoplane of rather unconventional form: the REP. 1. This plane had wings with slight negative dihedral (anhedral), a very short fuselage, a tailplane and an elevator, but no rudder. Control was achieved by warping the wings (down only) and through the elevator, operated by one control lever. The engine drove a four-bladed metal propeller.

Tests made between November and December 1907 showed that the plane was deficient in longitudinal and directional stability. The engine had not been properly tuned and developed problems with cooling. Following its five take-offs, the REP. 1 was unable to perform more than a 'hop', the longest being 1,968 feet (600 m) on November 16.

De Pischoff I

Like so many other designs of the period, de Pischoff's biplane was a failure in practice. But it did have one great merit: it carried forward the formula of the tractor biplane, a formula that was only fully worked out in 1910–11. Up to then, in fact, biplane builders usually followed the Wright brothers' pattern, with forward elevators and box-kite wings. De Pischoff's biplane, built in Lucien Chauvière's factory, anticipated the layout that was to become classic for biplanes: front engine and propeller, biplane/sesquiplane wings, and control surfaces in a rear 'tail'. The cruciform empennage included the fin, the rudder, the tailplane and the elevator. But there was no lateral control. The landing gear had bicycle-type wheels and a wide track, to guarantee better stability on the ground. The engine

Aircraft: **De Pischoff I**
Manufacturer: **Lucien Chauvière**
Year: **1907**
Engine: **Anzani 3-cylinder air-cooled radial, 25 hp**
Wingspan: **21 ft 4 in (6.50 m)**
Wing area: **269 sq ft (25 sq m)**
Weight (empty): **120.1 lbs (54.5 kg)**
Frame: **wood and bamboo**
Covering: **fabric**

and propeller were also forerunners in a sense. The Anzani engine and the Chauvière propeller were to become famous all over the world with the Blériot XI's English Channel flight in 1909.

De Pischoff was not discouraged by the failure of this plane and built another one, in conjunction with Koechlin in 1908. It was an unusual monoplane with three tandem wings for a total of 269.05 sq feet (25 sq m) of wing area, a tractor propeller, and a 2-cylinder, 20-hp Dutheil-Chalmers engine. It was tested at Villacoublay and gave its best performance on October 29, 1908 with a hop of 1,640 feet (500 m).

Wright Model A

After the last flight of the Flyer III, on October 16, 1905, 30 months passed before Orville and Wilbur Wright flew again. But this period was not one of inactivity. The Wright brothers spent the time perfecting their last plane, the Flyer III, so that it could carry a passenger as well as the pilot. The Wrights also perfected their engine and built half a dozen that were more powerful and more reliable. The new plane (of which several were built, including some under licence in other countries) is generally known as the '1907–1909 type', or Wright Flyer Model A.

The Model A had the general configuration of the Flyer III, but it was a two-seater, with upright seats, a much improved control system, and a far more powerful engine. It had a derrick-and-weight assisted take-off system, but if necessary it could also take flight from using its own launching-rail on engine power alone.

The plane was so successful in tests that the United States government, after a first refusal and extended negotiations, contracted for one plane for testing purposes. The plane was ready in February 1908. In March, the Wright brothers received another order, this time from a French company. The brothers decided that Orville would carry out the tests for the US Army, and Wilbur would go to France. But first the brothers went back to Kill Devil Hills, from May 6 to 14, 1908, and made a series of flights to get back in training and master their plane completely. Wilbur then left for France and, until the end of August, supervised the assembly and tuning of his plane in a workshop in Le Mans. His meeting with European aviation enthusiasts took place on August 8, 1908, at the Hunaudières race-track near Le Mans.

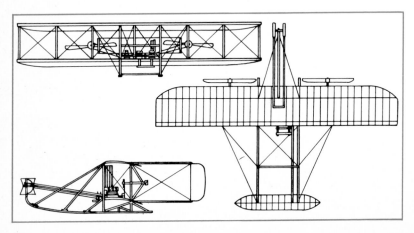

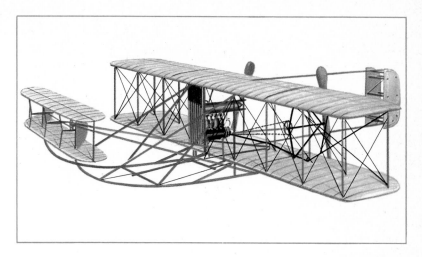

It was an enormous success. The scepticism and suspicion that had developed in previous months among French pilots (with the encouragement of the press) turned to excitement as soon as Wilbur took off, flew two beautifully controlled circles and then eased his plane down to land. He then made other demonstration flights for several days before receiving permission to use the military field at Camp d'Auvours, where he gave one demonstration after another. He carried passengers as well, set an endurance record (on December 31, with 2 hours 20 minutes 23 seconds in the air), and set an altitude record (on December 18, about 361 feet or 110 m). Camp d'Auvours became the mecca for pilots and flying enthusiasts. Construction licences for the Model A were sold to Great Britain, France, and Germany.

In the meantime, in the United States, Orville Wright had begun ac-

Aircraft: **Wright Model A (modified Signal Corps)**
Manufacturer: **Wright Brothers**
Year: **1908**
Engine: **Wright 4-cylinder water-cooled inline, 30 hp**
Wingspan: **36 ft 6 in (11.13 m)**
Length: **28 ft 11 in (8.81 m)**
Height: **8 ft 1 in (2.46 m)**
Wing area: **415 sq ft (38.55 sq m)**
Weight: **1,200 lbs (544 kg)**
Speed: **44 mph (71 kph)**
Frame: **spruce, ash**
Covering: **cotton**

(The data above refer to the 'one-off' special Wright Model A tested at Fort Myer in July 1909.)

ceptance flights for the army, at Fort Myer. These tests were clouded by the first fatal accident in the history of powered flight. At 5 pm on September 17, a propeller broke and the plane crashed. Orville Wright was seriously injured, and his passenger, Lieutenant Thomas Selfridge, was killed. Testing was resumed a year later, with a new and slightly modified plane. The army bought this Model A and gave it the designation of Signal Corps No. 1.

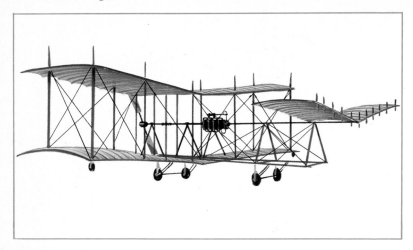

Roe Biplane I

Aircraft: **Roe Biplane I**
Manufacturer: **Alliott Verdon Roe**
Year: **1908**
Engine: **Antoinette 8-cylinder water-cooled inline, 24 hp**
Wingspan: **30 ft (9.14 m)**
Length: **23 ft (7 m)**
Weight: **600 lbs (272 kg)**
Frame: **wood**
Covering: **cotton**

With the £75 which he had won as prize money in a *Daily Mail* competition for model aircraft, Alliott Verdon Roe – the founder and principal driving force of the future A. V. Roe and Company Limited (Avro) – built his first full-size aircraft. It was basically a scaled-up version of his prize winning model: a canard biplane with a pusher propeller, clearly inspired by the Wrights. Roe intended to try for the prize of £2,500 for the first flight round Brooklands race track in 1907. Power was provided by a 9-hp J.A.P. engine, and at first Roe fitted a four-bladed propeller. This was then changed for a two-bladed aluminium unit. Proof of the insufficient power of the current engine was provided by the fact that the best Roe could manage was track-bound taxiing.

Not deterred, Roe now fitted a 24-hp Antoinette engine. But he had no better success with this power unit in May 1908. Small extra winglets between the main wings were also added at the inner ends of the main wings, still to no avail. In June 1908 the Roe I was tested in the air with the aid of a towing car, and a few short hops under the power of the Antoinette were made along the finishing straight of the motor race track.

Since that time there has been considerable controversy about whether or not Roe actually flew, although it seems that the best he did was 'hop'.

Ellehammer IV

Jacob Christian Hansen Ellehammer, the son of a carpenter, was a versatile Danish designer, and aviation was just one of his many interests. Although his planes made only a limited contribution to aeronautics, it is significant that he achieved some fairly important results working on his own, without the slightest contact with the work of contemporary pioneers in the field. His first plane was built in 1905, and had a 9-hp engine built by Ellehammer himself. The plane did not fly in the true sense of the word, being designed to fly in circles while attached to a central pole. It had a semi-automatic control system, and only made small hops around the circle. The longest (138 feet or 42 m) was made on September 12, 1906. For some time this achievement was cited against Santos-Dumont's claim to have made the first

Aircraft: **Ellehammer IV**
Manufacturer: **Jacob C. H. Ellehammer**
Year: **1908**
Engine: **Ellehammer 5-cylinder air-cooled radial 35 hp**
Wingspan: **39 ft 4.5 in (12 m)**
Wing area: **398.3 sq ft (37 sq m)**
Weight: **287 lbs (130 kg)**
Speed: **approx. 42 mph (67.5 kph)**
Frame: **mahogany, steel tube**
Covering: **fabric**

flight in Europe.

Ellehammer built several other aircraft, including a 'semi-biplane' and a triplane, equipped with more powerful engines of his own design. In 1908 he designed his model IV, a tractor biplane. This plane was tested in Germany and made a very short flight in June, the first flight ever made in Germany. At Kiel, on June 28, it remained in the air for 11 seconds and won a prize of 5,000 marks for the designer. The plane's longest flight, over a distance of 558 feet (170 m), was made on January 14, 1909. Ellehammer built other aeroplanes but finally went out of business.

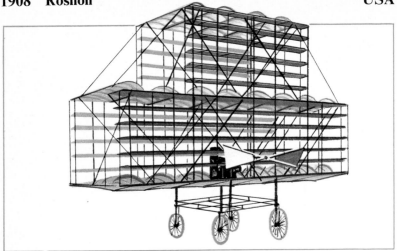

Roshon

Aircraft: **Roshon**
Manufacturer: **Roshon**
Year: **1908**
Engine: —
Wingspan: —
Length: —
Height: —
Weight: —
Frame: **wood, metal tube**
Covering: **fabric**

All that remains today of this intricate flying machine, with its frail, thread-like structure, is a photograph and a date. Four bicycle wheels attached to a framework of thin metal tubing supported a complicated trelliswork of lifting surfaces. In the photograph, the aircraft seems to have a large, metal, two-bladed propeller, and there is a vague shadow of an engine. Next to the plane there is a man wearing a jacket, a white shirt and a hat, with his hands in his pockets. He must have been the designer of the plane. We know nothing else about him or his plane.

The photograph of the Roshon Multiplane appears twice in the world's most authoritative aeronautical publication: in the 1909 and 1913 editions of Jane's *All the World's Aircraft*. There is no comment, however,

not the least description of the aircraft. In the preface to the historical section of the 1913 edition, however, the following remark is made: 'While many are freak machines, which in the light of present knowledge seem ridiculous, the germ of modern practice is to be found in many other aircraft illustrated in this cemetery of dead ideals' – good enough reason to remember these planes. Roshon must certainly have understood the basic principles of aerodynamics. He must have read and studied, and come into contact with the many aviation enthusiasts in the America of 1908. And he probably knew of Phillips' 1904 Multiplane.

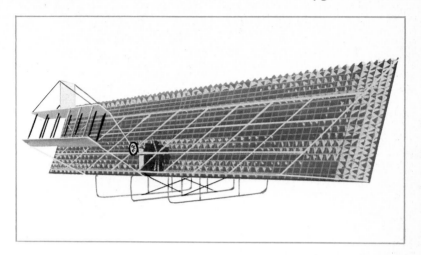

A.E.A. Cygnet II

Aircraft: **Cygnet II**
Manufacturer: **Aerial Experiment Association**
Year: **1908**
Engine: **Curtiss 8-cylinder water-cooled inline V, 50 hp**
Wingspan: **52 ft 6 in (16 m)**
Length: **13 ft 1.5 in (4 m)**
Height: **—**
Wing area: **—**
Weight: **950 lbs (431 kg)**
Frame: **wood, metal tube**

A beehive airframe made up of 3,610 tetrahedrons was the main characteristic of the Cygnet II, designed towards the end of 1908 by Alexander Graham Bell and built by the Aerial Experiment Association, the aeronautical society Bell founded in September 1907. The plane – equipped with a 50-hp Curtiss engine, a pusher propeller and three skids – was tested early in 1909 on the frozen surface of Lake Keuka, near New York, but never managed to take to the air. This was the Aerial Experiment Association's last experiment before disbanding in March of that year. It was also Bell's last attempt to build a flying machine with multicellular-type supporting surfaces.

Bell had studied the problems of this type of plane long and thoroughly. His main purpose in creating the

Aerial Experiment Association (along with Glenn Curtiss, Lieutenant Thomas Selfridge, John Douglas McCurdy, and Frederick Baldwin) had been to develop a working group to help him in his research. The Association's first project had been another Cygnet – the Cygnet I – tested by Selfridge with some success. The second design brutally dashed Bell's theories. By 1909, the 'heavier-than-air' machine had gone beyond the merely experimental stage and reached the basic configuration that was to lead to future developments.

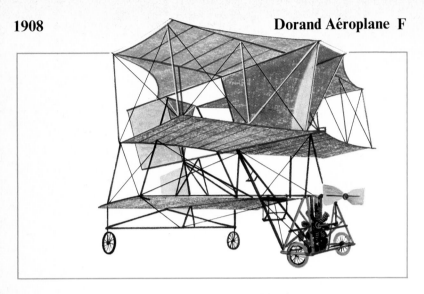

Dorand Aéroplane

Aircraft: **Aéroplane**
Manufacturer: **Dorand**
Year: **1908**
Engine: **Anzani 6-cylinder air-cooled radial, 43 hp**
Wingspan: **37 ft 8.75 in (11.50 m)**
Length: —
Height: —
Wing area: **968.8 sq ft (90 sq m)**
Weight: **611 lbs (300 kg)**
Frame: **wood, metal tube**
Covering: **fabric**

The first aeroplane expressly designed for military use was built in France in 1908. The chief concern was to provide the pilot with maximum visibility. The plane was constructed by an officer in the French Army, Captain Dorand, who thought his plane satisfied all the army's needs. But despite the many trials that were run, the *Aéroplane* never got off the ground.

Dorand's idea was simple but rather ingenious. He installed the lifting surfaces above and well away from a framework that carried the landing gear, the engine, and the pilot. This platform was more or less triangular in shape, and the two front wheels were attached to a structure that bore the engine, while the two rear ones were placed at the base of the broad triangle to ensure stability. The engine was a 6-cylinder Anzani radial driving

a two-bladed adjustable metal propeller. The wing cellule itself was of the biplane type, with the two broad-chord lifting surfaces attached in the centre to a triangular 'box'. A similar structure to the rear acted as the tailplane. The wing cellule had a marked positive angle of attack in respect to the platform base, so as to increase lift during take-off. But Captain Dorand's idea was too unorthodox. It deviated too far from the canons that had begun to assure the future of the heavier-than-air machine.

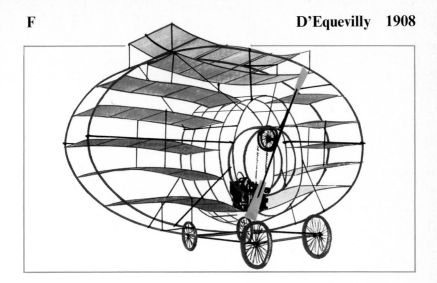

D'Equevilly

Aircraft: **D'Equevilly**
Manufacturer: **D'Equevilly**
Year: **1908**
Engine: **3-cylinder air-cooled semi-radial, 7-8 hp**
Wingspan: **16 ft 5 in (5 m)**
Length: **6 ft 6.75 in (2 m)**
Height: —
Wing area: **269.1 sq ft (25 sq m)**
Weight: **309 lbs**
Frame: **wood, metal tube**
Covering: **fabric**

The early successes of the European aviation pioneers set off a kind of chain reaction, especially in France, the fatherland of European aviation. Enthusiasts turned out hundreds of machines. Most of them were products of fantasy alone and too far removed from any technically sound principles to have any success. One such machine, built in France in 1908, was the multiplane constructed by the Marquis d'Equevilly, who wanted to try his hand at building a heavier-than-air machine.

This strange machine demonstrated a certain amount of originality and a good bit of imagination. Photographs of the time show an elliptical structure resting on four bicycle-type wheels, with a narrow metal propeller in front, a 3-cylinder air-cooled engine, and a man – evidently the pilot – standing inside an inner oval framework. The Marquis d'Equevilly was clearly inspired by the principle of multiple, superimposed wing surfaces. His multiplane's wing cellule was made up of 12 elements, five on each side, supported by the two concentric elliptical frames, with two more elements mounted above. The installation of the engine and propeller was also ingenious. The engine drove the propeller by means of a transmission chain reduction gear, which reduced the rpm from the 1,500 of the engine to the 500 of the propeller.

Blériot XI

'England's isolation has ended once and for all.' So wrote one English newspaper the day after Louis Blériot flew across the English Channel from France. The French aviation pioneer, in his modified type XI monoplane, took off from Les Baraques, near Calais, at 4.41 am on July 25, 1909 and landed at 5.17 am in Northfall Meadow, near Dover. He had flown almost 24 miles (38.6 km), almost entirely over water, in a fragile plane powered by a weak and unreliable engine. This daring exploit made Louis Blériot famous as a pilot and as a designer and builder of aircraft. His type XI established the classic formula of the tractor monoplane, a formula that remained unchanged until the start of the First World War.

The Blériot XI made its debut at the Paris *Salon de l'Automobile et de l'Aéronautique* in December 1908, in the aeronautical section, along with two other Blériot planes: the type IX (another tractor monoplane) and the type X (a pusher biplane). But these latter two models never flew, although the Blériot IX managed to make a few 'hops' in the following January and February. But the third plane, the XI, was another story. It made its first flight at Issy on January 23, 1909, and was clearly an efficient, if still not perfect, aircraft.

Raymond Saulnier made a fundamental contribution to the plane's design. The plane was first equipped with a 30-hp REP engine, which drove a four-bladed metal propeller. During testing, however, the engine was replaced by a 22/25-hp Anzani, and a Chauvière two-bladed propeller was installed. Other changes involved the control system: the rudder was enlarged, while the elevons at the outer ends of the tailplane were made to function only as elevators. Their lat-

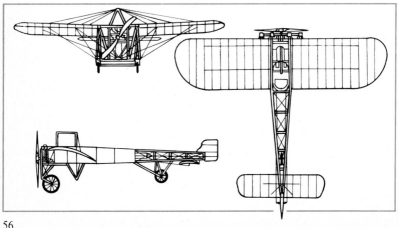

eral function was taken over entirely by warping the trailing edges of the wings. This modified Blériot XI gave excellent performance. Between May 27 and the historic Channel crossing, Louis Blériot made some remarkable flights at Issy and Toury; the best was on July 4, a flight lasting 50 minutes 8 seconds.

Blériot was already thinking about flying across the Channel. In October 1908, the London *Daily Mail* had offered a prize of £1,000 to the first aviator to cross the Channel in either direction. Blériot's exploit was preceded by the unsuccessful attempt of another aviation pioneer, Hubert Latham. Latham flew a stronger and heavier plane, the Antoinette IV, powered by a 50-hp Antoinette engine, considered the best engine of its time. Latham took off from Sangatte (Calais) on July 19, but after less than 8 miles (12.9 km), the engine broke down and he was forced down on the

Aircraft: **Blériot XI**
Manufacturer: **Louis Blériot**
Year: **1909**
Engine: **Anzani 3-cylinder air-cooled radial, 22-25 hp**
Wingspan: **25 ft 7 in (7.8 m)**
Length: **26 ft 3 in (8 m)**
Height: **8 ft 6.5 in (2.6 m)**
Wing area: **150.7 sq ft (14 sq m)**
Weight: **661 lbs (300 kg)**
Speed: **36 mph (58 kph)**
Frame: **ash, bamboo, steel tube**
Covering: **rubberized fabric**

water. Pilot and plane were picked up by a French destroyer.

The Blériot XI had an outstanding career. Apart from its sporting activities, it was also the first plane sold to the French Army and the first to serve during military operations. It was flown by Captain Carlo Piazza on October 23, 1911, during the Italo-Turkish War.

The type was used quite extensively by the French and British in the 1914–15 period.

Curtiss Golden Flyer

The Golden Flyer won the Gordon Bennett Trophy on August 28, 1909, and the *Prix de la Vitesse* the day after. With these two important victories at the first aviation rally in Reims, Glenn Hammond Curtiss' Golden Flyer established its claim to being one of the best planes of its era. The plane's series of successes was capped, slightly more than a year after the plane's debut, when a modified Golden Flyer made the first take-off in history from the deck of a warship, and the first deck landing a couple of months later. These tests – which opened the way to the development of the aircraft carrier – were made on November 14, 1910, on the light cruiser *Birmingham* at Hampton Roads in Virginia, and on January 18, 1911, on the armoured cruiser *Pennsylvania*, anchored in San Francisco Bay. Eugene Ely was at the controls during both events.

Glenn Hammond Curtiss, the great American aviation pioneer and de-signer of the Golden Flyer, was already famous as a builder and pilot of motorcycles when, in 1907, he decided to join the A.E.A. (Aerial Experiment Association), the aeronautical group founded by Alexander Graham Bell. Curtiss first built an engine; then he designed a plane. This first plane was the June Bug. On July 4, 1908, it won the Scientific American Prize for the first official flight made in the United States to cover a distance of more than one mile (1.61 km). The second Curtiss plane, the Gold Bug, was built in partnership with Augustus M. Herring, after Curtiss left the A.E.A. to devote himself to the commercial manufacture of aircraft. Built early in 1909, it was the direct predecessor of the Golden Flyer.

The Gold Bug was a great success. From its first flights, in Morris Park, it proved to be strong, fairly fast, and highly manageable. This last trait was due to the installation of ailerons be-

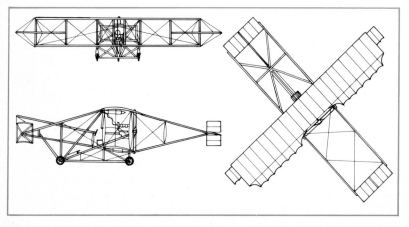

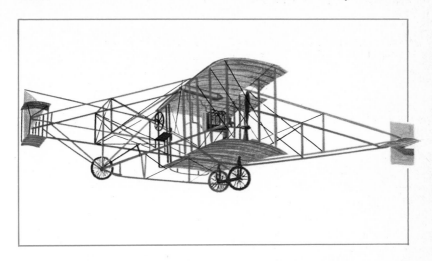

tween the two wings. Curtiss favoured these instead of the wing-warping system. As soon as the new Curtiss-designed engine – an 8-cylinder inline V of 50 hp – was ready it was installed in a similar machine. This modified aircraft was the Golden Flyer. It was one of the stars of the *Grande Semaine d'Aviation de la Champagne*, held in Reims in August 1909.

After his sports triumphs, Glenn Curtiss began a series of demonstration flights throughout Europe. His main purpose was to convince military authorities of the potential contribution the aeroplane could make to military technology. In 1910, during tests carried out for the United States Army and Navy, the Golden Flyer was the first plane to test out a rudimentary kind of bombing. It was also the first to make use of radio contact with the ground while in flight. In 1911 Curtiss built a seaplane version of the plane. This 'navalized'

Aircraft: **Curtiss Golden Flyer**
Manufacturer: **Herring-Curtiss Co.**
Year: **1909**
Engine: **Curtiss 8-cylinder water-cooled inline, 50 hp**
Wingspan: **28 ft 9 in (8.76 m)**
Length: **28 ft 6 in (8.69 m)**
Height: **9 ft (2.74 m)**
Wing area: **258 sq ft (23.97 sq m)**
Weight: **830 lbs (376 kg)**
Speed: **45 mph (72 kph)**
Frame: **spruce, bamboo**
Covering: **rubberized silk**

Golden Flyer – with a central float and small stabilizing floats at the wing-tips – showed that the ship-plane mix was absolutely feasible. The US Navy ordered one Golden Flyer float-plane, which took the official designation A.1, as its first plane. The Wright A (Military Flyer) called Signal Corps No. 1, had been the US Army's first aircraft.

After this Curtiss went from strength to strength as a US Navy aircraft supplier.

Antoinette VII

Like the Blériot XI, the Antoinette IV was the first of a series of monoplanes that made history in the pioneering years of aviation, The Antoinette company – named for the daughter of the director, Jules Gastambide – owed much of its fame to the designer Léon Levavasseur. His contribution to the development of European aviation was not only in aircraft design, but in the excellent quality of his engines. The Antoinette 8-cylinder inline V – from the first, 24-hp version to the final, 100-hp one – powered practically all the planes built in Europe up to 1909, starting with the Santos-Dumont 14-*bis* of 1906. Thanks to Levavasseur's engines, European aviation was able to catch up with America.

The Antoinette IV made its first flight at Issy on October 9, 1908, but Levavasseur waited until January–February of the following year before giving the plane its final touches. The basic modification consisted in adding a further 66 per cent to

the monoplane's wing area, from the prototype's 322.9 square feet to the 538.2 square feet (30 sq m to 50 sq m) of the final plane. This change was fundamental, and the next four versions of the Antoinette had the same size wings.

From the moment it first appeared, the Antoinette was considered an extremely elegant design, with its slim fuselage, trapezoidal wings with marked dihedral, amd cruciform tail surfaces. Only one aesthetic feature (a functional one as well) was changed in later models, starting with the type VI: the ailerons at the wing-tips were replaced by a warping control system on the trailing edges of the wings. In its definitive form, the plane showed its merits at once, flying 3.1 miles (5 km) at Mourmelon, on February 19, 1909. A month later, the plane was turned over to Hubert Latham, whom the French called 'the gentleman of the air', and this pilot gradually developed the plane's highest performance cap-

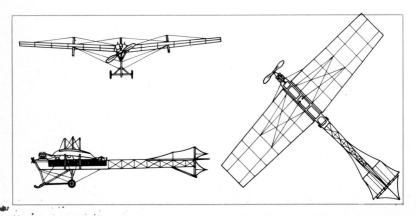

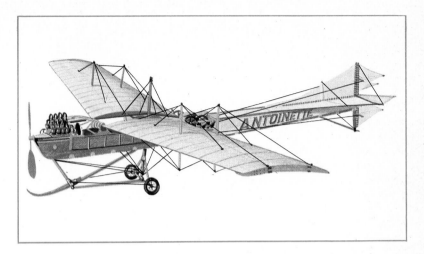

abilities. He made two unsuccessful attempts to cross the English Channel. The first took place on July 19, 1909, just six days before Blériot's successful flight. Latham took off from Sangatte, near Calais. His engine failed and he was forced down in the sea. The plane remained afloat until both it and the pilot were rescued by the French destroyer *Harpon*. The plane was repaired and gave a brilliant performance in the Reims aviation rally, winning second place in the Grand Prix for distance. Latham's second attempt to cross the Channel took place on July 27, two days after Blériot's, this time in a newer Antoinette, the type VII. The main difference between the two was that the type VII had a warped-wing control system, and had been specially built for Latham. This plane also went down into the sea (1 mile, or 1.61 km, from England this time). It was picked up, repaired, and taken to Reims,

Aircraft: **Antoinette VII**
Manufacturer: **Société Antoinette**
Year: **1909**
Engine: **Antoinette 8-cylinder water-cooled inline V, 50 hp**
Wingspan: **42 ft (12.8 m)**
Length: **37 ft 8 in (11.50 m)**
Height: **9 ft 10 in (3 m)**
Wing area: **538.2 sq ft (50 sq m)**
Weight (loaded): **1,301 lbs (590 kg)**
Speed: **43.5 mph (70 kph)**
Frame: **spruce, ash**
Covering: **wood panels, rubberized fabric**

where it won the *Prix de l'Altitude* (508.5 feet or 155 m) and came in second in the *Prix de la Vitesse* on August 29.

The Antoinette engines so essential for the development of practical aviation in Europe originated in the high-power, low-weight units built by Léon Levavasseur for racing power boats at the beginning of the century.

Santos-Dumont 20
Demoiselle

The world's first light plane was Alberto Santos-Dumont's final contribution to the history of aviation. A small, tractor monoplane, the *Demoiselle* became famous in the hands of flying enthusiasts and sportsmen at the leading airfields of the time. It had its limitations when compared with other contemporary planes, which were more efficient. It was, however, the first really successful plane built by the Brazilian pioneer, after the several unsuccessful attempts he made after the 1906 flights of his 14-*bis*.

The prototype of the *Demoiselle* was project No. 19, which made its first flight in November 1907, almost two years before the appearance of the No. 20. The No. 19, the first to be nicknamed *Demoiselle*, had a 20-hp engine, a bamboo fuselage with cruciform tail surfaces, and a framework beneath the wings that carried the

pilot and the landing gear. The plane was very light, weighing just over 235.9 pounds (107 kg) empty. Its flights were not exceptional (656 feet, or 200 m, at Issy on November 17, 1907, and 492 feet, or 150 m, on the 21st at Buc) and came to an abrupt halt after a landing accident. Santos-Dumont had the plane repaired but did not fly it again. The 19-*bis* had a more powerful, 24-hp, Antoinette engine. It was only in March 1909, that the No. 20 made its debut; it flew at Issy on March 6.

There were various innovations in the *Demoiselle*. There was a new engine, a 2-cylinder, 35-hp water-cooled Dutheil-Chalmers, which drove a mahogany Chauvière propeller. The fuselage, still of bamboo but triangular in section, was strengthened. And the wing area was somewhat enlarged. The control system was typical of Santos-Dumont: wing-warping,

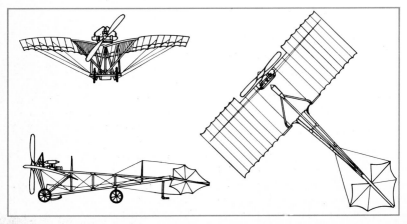

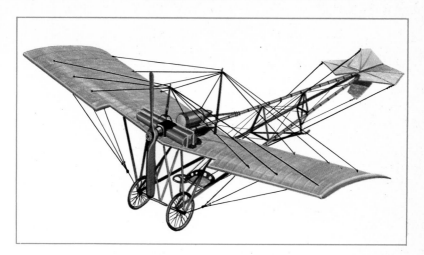

worked by wires connected to a vertical rod attached to the pilot's belt. The pilot simply shifted his position to correct the plane's balance. This system was too delicate, and many pilots found, to their dismay, that unless the weather was absolutely calm, the plane was very hard to control.

Santos-Dumont went on testing the *Demoiselle* after its first flight. In April he managed to fly a distance of 1.24 miles (2 km), and in September he remained in the air for 16 minutes, covering 11.18 miles (18 km). In the same month, the plane was exhibited at the Grand Palais in Paris, at the Clément-Bayard engine stand, and enjoyed great success. By 1910 about a dozen planes had been ordered.

Alberto Santos-Dumont ended his piloting career before his plane ended its flying career. His last flight took place in November 1909. A few months later he developed a serious

Aircraft: **Santos-Dumont No. 20 Demoiselle**
Manufacturer: **Alberto Santos-Dumont**
Year: **1909**
Engine: **Dutheil-Chalmers (Darracq) 2-cylinder air-cooled horizontally opposed, 35 hp**
Wingspan: **16 ft 8.75 in (5.1 m)**
Length: **26 ft 3 in (8 m)**
Height: **7 ft 10.5 in (2.4 m)**
Wing area: **110 sq ft (10.2 sq m)**
Weight: **315 lbs (143 kg)**
Speed: **56 mph (90 kph)**
Frame: **bamboo, steel tube**
Covering: **silk**

form of sclerosis which plagued him until his suicide in 1932. This Brazilian aviation pioneer established another record before he was forced to give up flying: he became the only aviator qualified to pilot four different types of flying machine: monoplanes, biplanes, balloons, and airships.

Santos-Dumont is perhaps more important in aviation for his knack of making the public 'air minded' than for this aircraft.

Henry Farman III

If the Voisin brothers had delivered the biplane Henri Farman ordered from them in 1908, this important aviation pioneer might never have decided to build a plane of his own! (Farman's parents were both British, but Farman lived in France most of his life and took French nationality in 1937. His baptismal name was Harry, but both Henri and Henry were used indiscriminately in France.) But Charles and Gabriel Voisin sold the aircraft Farman had ordered to J. T. C. Moore-Brabazon. Farman was highly offended, cancelled his order at once, and decided to set up a small factory in which to build a new plane of his own design. The result of this impulsive decision was one of the classics of aviation history, the world's most popular biplane between 1909 and 1911. At the Reims aviation rally in August 1909 the Henry Farman III carried off the highest awards, winning the Grand Prix (with a distance of

112 miles flown in 3 hours 4 minutes 56 seconds), the *Prix des Passagers* (with two passengers on board, plus the pilot) and second place in the *Prix de l'Altitude* (with 361 feet, or 110 m.), after H. Latham's Antoinette VII.

Farman's plane had the general features of the Voisin biplane. The most important innovation was the system of lateral control. Farman abandoned the idea of inherent lateral stability followed by the Voisin brothers and adopted aileron control, which he installed in a very advanced and efficient fashion. The aircraft, powered by a 4-cylinder 50-hp Vivinus engine, made its first flight on April 6, 1909, at Châlons. Then followed months of intense testing, during which the plane was improved and some changes were made in the ailerons and empennage. The tail section was radically altered. The original 'box-kite' structure was replaced by a much more complex biplane type with

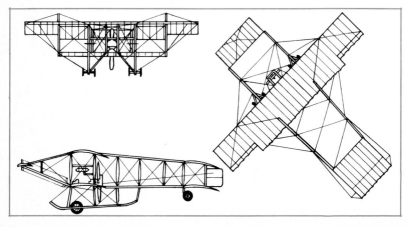

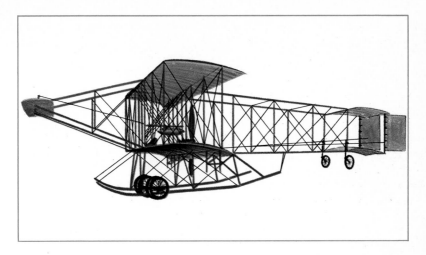

two projecting rear rudders.

Several outstanding flights were made, including one on July 19, when the plane remained in the air for 1 hour 23 minutes. And then the plane was taken to Reims. During the first tests, there was trouble with the Vivinus engine, and Farman asked permission of the meeting authorities to change it. He then installed a 50-hp Gnome rotary engine, a wise decision as it turned out. The plane was grounded for this repair work from August 23 to 27. When it competed again, it was one of the best in the field. Apart from the one piloted by Farman, two others of the same type took part in the rally. The first had been built for the Frenchman Roger Sommer, the second for the Englishman George Cockburn. Sommer's plane, powered by a Vivinus engine, made its first flight at Châlons on July 4. Cockburn's plane, with a Gnome rotary, took to the air on July 20. Piloted by

Aircraft: **Henry Farman III**
Manufacturer: **Henry Farman**
Year: **1909**
Engine: **Gnome 7-cylinder air-cooled rotary, 50 hp**
Wingspan: **32 ft 9.75 in (10 m)**
Length: **39 ft 4.5 in (12 m)**
Height: **11 ft 6 in (3.5 m)**
Wing area: **430.5 sq ft (40 sq m)**
Weight: **1,213 lbs (550 kg)**
Speed: **37 mph (60 kph)**
Frame: **mahogany, ash**
Covering: **cotton**

their owners, these two planes did not win any prizes in Reims. The best of Cockburn's three flights was 6.2 miles (10 km) covered in 11 minutes 28 seconds, while Sommer's best performance, in about 10 flights, was a distance of 37.3 miles (60 km).

After Reims, Henry Farman made further improvements on his biplane. He enlarged it, increased its wing area, and generally improved its performance. This modified version was an enormous success and became the most widely used aircraft in the years prior to World War 1.

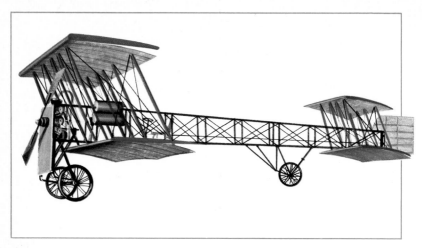

Goupy II

Inspired by the same idea that had led de Pischoff to build a tractor biplane in 1907, Ambroise Goupy designed his own model II in 1909. Unlike de Pischoff's biplane (which was a total failure), the Goupy II was a fairly successful machine, and it made a great contribution to the later development of the basic tractor biplane layout. In designing the plane, Goupy had the assistance of an Italian, Lieutenant Mario Calderara, one of Wilbur Wright's first two Italian pupils. The aircraft was built in the Blériot workshop at Buc, and reflected the building techniques of the French pioneer, especially in the structure of the fuselage, the empennage and the landing gear, which bore a marked resemblance to the Blériot XI monoplane. The Goupy II made only two flights before it was revised in 1909.

Aircraft: **Goupy II**
Manufacturer: **Louis Blériot**
Year: **1909**
Engine: **REP 7-cylinder air-cooled radial, 24 hp**
Wingspan: **20 ft (6.1 m)**
Length: **23 ft (7.01 m)**
Height: **8 ft (2.44 m)**
Wing area: **236 sq ft (22 sq m)**
Weight: **639 lbs (209 kg)**
Speed: **60 mph (97 kph)**
Frame: **spruce, ash**
Covering: **cotton**

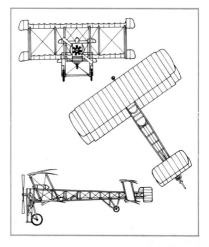

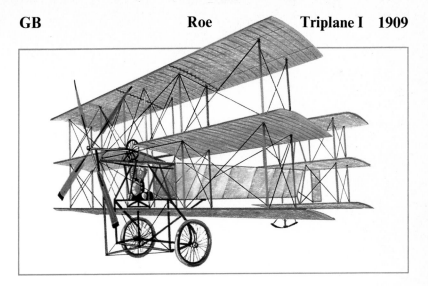

Roe Triplane I

The first flight made in England by a British-designed plane equipped with a British engine took place on July 23, 1909, with Alliott Verdon Roe at the controls. The aircraft was a triplane, the first of four that Roe built during those years before turning with greater success to the biplane formula. Roe's triplane turned out to be under-powered. The best it could do on July 23 with its 9-hp J.A.P. engine was a 'hop' of about 886 feet (270 m). A. V. Roe went on to build a second model with a 35-hp engine. It was introduced at the Olympia air salon in July 1909.

Roe's greatest successes, however, were to be a series of small biplanes. All these were not only notable for the excellence of their detail design but also their well-balanced and pleasing appearance.

Aircraft: **Roe Triplane I**
Manufacturer: **A. V. Roe**
Year: **1909**
Engine: **J.A.P. 4-cylinder air-cooled V, 9 hp**
Wingspan: **20 ft (6.1 m)**
Length: **23 ft (7.01 m)**
Height: **11 ft (3.35 m)**
Wing area: **320 sq. ft (29.73 sq m)**
Weight (empty): **200 lbs (90.72 kg)**
Weight: **400 lbs (181.45 kg)**
Speed: **25 mph (40 kph)**
Frame: **pine, spruce, ash, steel tube**
Covering: **paper**

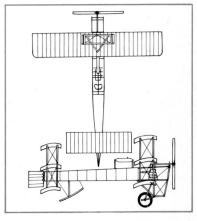

Ponzelli-Miller *Aerocurvo*

Aircraft: **Ponzelli-Miller Aerocurvo**
Manufacturer: **Franz Miller (Turin)**
Year: **1909**
Engine: **Miller 4-cylinder air-cooled in-line, 50 hp**
Wingspan: **23 ft (7 m)**
Length: **23 ft (7 m)**
Wing area: **236.8 sq ft (22 sq m)**
Weight: **551 lbs (250 kg)**

Italy entered European aviation late. Although the *Società Aeronautica Italiana* was founded at the beginning of the century, it was not until July 1908 that Italy witnessed its first flight by a heavier-than-air machine (with the flights of Léon Delagrange's Voisin in Turin). It was not until 1909 that the first planes which had been designed and built in Italy got into the air.

The first flight was made on January 13, 1909, by a triplane built in Turin by Aristide Faccioli. The plane crashed at the end of a hop-flight of a few dozen yards. About the same time the *Aerocurvo* made its debut. Another aviation enthusiast, Franz Miller from Messina, had established the first Italian aircraft factory in Turin. One of his first products was the *Aerocurvo*. Although this unusual plane, with its curved wings, was unsuccessful, it did help to arouse public interest in flying. The plane was designed in collaboration with Riccardo Ponzelli and built early in 1909. After a series of tests in Turin, it was taken in Brescia for the International Air Circuit. But the plane could not get off the ground. Only after modifications had been made and weight reduced did it manage to make a few 100-foot (30-m) hops at Mirafiori in 1910. The designers then moved on to other projects.

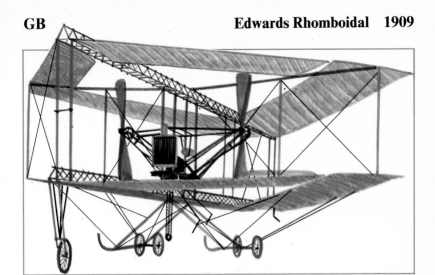

Edwards Rhomboidal

The Edwards Rhomboidal was one of the most unorthodox planes to appear during the early years of aviation in Great Britain. It got its name from the unusual structure of the two wing surfaces, rhomboidal in shape and biplane in configuration. The pilot, the engine, and the two propellers were in the middle. This machine never got off the ground. It represents a certain anachronistic tendency that developed in Great Britain around 1909 and 1910. A host of strange aircraft appeared on British airfields at the time. Fantastic and grotesque, these planes completely ignored the technical and structural principles that were already making possible the first triumphs of the 'classic' aeroplane and laying the basis for its future development.

The Rhomboidal was a failure in

Aircraft: **Edwards Rhomboidal**
Manufacturer: **Edwards**
Year: **1909**
Engine: **Humber 4-cylinder water-cooled inline, 50 hp**
Wingspan: **38 ft (11.58 m)**
Length: **48 ft (14.62 m)**
Wing area: **approx. 1,200 sq ft (111.48 sq m)**
Weight: **1,600 lbs (726 kg)**

tests carried out at Brooklands. Its structure was based on two triangular-section longitudinal frames supporting the wings, the engine, and the pilot. The two wings surfaces were linked by vertical struts braced by wires. Wires were also used as the 'spars' of the wings, stretched between the ends of the fuselage frames and four lateral, horizontal struts. The wings had a single canvas surface, kept rigid and curved by wooden battens inserted lengthwise, like those used for sails. The engine was mounted in the middle, in front of the pilot, and drove two propellers through transmission chains. A rudder was set above the upper wing, where it was useless.

Givaudan

Aircraft: **Givaudan**
Manufacturer: **Vermorel Compagnie**
Year: **1909**
Engine: **Vermorel 8-cylinder air-cooled inline V, 40 hp**
Length: **19 ft (5.79 m)**
Frame: **metal tube, wood**
Covering: **fabric**

Of the many projects carried out in France in 1909, in the wake of those of the great pioneers, Givaudan's was one of the most original. His plane never managed to get off the ground, but the designer's remarkable innovations in structure and aerodynamics aroused considerable interest. The plane was built in May 1909 at the Vermorel factory in Villefranche (Rhône). The aircraft had a cylindrical wing design, with the wing contours inserted into two concentric drums of the type invented by Lawrence Hargrave at the end of the nineteenth century. There were two cylinders – each made up of two concentric sections – set at the nose and tail of the plane. They were connected to each other by a framework of metal tubing. There was also a highly original control system, depending on the movement of the front cylinder, which could be moved in any direction since it was connected to the fuselage by a universal joint. The engine – an 8-cylinder air-cooled inline V Vermorel of 40 hp – was installed just behind the front cylinder and drove a propeller 7 feet 10.5 inches (2.4 m) in diameter, through a transmission that protruded outside the structure. The pilot sat behind the engine. The landing gear had four bicycle-type wheels, two attached to the rear cylinder and two to the forward part of the fuselage.

This original aircraft never got off the ground. It was one of many efforts made outside 'official' aviation and its teachings, and, for that very reason, was doomed to failure.

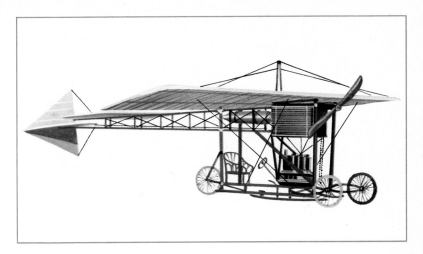

Blackburn Monoplane

Robert Blackburn, an English civil engineer, became a convert to aviation after seeing Wilbur Wright fly at Issy in 1908. Blackburn's first plane was designed in Paris, but as soon as the plans were completed, he returned to Great Britain and built the aircraft in a Leeds workshop, with the help of two mechanics. It was a high-wing monoplane, so strongly built as to merit its nickname, the 'heavy monoplane'. It was fairly solid, especially at the front. A metal structure suspended beneath the rectangular wings housed the engine, the three-wheeled undercarriage, and the pilot's seat. The wicker seat was set on a sliding base, so that the pilot could move his weight to control the plane in the longitudinal axis by shifting the centre of gravity. The engine drove the propeller above it by means of a transmission chain, and the

Aircraft: **Blackburn Monoplane**
Manufacturer: **Blackburn Aeroplane Co.**
Year: **1909**
Engine: **Green 4-cylinder water-cooled inline, 35 hp**
Wingspan: **30 ft (9.14 m)**
Length: **26 ft (7.92 m)**
Height: **9 ft 6 in (2.9 m)**
Wing area: **170 sq ft (15.79 sq m)**
Weight: **800 lbs (363 kg)**
Speed: **60.3 mph (97 kph)**
Frame: **spruce, ash, steel tube**
Covering: **cotton**

fuel tank was housed above the pilot's head. The cruciform empennage had a tailplane, elevators, and a triangular rudder. The trailing edges of the wings could be warped for lateral control.

The plane was tested at Marske, on the Yorkshire coast, in the spring of 1909. It managed to take off after some taxiing tests: Blackburn got off the ground, but lost control of the plane when he tried to make a turn. The 'heavy monoplane' crashed into the sand dunes and was never repaired.

71

Mortimer and Vaughan Safety

Aircraft: **Safety**
Manufacturer: **Mortimer and Vaughan**
Year: **1910**
Wingspan: —
Length: —
Height: —
Wing area: —
Weight: —
Frame: **wood, metal tube**
Covering: **fabric**

If the Safety had managed to fly, it would certainly have gone down in history as the first flying saucer! But the Safety biplane never got off the ground under its own power, although there are pictures of it suspended from cables. This fantastic flying machine was designed and built by Mortimer and Vaughan, two English enthusiasts from Edgware in Middlesex. Carried away by the general excitement about aviation, they were caught up in the eccentric craze to build fantastic aircraft that invaded England in 1909–10.

The distinguishing feature of the Safety was its two pairs of semi-circular wings, which gave the plane its remarkable doughnut shape. The double lifting surfaces were linked by a series of vertical struts and were based on the two ends of the fuselage.

The almost completely enclosed fuselage was rectangular in section, and the forward part was sharply tapered. The landing gear had four wheels attached to supports under the fuselage. Propulsion was to come from three four-bladed propellers, one in the nose and the other two inside the wing-circle, on the leading edge of the rear wings. The Safety was tested without success, and was finally wrecked and burned. Mortimer and Vaughan did not give up. In 1911 they built a second, modified aircraft, which turned out to be as impractical as the first.

De Havilland Biplane (No. 1)

Geoffrey de Havilland, who was to become one of the world's most famous designers and builders of aeroplanes, began building his first aircraft in 1908. He was helped by a friend, F. T. Hearle, and they turned out a fairly original-looking biplane. De Havilland also designed the engine, a four-cylinder horizontally opposed unit generating 45 hp. This biplane was completed early in 1910 and taken to Crux Easton for testing. The plane's first and only flight took place in April. The machine, with de Havilland at the controls, managed to leave the ground, but after flying about 100 feet the left wing collapsed and the plane crashed. The engine was saved and installed in de Havilland's second biplane. This new one was so good that the British War Office bought it in December 1910 as the F.E.1.

Aircraft: **De Havilland Biplane (No. 1)**
Manufacturer: **De Havilland-Hearle**
Year: **1910**
Engine: **Iris-built de Havilland water-cooled 4-cylinder horizontally opposed, 45 hp**
Wingspan: **36 ft (10.97 m)**
Length: **29 ft (8.84 m)**
Height: **9 ft 10 in (3 m)**
Wing area: **408 sq ft (37.9 sq m)**
Weight: **850 lbs (386 kg)**
Frame: **pine, spruce, ash**
Covering: **cotton**

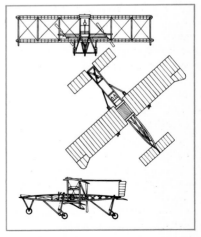

Wright Model B

With the universal success of the Model A biplane, it was not until 1910 that Wilbur and Orville Wright decided to make radical changes in their design. The new plane, designated Model B, was the first Wright biplane without forward elevators, these now being placed more conventionally to the rear. The earlier skids were replaced by a four-wheeled landing gear. This aircraft won immediate acclaim, and two planes were even ordered by the United States Army. A smaller single-seat version, the EX, was also developed. Other variations were the racing Model R, or 'Roadster', otherwise known as the 'Baby Wright', and the smaller 'Baby Grand'. Orville flew the Baby Grand in the Belmont Park meeting in 1910, reaching speeds between 71 and 75 mph (115 and 120 kph).

Aircraft: **Wright Model B**
Manufacturer: **Wright Brothers**
Year: **1910**
Engine: **Wright 4-cylinder water-cooled inline 30 hp**
Wingspan: **39 ft (11.89 m)**
Length: **31 ft (9.45 m)**
Wing area: **500 sq ft (46.45 sq m)**
Weight: **1,250 lbs (567 kg)**
Speed: **46.6 mph (75 kph)**
Frame: **spruce, ash**
Covering: **cotton**

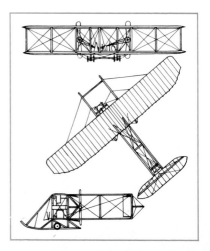

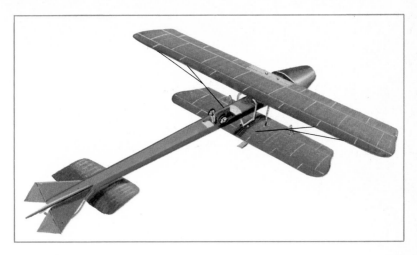

Coanda

The Coanda was the first 'jet' plane in history, a forerunner of modern aviation. It never managed to fly, but was superb evidence of the talent of its young designer, the Romanian Henri Coanda, who was only 24 when he built the plane. It was presented at the *Salon de l'Aéronautique* in Paris in October 1910. Through a series of multiple gears, the plane's piston engine drove a centrifugal blower installed in the forward part of the fuselage. Apart from this revolutionary form of propulsion, the plane also impressed those who saw it with its elegance and its structural features. Struts and bracing wires were reduced to a minimum, and for the first time, a plane was completely covered with wood. The chief reason it never got off the ground was the weak thrust supplied by the blower.

Aircraft: **Coanda**
Manufacturer: **Henri Coanda**
Year: **1910**
Engine: **Clerget 4-cylinder water-cooled inline, 50 hp**
Wingspan: **33 ft 1.5 in (10.08 m)**
Length: **39 ft 7.25 in (12.7 m)**
Height: **9 ft 0.25 in (2.74 m)**
Wing area: **344.45 sq ft (32 sq m)**
Weight: **926 lbs (420 kg)**
Frame: **steel tube**
Covering: **plywood**

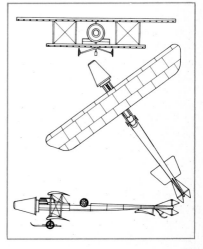

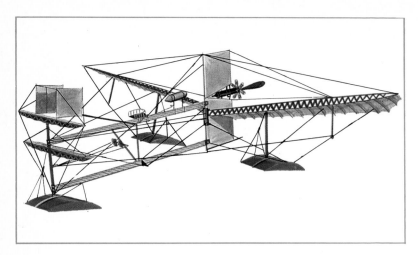

Fabre *Hydravion*

The French engineer Henri Fabre was the father of the seaplane. While every-one else in Europe and America was working on machines that could take off and land again on solid ground, Fabre set out in 1909 to develop a seaplane. His first model failed to rise from the water, but his second plane succeeded on March 28, 1910, in the port of La Mède. It flew about 1,640 feet (500 m) at an altitude of about seven feet (2 m) and made a satisfactory landing. Fabre's *Hydravion* looked extremely fragile and clumsy, but it was the first seaplane in aviation history, appearing a year before Glenn Curtiss's seaplane. Fabre continued his efforts until March 1911, when his seaplane crashed during landing. He lacked funds to continue, and from then on he devoted his talents to the design and building of floats.

Aircraft: **Fabre Hydravion**
Manufacturer: **Henri Fabre**
Year: **1910**
Engine: **Gnome 7-cylinder air-cooled rotary, 50 hp**
Wingspan: **45 ft 11 in (14 m)**
Length: **27 ft 10.5 in (8.5 m)**
Height: **12 ft 1.75 in (3.66 m)**
Wing area: **182.99 sq ft (17 sq m)**
Weight: **1,047 lbs (475 kg)**
Speed: **55 mph (89 kph)**
Frame: **ash**
Covering: **cotton and plywood (for the floats)**

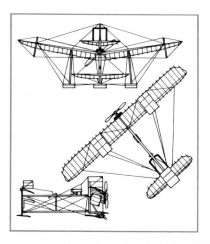

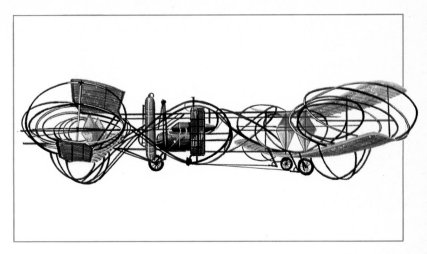

Seddon

Aircraft: **Seddon**
Manufacturer: **Accles and Pollock**
Year: **1910**
Engine: **Two N.E.C. water-cooled inlines, 65 hp each**
Wing area: **1,000 sq ft (93 sq m)**
Weight: **2,600 lbs (1,178 kg)**
Frame: **steel tube**
Covering: **fabric**

Like the Edwards Rhomboidal, the Seddon was another of those freak flying machines that appeared in Great Britain during 1909–10. The designers of this complicated steel-tube structure were Lieutenant J. W. Seddon, R.N. and A. G. Hackett, and they had the plane built in 1910 at the Accles and Pollock works in Oldbury. The machine was basically a tandem biplane. The front wing surfaces also served as elevators, for longitudinal control, while the rear ones were purely for lift. A pair of rudders was set between both the fore and aft sets of wings. The fuselage, which housed the engine, propellers, passengers, and landing gear, and also connected the wings, was a fantastic structure of steel tubing formed into hooplike, geodetic shapes. The wing struts were metal hoops. Some 2,000 feet (600 m) of steel

tubing, weighing almost a ton (1,016 kg), were used to build this machine. Power was supplied by a pair of 65-hp N.E.C. engines driving two large Beedle-type tractor propellers. The plane was designed to carry five passengers plus the pilot.

The plane was completed late 1910 and taken to Dunstall Park, Wolverhampton, for testing (the airfield of the Midland Aero Club). It failed to fly and was broken up. Its only claim to fame, and a dubious one at that, was that for some time the Seddon was considered the world's largest aeroplane.

Dunne D.5

As soon as John William Dunne, an officer in the British Army, became interested in aviation, he concentrated on the problem of inherent aircraft stability. He made several attempts, at the Farnborough Balloon Factory, to give concrete form to his ideals in machines with arrow-shaped wings and no tails. The first 'flying wing' plane in history that managed to fly was the Dunne D.5, built by Short Brothers in 1910. Test flights began at Eastchurch on March 11. In May, the D.5 flew two miles (3.22 km) with such perfect stability that the pilot was able to remain aloft without touching the controls.

Test flights continued throughout 1911 and repeatedly demonstrated the soundness of the designer's theories. The D.5 was destroyed in an accident, but was rebuilt in 1912 as the D.8.

Aircraft: **Dunne D.5**
Manufacturer **Short Brothers**
Year: **1910**
Engine: **Green 4-cylinder water-cooled inline, 60 hp**
Wingspan: **46 ft (14.02 m)**
Length: **20 ft 4.5 in (6.21 m)**
Height: **11 ft 6 in (3.5 m)**
Wing area: **527 sq ft (48.96 sq m)**
Weight: **1,550 lbs (70 kg)**
Speed: **45 mph (72 kph)**
Frame: **spruce, ash, pine, steel tube**
Covering: **linen**

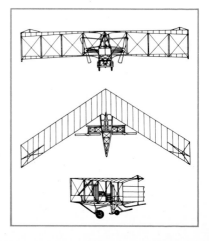

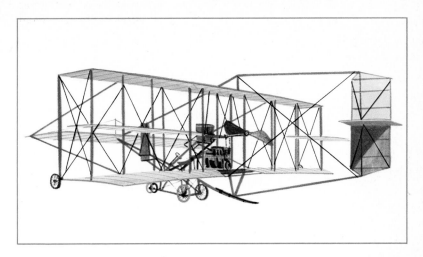

Cody Michelin Cup Biplane

Samuel Franklin Cody, an American expatriate, made the first powered heavier-than-air flight in Great Britain, at Farnborough on October 16, 1908. The plane was a Wright-type biplane, built by Cody at the Balloon Factory and designated the British Army Aeroplane No. 1. After more than a year of test flights, Cody decided to build another biplane, to compete for the first Michelin Cup. It resembled his first machine, but had improved controls and was equipped with ailerons. Before the competition, Cody replaced the original 60-hp Green engine with an E.N.V. of equal power and set British records for endurance and distance: 94.5 miles (152.08 km) in 2 hours 24 minutes. On December 31, 1910, he won the Michelin Cup: 185.5 miles (298.47 km) in 4 hours 47 minutes.

Aircraft: **Cody Michelin Cup Biplane**
Manufacturer: **Cody**
Year: **1910**
Engine: **E.N.V. 8-cylinder water-cooled inline V, 60 hp**
Wingspan: **46 ft (14.02 m)**
Length: **38 ft 6 in (11.73 m)**
Height: **13 ft (3.96 m)**
Wing area: **640 sq ft (59.46 m)**
Weight (empty): **2,200 lbs (996 kg)**
Weight (loaded): **2,950 lbs (1,138 kg)**
Speed: **65 mph (105 kph)**
Frame: **spruce, bamboo**
Covering: **fabric**

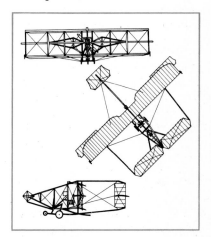

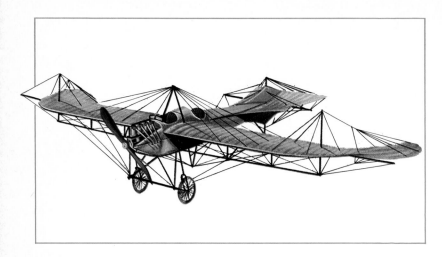

Etrich *Taube*

The *Taube* (Dove) monoplane, which
saw military service at the beginning
of the First World War, was built in
1910 from the plans of the Austrian
engineer Igo Etrich. After extensive
studies in aerodynamics, Etrich designed a plane whose wing planform
closely resembled that of a bird. The
Taube was a tractor monoplane, the
basic formula for which was obviously
inspired by the planes of Vuia and
Blériot. The *Taube* was immensely
successful. After his first flights Etrich
granted construction rights to the
Rumpler factory in Johannisthal, but
later gave up his rights in the plane
altogether. Ten different firms then
began building *Taubes* in various
shapes and sizes. The success of the
Taube can be seen in the enormous –
for that period – number of examples
built: some 500.

Aircraft: **Etrich Taube**
Manufacturers: **various**
Year: **1910**
Engine: **Mercedes 6-cylinder water-
    cooled inline, 100 hp**
Wingspan: **47 ft 1 in (14.35 m)**
Length: **32 ft 3.75 in (9.85 m)**
Height: **10 ft 4 in (3.15 m)**
Wing area: **418 sq ft (38.84 sq m)**
Weight: **1,918 lbs (870 kg)**
Speed: **71.5 mph (115 kph)**
Frame: **spruce, steel tube**
Covering: **aluminium, plywood, cotton**

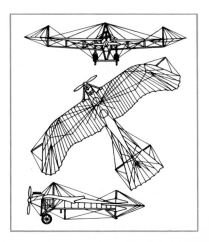

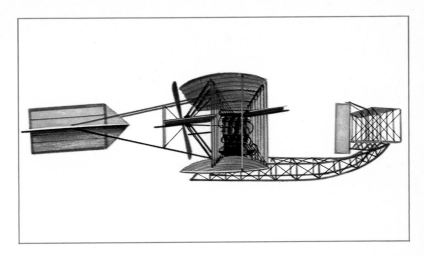

Short No. 3

The Short No. 3 was designed as an improved version of a successful plane, but it never managed to get off the ground. The third plane built by the Short brothers (Horace, Eustace and Oswald) represented an unusual case of technological regression. Its immediate predecessor was the Short No. 2, a Wright-type biplane that J. T. C. Moore-Brabazon flew on October 30, 1909, to win the £1,000 *Daily Mail* prize for the first circular flight of one mile (1.61 km) made in Great Britain. The Short No. 3 was designed and built in the wake of this success and was exhibited at the Olympia Aero Show in 1910. The 35-hp engine drove a single pusher propeller. (The two earlier Short models had had two propellers.) And the plane had a retractable landing gear. Nevertheless the plane failed to get off the ground.

Aircraft: **Short No. 3**
Manufacturer: **Short Brothers**
Year: **1910**
Engine: **Green 4-cylinder water-cooled inline, 35 hp**
Wingspan: **31 ft 8 in (9.65 m)**
Length: **31 ft (9.45 m)**
Height: **8 ft 8 in (2.64 m)**
Wing area: **282 sq ft (26.2 sq m)**
Weight (empty): **655 lbs (297 kg)**
Weight (loaded): **857 lbs (389 kg)**
Frame: **spruce**
Covering: **rubberized cotton**

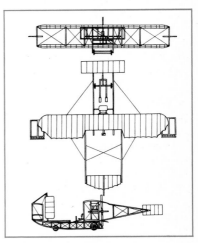

Fokker *Spin*

Spin is the Dutch word for spider. This is the name which has been given to all the planes that Anthony Fokker, the great aircraft designer, produced between 1910 and 1913, although properly only the third and later craft were *Spins*. This series of planes used the same basic format, with constant improvements. Fokkers were used in the civilian and military flying schools of the time. In the spring of 1911, Anthony Fokker himself learned to fly and qualified for his pilot's licence at the controls of his second *Spin*.

Although Fokker only became world-famous during the First World War, when he was credited with the design of several outstanding fighting planes, the *Spin* made an important contribution to the early success of the 'Flying Dutchman'. This pioneering period saw his initial trials and risky experiments carried out almost clandestinely in order to avoid the sarcastic comments of his critics.

Anthony Fokker found his aeronautical vocation in 1908, when Wilbur Wright took his Model A to France. Two years later, in Wiesbaden, Germany, Fokker went into partnership with another aviation enthusiast, Franz von Daum. Together they built Fokker's first plane, the plane which is commonly called the *Spin* I. It was a monoplane, with a 50-hp Argus engine. The young Fokker managed to make a few 100-yard (100-m) 'hops' in December. While Fokker was in Holland for the Christmas holidays, von Daum tried his hand at flying the plane himself. The plane crashed into a tree and was demolished. Fokker managed to salvage the engine and, with the help of Jacob Goedecker, a boat-builder who had turned to aviation, built a second aeroplane. The *Spin* II was a great improvement over its predecessor: structural changes were made, ailerons were fitted, and the plane could carry two people. Flying this plane, Fokker

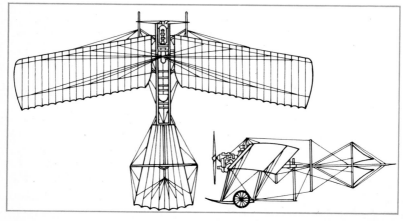

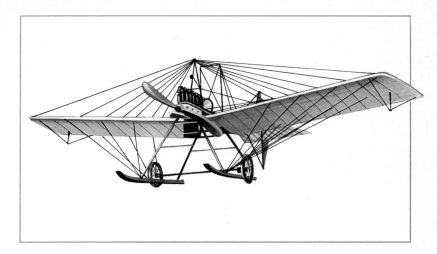

earned his pilot's licence on May 16, 1911. A month later, the *Spin* II crashed, again with von Daum at the controls.

And again Fokker built a new plane. He ended his partnership with von Daum and went into business with Jacob Goedecker, with whom he produced the third *Spin* in August 1911. The *Spin* III was smaller but superior to its predecessor. Fokker decided to take it to Holland and give exhibition flights in Haarlem. The success of these flights and later flights in Germany encouraged the young Dutchman to start building aircraft commercially. He ended his partnership with Goedecker, and early in 1912 he founded the Fokker *Aeroplanbau G.m.b.H.* at Johannisthal, near Berlin. This was the official start of his career.

New variations of the *Spin* were turned out, with structural modifications and different engines. The

Aircraft: **Fokker Spin III**
Manufacturer: **Anthony Fokker**
Year: **1911**
Engine: **Argus 4-cylinder water-cooled inline, 50 hp**
Wingspan: **36 ft 1 in (11 m)**
Length: **25 ft 5 in (7.75 m)**
Height: **9 ft 10 in (3 m)**
Wing area: **236.8 sq ft (22 sq m)**
Weight: **882 lbs (400 kg)**
Speed: **56 mph (90 kph)**
Frame: **bamboo, ash, steel tube**
Covering: **cotton**

second 1913 variation had a faired fuselage. Two of them were sold to the German military authorities, who designated the plane the M.1. Most of Fokker's planes were used at that time for training, both civilian and military. The flying school that Fokker founded in Schwerin used them for a long time, and many German aviation enthusiasts learned to fly in the various *Spins*, including many of the men who were to pilot the immortal Fokker fighters during the First World War.

Curtiss A-1

After becoming a success in the world of aviation with the 1909 Golden Flyer, Glenn Hammond Curtiss spent a number of years developing seaplanes. The results he achieved were so outstanding that Curtiss has gone down in history as the first major designer, builder and pilot of seaplanes.

In 1908 Curtiss began testing a seaplane version of his first plane, the June Bug, built for the Aerial Experiment Association of which he was one of the founders. Two years went by before he succeeded in making a take-off from water. The date was January 26, 1911. The place was San Diego, California. The plane was a modified Golden Flyer equipped with a central float and two stabilizers under the wingtips. The plane was frequently modified after its first successful tests, and in its final form was ordered by the United States Navy, which designated

it the A-1. The US Navy made up its mind after Curtiss flew his seaplane on February 17, 1911, from a naval base on the coast to the armoured cruiser *Pennsylvania*, anchored off San Diego. In later demonstrations Curtiss showed that a seaplane could easily operate from a warship.

The purchase of the Curtiss A-1 by the U.S. Navy was followed by a period of intense activity, aimed at developing and broadening co-operation between ship and plane. The first US Navy pilot was Lieutenant Theodore G. Ellyson, who was trained at the Curtiss Flying School in Hammondsport. Ellyson made numerous test flights, the most important of which were concerned with perfecting launching techniques. Various systems were tried, including that of catapulting the plane with a compressed-air launcher developed for torpedoes. During these tests El-

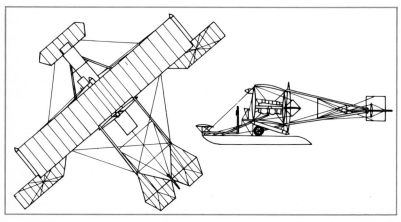

lyson set several records, including a flight of 112 miles (180 km) from Annapolis, Maryland, to Milford Haven, Virginia, with one passenger on board, in 2 hours 2 minutes.

The Curtiss A-1, which was converted into an amphibious plane by adding two retractable wheels to the floats, was followed by three other models, the A-2, A-3, and A-4, each incorporating minor improvements. The A-2 built as a landplane. In October 1912, the plane was modified, and a superstructure was added to the central float that had been fitted, making the A-2 a flying boat. On June 13, 1913 the A-3 won the American seaplane altitude record, reaching a height of 6,200 feet (1,890 m). In the meantime, Glenn Curtiss had given up the float formula and had begun working on a central-hulled seaplane (flying boat) that was to set the pattern for most future developments in the field.

The Curtiss seaplane's history-

Aircraft: **Curtiss A-1**
Manufacturer: **Curtiss Aeroplane and Motor Co., Inc.**
Year: **1911**
Engine: **Curtiss 8-cylinder water-cooled inline V, 75 hp**
Wingspan: **37 ft (11.28 m)**
Length: **28 ft 7 in (8.71 m)**
Height: **9 ft 4 in (2.84 m)**
Wing area: **286 sq ft (26.57 sq m)**
Weight: **1,575 lbs (714 kg)**
Speed: **approx. 65 mph (105 kph)**
Frame: **spruce, bamboo, steel tube**
Covering: **rubberized fabric, wood**

making flight of January 26, 1911, was not without precedents. Attempts had been made in Europe since the beginning of the century. The first successful water take-off was made on June 6, 1905, by Gabriel Voisin on the Seine in Paris. Voisin's aircraft was not powered, but was rather a float-glider towed into the air by a motorboat. The first independent water take-off was made by Henri Fabre on March 29, 1910.

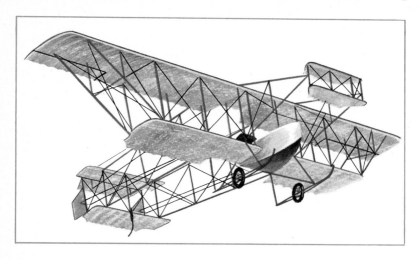

Asteria No. 3

The first warplane designed and built in Italy was the Asteria No. 2. The Italian government bought it in October 1911, and sent it to Benghazi for operations against the Turks. The plane was designed and built by Francesco Darbesio, who founded the *Società Aeronautica* Asteria in Turin in 1909. From what was basically a Farman-type biplane, Darbesio and his partner Origoni developed a slightly larger model, with pilot and passenger in a small nacelle. This aircraft, called the Asteria No. 3, did a great deal of flying at the flying school Darbesio founded in Mirafiori. On September 20, 1911, it set an Italian endurance record. In far from ideal weather conditions, pilot and passenger managed to stay in the air for 2 hours 2 minutes 29 seconds, a very creditable effort.

Aircraft: **Asteria No. 3**
Manufacturer: **Società Aeronautica Asteria**
Year: **1911**
Engine: **Gnome 7-cylinder air-cooled rotary, 50 hp**
Wingspan: **49 ft 3 in (15 m)**
Length: **34 ft 5 in (10.5 m)**
Wing area: **516.67 sq ft (48 sq m)**
Frame: **wood, steel tube**
Covering: **fabric**

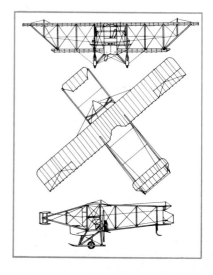

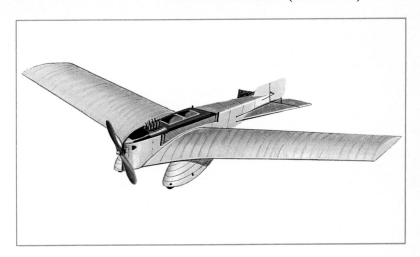

Antoinette Latham

Although the *Monobloc* monoplane that the Antoinette company built for Hubert Latham never managed to fly, it anticipated technical and structural innovations that were adopted years later. Latham ordered the plane, known as the *Monobloc*, for the 1911 *Concours Militaire* in Reims. It was a three-seater monoplane, with the crew accommodated in a completely enclosed fuselage. To obtain maximum performance the aerodynamic characteristics of the aircraft were developed in every possible way. The wings were cantilevered, with internal control cables, and the landing gear was faired. Unfortunately the *Monobloc*, with its 50-hp engine, was underpowered and only managed to get off the ground for a few feet at most. Attempts were made to modify the plane but met with no success.

Aircraft: **Antoinette Latham (Monobloc)**
Manufacturer: **Société Antoinette**
Year: **1911**
Engine: **Antoinette 8-cylinder water-cooled inline V, 50 hp**
Wingspan: **52 ft 2 in (15.9 m)**
Length: **37 ft 8 in (11.50 m)**
Height: **8 ft 2 in (2.5 m)**
Wing area: **602.78 sq ft (56 sq m)**
Weight: **2,976 lbs (1,350 kg)**
Frame: **ash, steel tube**
Covering: **aluminium, linen**

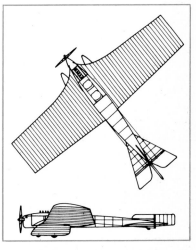

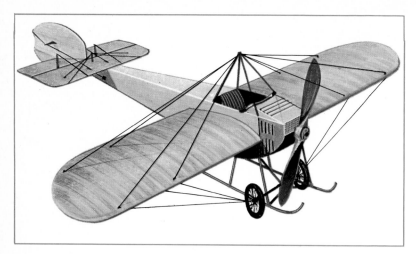

Chiribiri No. 5

The aircraft Antonio Chiribiri produced in Turin between 1911 and 1913 were among the first monoplanes designed and built in Italy. The No. 5 was the last of the series and was, in a certain sense, the peak of the designer's output. The No. 5 made its debut early in July, and from the very first tests, made by Maurizio Ramassotto, it demonstrated excellent qualities. The Chiribiri No. 5 was a mid-wing monoplane. The fuselage was entirely covered with canvas and could accommodate two persons. Chiribiri himself designed and built the engine. After taking part in a campaign to promote air-mindedness in Italy and operations the Mirafiori flying school, the aircraft was tested at the 1913 military competition, where it failed to secure orders despite its good performance.

Aircraft: **Chiribiri No. 5**
Manufacturer: **A. Chiribiri & Compagnia**
Year: **1912**
Engine: **Chiribiri 4-cylinder water-cooled inline, 50 hp**
Wingspan: **31 ft (9.45 m)**
Length: **24 ft (7.32 m)**
Wing area: **226 sq ft (21 sq m)**
Weight: **772 lbs (350 kg)**
Speed: **approx. 56 mph (90 kph)**
Frame: **wood, steel tube**
Covering: **fabric**

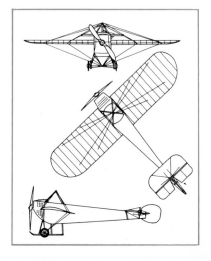

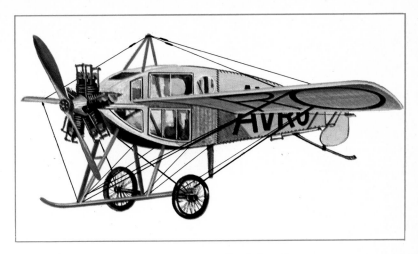

Avro F

Alliot Verdon Roe, who had founded
A. V. Roe & Co. in 1910, wanted to
build a plane in which the passengers
could be completely protected from
the elements. This project resulted in
two planes, a monoplane and a biplane. Both aircraft had completely
enclosed fuselages with celluloid vision
panels for the pilot. The monoplane,
the Avro F, was the first to be built
and also the world's first cabin aircraft
to fly. Successful tests took place on
May 1, 1912, at Brooklands, although
critics had predicted that the pilot's
visibility would be totally obscured by
oil and exhaust fumes from the engine.
Successful flights continued until, on
September 13, the Avro F was damaged beyond repair.

The biplane Avro G was the second
British aircraft definitely known to
have recovered from a spin.

Aircraft: **Avro F**
Manufacturer: **A. V. Roe & Co.**
Year: **1912**
Engine: **Viale 5-cylinder radial, 40 hp**
Wingspan: **29 ft (8.53 m)**
Length: **23 ft (7.01 m)**
Height: **7 ft 6 in (2.31 m)**
Wing area: **158 sq ft (14.68 sq m)**
Weight (loaded): **800 lbs (363 kg)**
Speed: **65 mph (105 kph)**
Frame: **spruce, ash, steel tube**
Covering: **aluminium, linen**

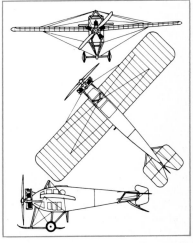

Breguet III

With the Breguet III, the tractor bi-plane attained its definitive form, the basic formula for all the planes the great French designer was to build. Until 1914 Louis Breguet's planes were simply developments of this original biplane. The aircraft attracted great interest chiefly because of its military possibilities. In 1912 alone, the French Army ordered 32 Breguet IIIs, the British Army ordered five, the Italian Army bought three, and Sweden took one. France and Great Britain used the plane extensively in the years just before the First World War, and even in the early months of the conflict.

Louis Breguet first became interested in aviation when he was attending the *Ecole Superieure de l'Electricité*. With his brother Jacques and an engineer named Charles Richet, he built a 'gyroplane' in 1907. A kind of helicopter with four large vertical propellers driven by an An-toinette engine, the gyroplane managed to rise a few inches from the ground on August 24. After a series of gyroplane projects (the model 2-*bis* rose just over 13 feet (4 m) into the air on July 22, 1908), Louis Breguet founded the *Société des Ateliers d'Aviation* Breguet-Richet and turned to fixed-wing planes. He produced his first biplane in 1909. It was an influential plane for, unlike the Goupy II biplane, it managed to fly. Although it only flew short distances at the Reims air meeting in 1909, it attracted a great deal of interest. The Breguet I also had some highly original technical and structural features, such as the wide use of metal components. The wing structure and struts were made of steel tubing. Wing-warping, in concert or differentially, was used for longitudinal and lateral control. The plane was seriously damaged while landing after its third flight at Reims, but it gave Louis Breguet some useful ex-

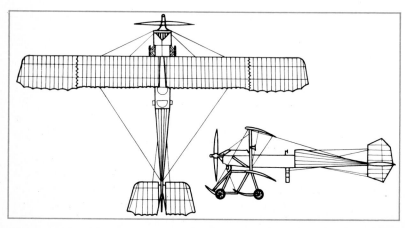

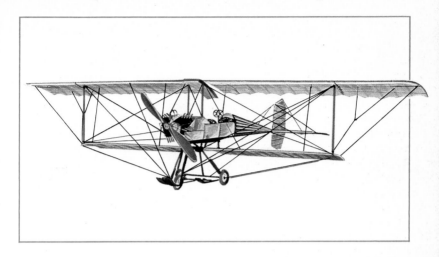

perience for designing the next model, from which the Breguet III was developed.

The designer used even more metal in his model III biplane. Apart from the steel-tube structure, Breguet used sheet aluminium to cover the front part of the fuselage. This gave the plane such an unusual look that Royal Navy pilots quickly nicknamed it the 'Tin Whistle'. (It also gave off metallic whistling noises in flight.) Different engines were installed in various models of this plane, each of which gave rise to a variant model with its own name. The most common engines were the 60-hp Renault (an air-cooled 8-cylinder V), the 50- or 80-hp Gnome rotary, and the Canton-Unné 80- or 110-hp 7-cylinder water-cooled radial. Some Breguets with Canton-Unné engines were still in service in a French squadron in August 1914.

The last biplane in the series – the Breguet X – came out in 1914. A

Aircraft: **Breguet III**
Manufacturer: **Louis Breguet**
Year: **1912**
Engine: **Canton-Unné 7-cylinder water-cooled radial, 80 hp**
Wingspan: **44 ft 8 in (13.61 m)**
Length: **29 ft (8.84 m)**
Height: **9 ft 10 in (2.99 m)**
Wing area: **387.5 sq ft (36 sq m)**
Weight: **2,095 lbs (949 kg)**
Speed: **62 mph (100 kph)**
Endurance: **7 hours**
Crew: **2-3**
Frame: **ash, steel tube**
Covering: **aluminium, linen**

tougher plane with a more powerful engine, the Breguet X saw extensive service in the first months of the war. Breguet himself flew a model X in a reconnaissance flight to observe enemy troop movements on the eve of the battle of the Marne, in September 1914. This exploit earned Breguet the *Croix de Guerre*.

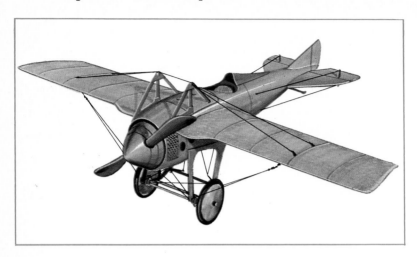

Deperdussin 'Monocoque' racer
Deperdussin 'Monocoque' floatplane racer

Aircraft: **Deperdussin 'Monocoque' racer**
Manufacturer: **Société pour les Appareils Deperdussin**
Year: **1912**
Engine: **Gnome 14-cylinder air-cooled rotary, 160 hp**
Wingspan: **21 ft 9.75 in (6.65 m)**
Length: **20 ft (6.1 m)**
Height: **7 ft 6.5 in (2.3 m)**
Wing area: **104 sq ft (9.66 sq m)**
Weight: **1,350 lbs (612 kg)**
Speed: **130 mph (209 kph)**
Frame: **ash**
Covering: **plywood, linen**

The first plane to break the 200 kph (124 mph) 'barrier', and the first Schneider Trophy winner, was Armand Deperdussin's monoplane. It was the 'speed phenomenon' of the years before the First World War. The plane was developed early in 1912 by Louis Béchereau, the designer for the *Société pour les Appareils* Deperdussin. Béchereau worked from an idea by Swedish engineer Ruchonnet, and developed a streamlined monocoque plywood fuselage with a large spinner. To achieve maximum power two Gnome rotaries were mounted on a common crankshaft. The first noteworthy achievement of this plane was the 1912 Gordon Bennett Cup, which it won with a

speed of 108.1 mph (174.01 kph). The plane won the cup again the following year, on September 29, 1913 in Reims, Maurice Prévost achieving an average of 124.6 mph (200.5 kph). During this race the plane beat the world speed record three times, and its maximum speed was 126.7 mph (203.85 kph).

A few months earlier, in April 1913, Prévost had won another exceptional victory at the controls of the floatplane version of the Deperdussin monoplane: first place in the first race for the Schneider Trophy in Monaco,

with an average speed of 45.75 mph (73.63 kph). The low speed was due to the fact that the judges made Prévost repeat his take-off and about six miles (10 km) of the course because of a supposed violation of the rules. This Deperdussin victory was the only time in the history of the Schneider Trophy (1912–31) that France won a race.

Aircraft: **Deperdussin 'Monocoque' floatplane racer**
Year: **1913**
Engine: **Gnome 14-cylinder air-cooled rotary, 160 hp**
Wingspan: **44 ft 3 in (13.49 m)**
Length: **32 ft 9 in (9.98 m)**
Wing area: **301 sq ft (27.96 sq m)**
Weight (loaded): **2,649 lbs (1,200 kg)**
Speed: **approx. 75 mph (120 kph)**
Crew: **2**
Frame: **ash**
Covering: **plywood, linen**

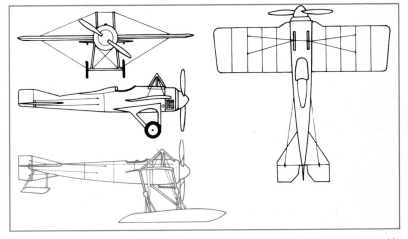

Sopwith Tabloid

A specially modified Sopwith Tabloid was the winner of the second Scheider Trophy race, in 1914. The modifications consisted of the installation of two floats and a more powerful engine. On April 20, 1914, at Monaco, Howard Pixton flew an average of 86.9 mph (139.6 kph). In two extra laps, he reached 92 mph (148 kph), establishing a new seaplane speed record. Thus the Sopwith biplane had its revenge on the Deperdussin monoplane and gave Great Britain its first major international success in aviation.

The special version of this plane prepared for Britain's first appearance at the Schneider Trophy was not substantially different from the model that had appeared the previous autumn. The land version of the Tabloid was designed by T. O. M. Sopwith and F. Sigrist, as a demonstration and racing aircraft. It was built in great secrecy, and preliminary tests were made at Brooklands in autumn 1913. These were followed by the official evaluation tests, and the plane immediately demonstrated its speed and manoeuvrability.

At the Royal Aircraft Factory at Farnborough, where the tests were conducted, the Tabloid reached a top speed of 92 mph (148 kph) in horizontal flight and showed a rate of climb in the order of 1,200 feet per minute (365.75 metres per minute). The same day, November 29, test pilot Harry Hawker flew the plane to Hendon, where one of the popular Saturday air meetings was being held. The new Sopwith was seen by more than 50,000 spectators, and flew two low-altitude laps round the course at more than 87 mph (140 kph). After that, the plane was ordered in large numbers by the

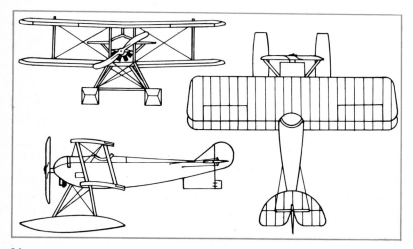

army and the navy as a single-seater reconnaissance aircraft.

Then the Sopwith company readied one of its single-seaters for the upcoming Schneider Trophy race. Since the race was restricted to seaplanes, the aircraft had to be modified. The landing gear was removed, and a large central float was installed in its place. The 100-hp Gnome engine was also modified for the occasion. The single float did not stand up to tests, the plane capsizing. There was very little time left before the race, so the Sopwith designers decided to slice the original float in half to make two new ones. This time flight and landing tests on the Thames were successful, and the Tabloid was sent off to Monaco on April 8, 1914. The final modification before the race was the installation of a better propeller. The rest is history.

Back in England after the race, the floats were removed at Sopwith's factory at Kingston-on-Thames, and a V-

Aircraft: **Sopwith Tabloid**
Manufacturer: **Sopwith Aviation Co. Ltd.**
Year: **1914**
Engine: **Gnome 9-cylinder air-cooled rotary, 100 hp**
Wingspan: **25 ft 6 in (7.77 m)**
Length: **20 ft 4 in (6.2 m)**
Height: **8 ft 5 in (2.57 m)**
Wing area: **241.3 sq ft (22.42 sq m)**
Weight (empty): **730 lbs (331 kg)**
Weight (loaded): **1,120 lbs (508 kg)**
Speed: **92 mph (148 kph)**
Frame: **spruce, pine**
Covering: **aluminium, linen**

strut landing gear was installed. Now the plane was ready for R. H. Barnwell to fly at the 1914 Aerial Derby. But because of poor visibility the plane did not complete the race. That was the end of the Tabloid's racing career. War broke out, and the Tabloid served as a reconnaissance plane during the first months of the conflict, when its speed and general handiness became very useful military assets indeed.

1908 A.E.A. Red Wing (USA) – Wingspan: 43 ft (13.1 m) – Wing area: 387.5 sq ft (36 sq m) – Weight: 385 lbs (174.5 kg) – Engine: Curtiss 8-cylinder, 30 hp. The first plane of the Aerial Experiment Association. Designed by Lieut. T. E. Selfridge, it was tested twice on Lake Keukba (near Hammondsport, N.Y.) on March 12, 1908. Before it crashed during a landing, it managed to 'hop' 319 feet (97 m).

1908 A.E.A. Silver Dart (USA) – Wingspan: 49 ft 1 in (14.96 m) – Wing area: 420 sq ft (39.02 sq m) – Weight: 860 lbs (390 kg) – Engine: Curtiss 8-cylinder, 50 hp. The fourth plane of the A.E.A., it flew for the first time on February 23, 1909, at Baddeck Bay in Nova Scotia, where it covered 2,400 feet (800 m). The designer-pilot was a Canadian, J. A. D. McCurdy.

1909 Curtiss Gold Bug (USA) – Wingspan: 28 ft 9 in (8.76 m) – Wing area: 258 sq ft (23.76 sq m) – Weight: 552 lbs (250 kg) – Engine: Curtiss 4-cylinder, 30 hp. Built in spring 1909 for the Aeronautic Society of New York, this was Glenn Curtiss's first independent design. On July 17 the plane made a nonstop flight of about 25 miles (40 km) and became the direct rival of the Wright planes.

1909 Blériot XII (F) – Wingspan: 32 ft 10.5 in (10 m) – Wing area: 237 sq ft (22 sq m) – Weight: 1,368 lbs (620 kg) – Engine: E.N.V. 8-cylinder, 35 hp. This plane was specially designed by Louis Blériot to carry a passenger as well as a pilot. It flew for the first time on May 21, 1909, at Issy, and was the first aircraft to carry three people when, on June 12, Blériot took with him Santos-Dumont and Fournier. The plane crashed at Reims on August 29.

1909 Breguet I (F) – Wingspan: 39 ft 5 in (12 m) – Wing area: 538 sq ft (50 sq m) – Weight: 1,325 lbs (600 kg) – Engine: Renault 8-cylinder, 50 hp. This was Louis Breguet's first plane. It managed to complete three flights (of 300, 1,500 and 900 feet, or 100, 500 and 300 metres) at Reims before it crashed in landing. Nevertheless the plane attracted much interest and influenced the development of the biplane formula.

1910 A.S.L. Valkyrie A (GB) – Wingspan: 34 ft (10.36 m) – Wing area: 190 sq ft (17.65 sq m) – Weight: 520 lbs (236 kg) – Engine: Green 4-cylinder, 35 hp. Designed by Horatio Barber, founder of the Aeronautical Syndicate Limited. This plane was one of a series of monoplanes that for two years did much to spread interest in aviation in Great Britain. It carried hundreds of passengers and had only two accidents.

1911 Bristol Boxkite (GB) – Wingspan: 46 ft 6 in (14.17 m) – Wing area: 517 sq ft (48.03 sq m) – Weight: 1,150 lbs (522 kg) – Engine: Gnome rotary, 50 hp. The first original design of the British & Colonial Aeroplane Co. and a great commercial success. The prototype flew on July 29, 1910, and by 1914, 66 planes had been built, 16 of them exported to Germany, Russia, South Africa and Spain.

1911 Vickers No. 1 (GB) – Wingspan: 47 ft 6 in (14.48 m) – Wing area: 290 sq ft (26.94 sq m) – Weight: 1,150 lbs (522 kg) – Engine: R.E.P. semi-radial, 60 hp. A modified version of the REP monoplane, production rights to which had been bought by Vickers; it marked the entrance of this British company into aeronautics. Changes mainly involved the front part of the fuselage, and the landing gear.

1911 Nieuport IVG (F) – Wingspan: 38 ft 1 in (11.6 m) – Wing area: 188.4 sq ft (17.5 sq m) – Weight: 772 lbs (350 kg) – Engine: Gnome rotary, 50 hp. Developed from the 1910 monoplane and one of the planes used by Italy during the Italo–Turkish War, the second occasion on which

aircraft were employed for military purposes. It broke a number of records and was also used by the French and British air forces.

1912 Morane Saulnier G (F) – Wingspan: 30 ft 6 in (9.3 m) – Wing area: 160 sq ft (14.86 sq m) – Weight: 816 lbs (370 kg) – Engine: Gnome, 80 hp. A prewar development of the excellent monoplanes built by Léon and Robert Morane and Raymond Saulnier, it served with French squadrons in various versions and to the number of 120.

It was involved in many sporting events and set an altitude record in 1912 of 16,830 feet (5,610 m).

1913 Borel Monoplane (F) – Wingspan: 36 ft 9 in (11.2 m) – Wing area: 204.5 sq ft (19 sq m) – Weight: 926 lbs (420 kg) – Engine: Gnome rotary, 80 hp. Designed by Gabriel Borel, who had been producing sea- and landplanes since 1911, this monoplane was designed for military use. It was a two-seater, pusher monoplane with an armour-plated nacelle and also had provision for armament, including a number of bombs.

1913 Sopwith Bat Boat (GB) – Wingspan: 41 ft (12.5 m) – Wing area: 428 sq ft (39.76 sq m) – Weight: 1,700 lbs (771 kg) – Engine: Austro-Daimler, 90 hp. The first all-British flying boat. It was exhibited at the 1913 Olympia Air Show and, after the installation of a pair of wheels, won the Mortimer-Singer Prize for amphibian planes. It was so successful that the British Admiralty purchased it.

1914 Pateras Guidoni seaplane (I) – Wingspan: 62 ft 4 in (19 m) – Length: 49 ft 3 in (15 m) – Engine: Gnome 18-cylinder rotary, 200 hp. A plane designed by Pateras Pescara and built by Captain Alessandro Guidoni of the Italian Naval Engineers Corps. This seaplane was of original design, with two propellers on the fuselage centre-line, and was the first aircraft in which the technique of torpedo-dropping was attempted.

MILANO
CIRCUITO AEREO
INTERNAZIONALE
24 SETT.^bre – 3 OTT.^bre 1910
PREMI L. 300.000

Flying Records 1906–1914

The impulse that led man to master the principles of flight continued to inspire him to finer achievements. It began in 1783, with the first balloon flight, and progress became more rapid with the arrival of heavier-than-air machines in 1903. Pioneers and early enthusiasts realized that the setting of records and continually improved performance attracted public interest to flying. For at the outset flying machines were looked on with suspicion and doubt. Designers and builders studied and experimented with new scientific solutions to structural and aerodynamic problems and continued to improve engines and their accessories.

The *Grande Semaine d'Aviation de la Champagne* held outside Reims in 1909 greatly stimulated the development of aviation. Enormous and enthusiastic crowds had a chance to see the achievements and progress that had been made in aviation. This meeting also put planes to a rigid test. Sensible designs proved their merits, while the last products of the 'fantastic' phase of aviation were rejected. Thus the lines of the future development of aviation were clearly established.

The International Aeronautical Federation (*Fédération Aéronautique Internationale* or F.A.I.) was founded for in Paris on October 14, 1905, to establish rules and procedures for the ratification of flying records and to homologate those records on the basis of the rules. The *Fédération* was founded by flying club representatives from the nations most involved in aviation development: France, Belgium, Great Britain, Italy, Spain, Switzerland and the United States. In 1910 the International Aeronautical Federation also concerned itself with the licensing of pilots, and in 1912 it laid down the first regulations for international air navigation.

From the outset, four categories of records were established: altitude, speed, endurance and distance. Endurance and distance were of particular importance in the early years of aviation. They were a direct gauge of the efficiency, safety, and engine reliability of an aircraft. It was no accident that the first flights were measured in minutes and seconds, and in terms of distance flown.

A quick glance at statistics shows that the records mirrored the extremely rapid evolution of the aeroplane: from the 82-foot (25-m) altitude Farman reached in 1908 to the 25,755 feet (7,850 m) touched by Oelerich in 1914; from Wilbur Wright's 27.2 mph (44 kph) in 1908 to Prévost's 126.75 mph (204 kph) in 1914; from Alberto Santos-Dumont's 21-second flight in 1906 to Bohem's 24-hour flight in 1914; from Santos-Dumont's first hop of about 25 feet (7.8 m) to the 1,181 miles (1,900 km) Landmann flew in 1914. All these advances were made in only eight years, the first years of modern flight.

Altitude

The Voisin biplane on which Henri Farman established the first properly homologated world altitude record on November 13, 1908

Date		Place
1908	13 XI	Issy (F)
1908	13 XI	Auvours (F)
1908	18 XII	Auvours (F)
1909	18 VII	Douai (F)
1909	29 VIII	Reims (F)
1909	20 IX	Brescia (I)
1909	18 X	Juvisy (F)
1909	1 XII	Chalons (F)
1910	7 I	Chalons (F)
1910	12 I	Los Angeles (USA)
1910	14 VI	Indianapolis (USA)
1910	7 VII	Reims (F)
1910	10 VII	Atlantic City (USA)
1910	11 VIII	Lanark (USA)
1910	29 VIII	Le Havre (F)
1910	3 IX	Deauville (F)
1910	8 IX	Issy (F)
1910	1 X	Mourmelon (F)
1910	31 X	Belmont Park (USA)
1910	9 XII	Pau (F)
1911	9 VII	Buc (F)
1911	5 VIII	Étampes (F)
		Chicago (USA)
1911	4 IX	St-Malo (F)
1911	6 IX	Dinard (F)
1912	17 IX	Issy, Villalonblay (F)
1912	11 XII	Tunisi (TN)
1913	11 III	Buc (F)
1913	29 XII	St-Raphaël (F)
1914	9 VII	Johannisthal (D)
1914	14 VII	Lipsia (D)

ilot	Aeroplane	Engine	Altitude (metres)	(feet)
Henri Farman	Voisin	40 hp Vivinus	25	82
Wilbur Wright	Wright	24 hp Wright	25	82
Wilbur Wright	Wright	24 hp Wright	110	360
Louis Paulhan	Voisin	50 hp Gnome	150	492
Hubert Latham	Antoinette	50 hp Antoinette	155	508
Rougier	Voisin	50 hp E.N.V.	193	633
De Lambert	Wright	24 hp Wright	300	984
Huberth Latham	Antoinette	50 hp Antoinette	453	1436
Huberth Latham	Antoinette	50 hp Antoinette	1.050	3444
Louis Paulhan	H. Farman	50 hp Gnome	1.269	4110
Walter Brookins	Wright	40 hp Wright	1.335	4379
Hubert Latham	Antoinette	50 hp Antoinette	1.384	4539
Walter Brookins	Wright	40 hp Wright	1.900	6237
Armstrong Drexel	Blériot	50 hp Gnome	2.013	6603
Léon Morane	Blériot	50 hp Gnome	2.150	7042
Léon Morane	Blériot	50 hp Gnome	2.582	8469
Geo Chavez	Blériot	50 hp Gnome	2.587	8484
Jan Wijnmalen	H. Farman	50 hp Gnome	2.780	9118
Ralph Johnstone	Wright	60 hp Wright	2.960	9600
Geo Legagneux	Blériot	50 hp Gnome	3.100	10,168
Loridan	H. Farman	70 hp Gnome	3.200	10,496
Cap. Félix	Blériot	70 hp Gnome	3.350	10,988
Lincoln Beachey	Curtiss	60 hp Curtiss	3.527	11,578
Roland Garros	Blériot	70 hp Gnome	3.950	12,824
Roland Garros	Blériot	70 hp Gnome	4.960	16,269
Geo Legagneux	Morane	80 hp Gnome	5.450	18,050
Roland Garros	Morane	80 hp Gnome	5.610	18,400
Édouard Perreyon	Blériot	80 hp Gnome	5.880	19,290
Geo Legagneux	Nieuport	60 hp Le Rhône	6.120	20,060
Gino Linnekogel	Rumpler	100 hp Mercedes	6.600	21,653
Harry Oelerich	D.F.W.	100 hp Mercedes	7.850	25,725

Speed

The speed of 27.2 mph (44 kph) achieved by a Wright Model A biplane flown by Wilbur Wright was the first noteworthy speed record. The Model A was in many respects the acme of the Wright brothers' work.

	Date	Place
	1908 21 IX	Auvours (F)
	1909 31 V	Juvisy (F)
	1909 3 IX	Juvisy (F)
	1909 28 VIII	Reims (F)
	1910 29 X	Belmont Park (USA)
	1911 1 VII	Eastchurch (GB)
	1912 9 IX	Chicago (USA)
	1913 29 IX	Reims (F)

Pilot	Aeroplane	Engine	Speed (kph)	(mph)
Wilbur Wright	Wright	24 hp Wright	44	27.2
Léon Delagrange	Voisin	45 hp Antoinette	45	27.9
Cap. Ferber	Voisin	45 hp Antoinette	48	29.7
Louis Blériot	Blériot	60 hp E.N.V.	77	47.7
Alfred Lèblanc	Blériot	100 hp Gnome	109	67.5
C. Weymann	Nieuport	100 hp Gnome	125	70.5
Jules Védrines	Deperdussin	100 hp Gnome	170	105
Marcel Prévost	Deperdussin	160 hp Le Rhône	204	124.5

Endurance

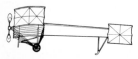

The Brazilian Alberto Santos-Dumont was the first man to stay in the air for a measurable time under official conditions, in an aeroplane of his own design.

Date		Place
1906	12 XI	Bagatelle (F)
1907	26 X	Issy (F)
1908	13 I	Issy (F)
1908	21 III	Issy (F)
1908	11 IV	Issy (F)
1908	30 V	Roma (I)
1908	6 VII	Issy (F)
1908	6 IX	Issy (F)
1908	21 IX	Auvours (F)
1908	18 XII	Auvours (F)
1908	31 XII	Auvours (F)
1909	27 VIII	Béthény (F)
1909	27 VIII	Béthény (F)
1909	3 XII	Mourmelon (F)
1910	9 VII	Reims (F)
1910	10 VII	Reims (F)
1910	28 X	Étampes (F)
1910	18 XII	Étampes (F)
1911	1 IX	Buc (F)
1912	11 IX	Buc (F)
1914	4 II	Johannisthal (D)
1914	24 IV	Étampes (F)
1914	24 VI	Johannisthal (D)
1914	28 VI	Johannisthal (D)
1914	10 VII	Johannisthal (D)

Pilot	Aeroplane	Engine	Time (hrs mins secs)
Santos-Dumont	Santos-Dumont	50 hp Antoinette	0 0 21
Henri Farman	Voisin	40 hp Vivinus	0 0 52
Henri Farman	Voisin	50 hp Antoinette	0 1 28
Henri Farman	Voisin	50 hp Antoinette	0 3 39
Léon Delagrange	Voisin	40 hp Vivinus	0 6 39
Léon Delagrange	Voisin	50 hp E.N.V.	0 15 26
Henri Farman	Voisin	50 hp Antoinette	0 20 19
Léon Delagrange	Voisin	40 hp Vivinus	0 29 53
Wilbur Wright	Wright	24 hp Wright	1 31 25
Wilbur Wright	Wright	24 hp Wright	1 54 53
Wilbur Wright	Wright	24 hp Wright	2 20 23
Louis Paulhan	Voisin	50 hp Gnome	2 43 24
Henri Farman	H. Farman	50 hp Gnome	3 4 56
Henri Farman	H. Farman	50 hp Gnome	4 17 53
Labouchère	Antoinette	50 hp Antoinette	4 19 0
Jan Olieslaegers	Blériot	50 hp Gnome	5 3 5
Maurice Tabuteau	M. Farman	70 hp Renault	6 0 0
Henri Farman	H. Farman	50 hp Gnome	8 12 23
Fourny	M. Farman	70 hp Renault	11 1 20
Fourny	M. Farman	70 hp Renault	13 17 57
Langer	L.F.G. Roland	100 hp Mercedes	14 7 0
Poulet	Caudron	50 hp Gnome	16 28 56
Basser	Rumpler	100 hp Mercedes	18 10 0
Landmann	Albatros	100 hp Mercedes	21 50 0
Boehm	Albatros	100 hp Mercedes	24 12 0

Distance

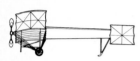

The Santos-Dumont 14-*bis* took the first world 'distance' record in France.

	Date	Place
	1906 14 IX	Bagatelle (F)
	1906 12 XI	Bagatelle (F)
	1907 26 X	Issy (F)
	1908 13 I	Issy (F)
	1908 21 III	Issy (F)
	1908 11 IV	Issy (F)
	1908 30 V	Roma (I)
	1908 6 IX	Issy (F)
	1908 17 IX	Issy (F)
	1908 21 IX	Auvours (F)
	1908 18 XII	Auvours (F)
	1908 31 XII	Auvours (F)
	1909 26 VIII	Reims (F)
	1909 3 XI	Mourmelon (F)
	1910 10 VII'	Reims (F)
		Reims (F)
	1910 28 X	Étampes (F)
	1910 30 XII	Étampes (F)
	1911 16 VII	Kiewitt (D)
	1911 1 IX	Buc (F)
	1911 24 XII	Pau (F)
	1912 11 IX	Étampes (F)
	1914 28 VI	Johannisthal (D)

Pilot	Aeroplane	Engine	Distance	
Santos-Dumont	Santos-Dumont	50 hp Antoinette	7,8 m	8.6 yd
Santos-Dumont	Santos-Dumont	50 hp Antoinette	220	244.4 yd
Henri Farman	Voisin	40 hp Vivinus	770	855.5 yd
Henri Farman	Voisin	50 hp Antoinette	1 km	0.625 mi
Henri Farman	Voisin	50 hp Antoinette	2	1.25
Léon Delagrange	Voisin	40 hp Vivinus	4	2.50
Léon Delagrange	Voisin	50 hp E.N.V.	13	7.7
Léon Delagrange	Voisin	40 hp Vivinus	24	15.3
Léon Delagrange	Voisin	40 hp Vivinus	67	41.5
Wilbur Wright	Voisin	24 hp Wright	97	60.9
Wilbur Wright	Wright	24 hp Wright	100	62
Wilbur Wright	Wright	24 hp Wright	125	77.5
Henri Farman	H. Farman	50 hp Gnome	180	112
Henri Farman	H. Farman	50 hp Gnome	210	150
Jan Olieslaegers	Blériot	50 hp Gnome	225	139.5
Jan Olieslaegers	Blériot	50 hp Gnome	393	245
Maurice Tabuteau	M. Farman	70 hp Renault	465	290
Maurice Tabuteau	M. Farman	70 hp Renault	585	362.7
Jan Olieslaegers	Blériot	50 hp Gnome	635	393.7
Fourny	M. Farman	70 hp Renault	723	448.3
Gobé	Nieuport	70 hp Gnome	740	460
Fourny	M. Farman	70 hp Renault	1.017	633
Landmann	Albatros	100 hp Mercedes	1.900	1178

Insignia of the Nations at War

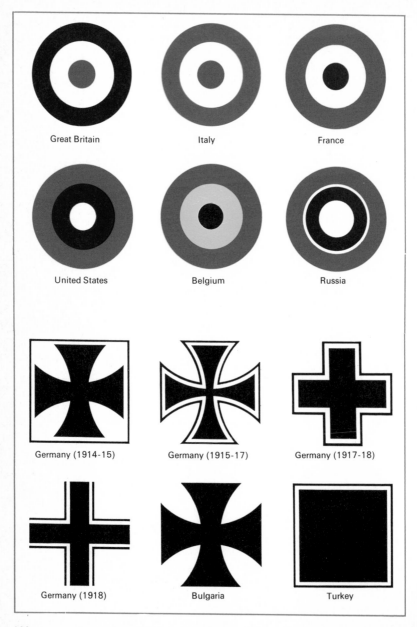

Great Britain

Italy

France

United States

Belgium

Russia

Germany (1914-15)

Germany (1915-17)

Germany (1917-18)

Germany (1918)

Bulgaria

Turkey

The Development of Aviation 1914–1918

When the First World War broke out in August 1914, the aeroplane was still in a transition phase. Many people had foreseen that the plane could be an effective instrument of war, and aircraft had already been used in military missions. But no clear idea had been formed of what actual tasks this new weapon could carry out. Military leaders were attached to the idea of a traditional army and could not wholeheartedly accept the prospects of the heavier-than-air machine. So at first the aeroplane was limited to reconnaissance work for army and navy. And the actual achievements of aircraft at the time did not warrant considering them for anything but quiet observation flights outside the enemy's range of fire and not too far from their own lines. The first military planes were built from prewar plans and were on the whole unarmed. They were slow (about 60 mph, or 96.7 kph) and fragile, with limited range and low ceiling.

But changes came about very rapidly. Reconnaissance planes, observing troop movements and gathering intelligence for artillery fire, came into conflict with enemy reconnaissance planes on similar missions. The only weapons at first available were the crew's pistols and rifles, but the imminence of aerial combat in a real sense was already clear in these early exchanges of small arms fire. Before the machine-gun turned the aeroplane into a real fighting machine, pilots and observers made use of a vast assortment of individual weapons, ranging from regulation to hunting rifles, from standard automatic pistols to specially modified ones with lengthened stocks and larger magazines. Some of these guns had a metal container to catch ejected cartridge-cases that might otherwise have ended up in the propeller blades. Some pilots found firearms unsatisfactory and used combat devices of their own making. A Russian, Captain Kazakov, attached a hook to a long metal cable to grapple enemy planes. French and British airmen dropped steel arrows on the wings and fuselages of enemy aircraft flying at a lower altitude.

Machine-guns appeared more frequently late in 1914, and thus was born the armed reconnaissance plane. The machine-gun was installed for the observer's use, and he could manoeuvre it as he pleased thanks to a movable mounting. Combat experience, however, showed that this kind of weapon was seriously limited. Except in pusher types, it was impossible for the gunner/observer to respond to attacks made from in front of the aircraft. A way had to be found to direct machine-gun fire towards the front of the plane without damaging the propeller. Various solutions were tried out. One solution was to install the gun on the upper part of the wing, so as to avoid the propeller disk. Several machines with pusher propellers were also designed, so that the machine-gun could be installed in the nose of the plane, with a forward field of fire free from all obstacles.

Meanwhile a new type of aircraft

was designed. This was the bomber. Most of the first bombers were simply modified reconnaissance planes. Since the original fuselages were usually amply dimensioned, they could carry small bombs, almost all anti-personnel.

What was still missing in the arsenal of military aircraft was the fighter plane, a fast, manoeuvrable, and well-armed machine in which all the flying and fighting could be done by a single man. The fighter plane evolved naturally when the problem of forward fire through the propeller disk was solved. The first fighter plane was the French Morane-Saulnier L, which appeared in 1915. A fixed forward-firing machine-gun was installed and the propeller blades were equipped with rudimentary deflector plates at the level where bullets might hit them. This was still a makeshift solution. The first genuine fighter plane appeared in the summer of 1915. It was the German Fokker monoplane, which was equipped with the first device to synchronize gunfire with propeller rotation.

It was then, perhaps for the first time in the history of aviation, that the importance of the plane as a fighting machine was fully appreciated. Military experts realized that whoever obtained aerial supremacy would have immense tatical and strategic advantages. The fighter plane, with its specialized characteristics, proved to be a decisive weapon in the air war. It could forestall all threats from the air, including bombing, reconnaissance flights, and sudden attacks on ground troops. Thus one of the major efforts of all the nations involved in the war

came to be the design and construction of better and yet better fighter planes.

The appearance of the Fokker monoplane was a bitter surprise for the Allies. What soon became the 'Fokker Scourge' began on August 1, 1915, when two German pilots, Oswald Boelcke and Max Immelmann, in their Fokker E Is, attacked nine British planes that had raided their airfield at Douai. Boelcke's machine-gun jammed, but Immelmann hit a British plane and forced it down behind the German lines. That was the beginning of the Fokker Scourge. The German fighters were allocated to reconnaissance units all along the front, and immediately demonstrated their superiority to the slow and poorly-armed Allied planes. The British B.E.2cs were particularly vulnerable, for the observer/gunner was located forward of the pilot and under the top wing, with a poor field of fire. They were clumsy planes as well, no match for the relatively nimble German single-seaters. The effects on morale were enormous. The Germans exploited their aerial feats to great psychological advantage by publicizing their achievements. The Allies were discouraged and could do little to offset the enemy's advantage, at least until a plane equal to that of the Germans could be produced.

The German pilots, backed up by their supremacy in the air, were the first to develop air combat tactics, tactics that were to set a standard for almost half a century. Max Immelmann, for example, was keenly aware of the Fokker's vulnerability to attack from the rear. He worked out a man-

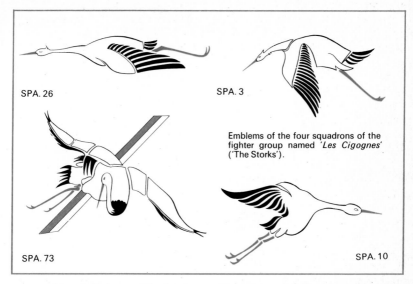

SPA. 26

SPA. 3

Emblems of the four squadrons of the fighter group named *'Les Cigognes'* ('The Storks').

SPA. 73

SPA. 10

oeuvre that made it possible for the pilot to get away from the enemy on his tail and reverse their positions. Fighter pilots soon became aware of the tactical advantages of altitude and having the sun behind one in combat. The pilots carefully studied the enemy's planes to discover the dead angles of their guns, to assess their manoeuvrability, and to evaluate their ability to make tight turns.

Fokker superiority reached its peak in February 1916, when a large number of the definitive Fokker monoplane, the E III, were in service.

But it was only a short time before the scales began to tip back again, thanks to the appearance of two British planes, the F.E.2b and the D.H.2. Both aircraft were pusher biplanes. They could outdo the Fokker in speed, and the D.H.2 in manoeuvrability, and rate of climb. The final blow to

German superiority came from two French fighters, the Nieuport 11 and 17, which had a chance to display their excellent features at the battle of Verdun from February 1916 onwards. The balance had begun to sway in favour of the Allies. Allied air superiority was consolidated by the appearance of the first planes equipped with forward-firing synchronized machine-guns. One of these planes was the Spad S.VII, the finest product of aviation know-how of the day.

The German response to all this was not long in coming. And it came on two fronts. The first was technical, with the production of fighters such as the Albatros D I, D II and D III, and the Halberstadt D II and D III. The second was organizational, with the complete overhauling of the structure of combat squadrons. On the advice of the great ace Oswald Boelcke, the

111

French insignia (1914-18)

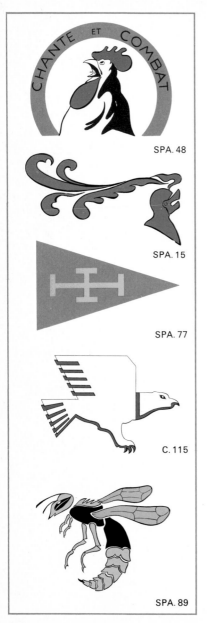

SPA. 48

SPA. 15

SPA. 77

C. 115

SPA. 89

German high command grouped all the fighting planes at the front into independent units, called *Jagdstaffeln* or *Jastas*, each with a basic allotment of 14 D-type planes. ('D' indicated single-seat, single-engined biplane fighters.) Seven units were in action by October 1, 1916. They were elite units manned by outstanding pilots who could exploit the virtues of their aircraft to the full.

When winter came, the Germans were again in command of the air. The most important single factor, apart from the intrinsic superiority of German aircraft, was the lethal firepower of the two synchronized machineguns, which had become standard armament, with 500 rounds per gun. The Allies had to wait till the spring and summer of 1917 to restore the balance again. It was in 1917 that the British Sopwith Camel and Triplane, the S.E.5 and the Bristol Fighter, together with the French Spad S. XIII, appeared on the scene. The Allies maintained control of the air until the end of the war, despite a final German production effort that turned out such superb planes as the Fokker D VII and D VIII, the Roland D VI, and the Pfalz D XII. These fighters supplied only temporary air superiority. At that point, it was no longer a matter of quality, but one of quantity. The German air force had about 2,390 fighting planes in the spring and summer of 1918, while the Allies had more than 10,000. It was just a question of time before the Allied victory.

It was not just the planes that counted in aerial warfare, but also the ability of the pilots. The Germans were the first to publicize the achievements of their air aces, chiefly for propaganda purposes, but the passion for the heroes of the air soon swept all the nations in the war. The public wanted heroes, and feats of outstanding pilots totally captured their imagination. Every country laid down stiff rules for confirming air victories, and every plane shot down was carefully listed on individual charts, except in Great Britain. When the war was over, it became a question of honour to publish the rolls of the leading aces country by country. The German Manfred von Richthofen, the 'Red Baron', was the 'ace of aces'. He shot down 80 planes. The Frenchman René Paul Fonck had 75; the Englishman Edward Mannock had 73; Godwin Brumowski of Austria had 40; the Belgian Willy Coppens de Houthulst had 37; Francesco Baracca of Italy had 34; the American Edward Rickenbacker had 26; and the Russian Alexander Alexandrovich Kazakov had 17.

Most of these fighter pilots were associated in the public mind with their planes. Thus von Richthofen was considered synonymous with his Fokker triplane, although he had fought in various types of aircraft, and Willy Coppens de Houthulst with his Hanriot and Francesco Baracca with his Spad became popular legends.

In this heroic atmosphere, the planes themselves became highly personalized aesthetic creations. In violation of all the laws of camouflage, the pilots decorated their planes with personal insignia and colours, pictorial designs and geometric patterns. This raised pilots' morale and was also an attempt at psychological warfare, a

French insignia (1914-18)

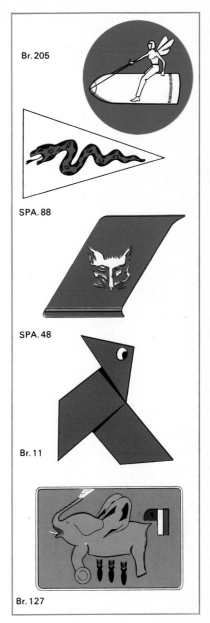

Br. 205

SPA. 88

SPA. 48

Br. 11

Br. 127

challenge to the enemy. The most stiking example was von Richthofen's 'Flying Circus'. The planes were decorated in bright colours from nose to tail, to emphasize the squadron's *esprit de corps* and flaunt its superiority over the enemy. The same phenomenon was repeated during the Second World War, albeit on a smaller scale. The Americans, for example, turned their planes into multi-coloured and highly visible objects. At times they looked like flying frescoes!

The need for camouflage had been understood from the beginning of World War I: on the ground it was important to avoid enemy observation planes; in the air it was important to get as close as possible to the target unseen. At first nothing was done. But as suitable paints were developed, warring nations carefully studied the problem of camouflage and came up with many ingenious solutions. Camouflage colours soon became standardized (albeit with some exceptions) in dark shades of green and brown for the upper surfaces of aircraft and in shades of beige and light blue for the under surfaces. Then it was discovered that the optical effect produced by stripes of two or more colours could 'split up' the outlines of a plane. This technique was particularly popular with the French and the Germans. The Germans also devised a complicated camouflage system of lozenges of four or five colours arranged in sequence and applied to both upper and under surfaces. At one point German researchers were even attempting to find a kind of invisible paint.

The only officially authorized exceptions to the rules of camouflage were national markings and squadron symbols. The first were almost always clearly painted on the camouflaged surfaces and often provided perfect targets for enemy guns.

For fast identification, the Allies settled on a circle as background for their national markings, while the Germans used a square with a black cross, the symbol of the Teutonic Knights. As the war went on, this German marking became more and more stylized. Squadron markings were sometimes combinations of letters and numbers, though they might be limited to the unit's general marking and nothing more.

The fighter plane proved to be a decisive weapon, and the war also demonstrated the tactical and strategic advantages of bombing from the air. The bomber developed alongside the fighter. At the start of the war, reconnaissance planes were adapted to carry a small load of light bombs. One of the very few planes that could really be considered a bomber was the French Voisin. France was the first of the countries at war to create separate bomber units, although their missions were limited to tactical bombing. Russia, which had developed the first 'jumbo' aircraft, the four-engined Sikorsky *Ilya Muromets*, followed France's example in 1915. The success of the *Vozdushnikh Korab* squadron's missions over Germany gave the final impulse to the production of heavy bombers. Italy, too, had its bombers in the form of several types of Caproni, and made intensive use of them when it entered the war in 1915. And

32nd Squadron   70th Fighter Squadron   1st Reconnaissance Section

76th Squadron   81st Fighter Squadron   80th Fighter Squadron

the Handley Page company in Great Britain also began manufacturing large 'strategic' bombers. Germany had used its Zeppelin dirigibles for heavy bombing but soon switched to the aeroplane. The first bombers were two-engined A.E.G., Gotha and Friedrichshafen planes, and then the gigantic Zeppelin (Staaken) aircraft appeared. It was the Germans who initiated a new kind of air assault, one that was to have more dramatic developments in the future, the prolonged strategic bombing of a single objective, which they began in the night-raids on London and southern England in 1917.

By the end of the war bombers had developed enormously. In 1914 converted reconnaissance planes were dropping small bombs weighing only a few pounds. By 1918 heavy bombers were dropping incendiary and frag-mentation as well as high-explosive bombs weighing from 220 pounds (100 kg) up to 2,205 pounds (1,000 kg). The 1918 Handley Page V/1500 could carry two bombs weighing 3,300 pounds (1,497 kg) each, veritable prototypes of the huge bombs of the Second World War.

The evolution of the bomber aircraft itself went hand-in-hand with the rapid development of bombs and mechanisms for carrying them, bomb-aiming, and dropping. The early improvised racks under the wings or fuselage were gradually replaced by automatic bomb racks. The Michelin bomb rack, for example, could release bombs at regular intervals. Later versions could accommodate bombs of all sizes from 22 to 441 pounds (10 to 200 kg). As heavy bombers became large enough to accommodate the bombs inside the fuselage, bomb racks

115

were designed to house a maximum of bombs ready for dropping. Bomb-aiming systems also became more sophisticated. The first bombers had rudimentary clockwork mechanisms, and the bombardier had to calculate his ground speed and approach angle with simple back-sights. But in the last two years of the war, bombers were equipped with telescopic sights.

The most important weapon, for both defence and offence was the machine-gun. And every country developed its own types. For the most part, they were modified versions of machine-guns used by ground troops, but special models were soon developed for aircraft.

Hotchkiss, Lewis, 'Spandau', Schwarzlose, Revelli, and Vickers were the leading machine-gun manufacturers. The Hotchkiss was the most commonly used machine-gun in France in the first years of the war. It was mounted on the Voisin and the Farman. This 8-mm (.315-in) weapon was fed from 25-shot metal strips or from belts rolled up in a drum magazine. The Lewis was designed by an American colonel, Isaac Newton Lewis, and built in Belgium. It became one of the Allies' standard weapons. For a weapon of .303-inch (7.7-mm) calibre it was light and efficient and had a 97-round double drum magazine. The Lewis gun had a rate of fire of 850 rounds per minute. The final model had a round-counter and electric heating for high altitudes. The Spandau, named for the place where it was manufactured, was the standard machine-gun of the German air force. It had a calibre of 7.62-mm (.3-in), could fire 550 rounds per minute and, when equipped with a synchronizer, made a fundamental contribution to German air supremacy. The 8-mm (.315-in) Schwarzlose was the standard Austrian weapon, while the 6.5-mm (.256-in) Revelli was standard

American Squadron Insignia (1914-18)

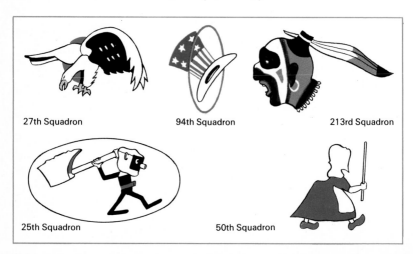

27th Squadron

94th Squadron

213rd Squadron

25th Squadron

50th Squadron

armament on most Italian reconnaissance planes. The Vickers .303-inch (7.7-mm) was the first machine-gun to be equipped with the Constantinesco hydraulic synchronizer, about the middle of 1917. This device greatly increased Allied fighters' efficiency.

Aero engines and construction techniques underwent great changes during the war. At the beginning of the war France and Germany had the best engines. Great Britain did not have an efficient aero engine of its own, and its planes were powered by French engines, either imported or built under licence. France and Germany were interested in different kinds of engines. French manufacturers had brought the rotary engine to a high level of efficiency. The rotary engine was a highly original idea, and many people considered it a revolutionary innovation. The cylinders and the crankcase rotated around a fixed crankshaft, turning the propeller bolted to them. It constituted a compact, lightweight engine with a power:weight ratio higher than any other types. It was the perfect engine for fast, light planes. German industry, on the other hand, concentrated on stationary, liquid-cooled inline engines. Companies like Mercedes, Benz, and Austro-Daimler produced high quality engines that were tough, powerful, and reliable. Some German companies also built rotary engines. The most popular German rotary, the Oberursel, was simply a copy of the French Le Rhône. Practical reasons made it impossible for Germany to ignore the rotary engine. With its high torque reaction and gyroscopic effect, the rotary engine made planes extremely agile. The stationary engines of the time could not match the rotaries' performance. The only way German planes could match the French and British was to adopt the rotary engine.

American Squadron Insignia (1914-18)

91st Squadron

Lafayette *Escadrille*

11th Squadron

Lafayette *Escadrille* (April 1917)

German pilots' personal markings (1914-18)

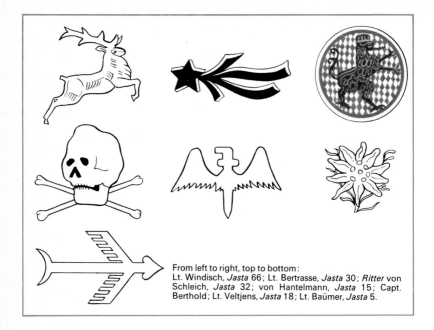

From left to right, top to bottom:
Lt. Windisch, *Jasta* 66; Lt. Bertrasse, *Jasta* 30; *Ritter* von Schleich, *Jasta* 32; von Hantelmann, *Jasta* 15; Capt. Berthold; Lt. Veltjens, *Jasta* 18; Lt. Baümer, *Jasta* 5.

Great Britain was a slow starter in the field of aero engine manufacture, but it too was soon producing first-rate powerplants. In 1915 Henry Royce introduced his first 12-cylinder inline V engine, the Eagle, the first of a long and successful line of engines. In the last two years of the war, the rotary engine began to betray its limitations. The cooling problem was crucial, especially where double-row radial engines were concerned. New production techniques and a greater variety of metals and light alloys resulted in ever better engines of a more conventional type. The Hispano-Suiza V-8 was a landmark in such engine development. It had an aluminium cylinder block with steel liners, which made possible a

power:weight ratio never obtained before. The prototype generated 140 hp. Later models reached 200 and finally 300 hp. The last Rolls-Royce engines were even more powerful. And the V-12 Liberty, designed in America in 1917 by the Packard Motor Company, reached the 400-hp mark. This was one of the most powerful engines used in the war.

The increase in engine power led to changes in the conception and construction of aircraft. Traditional materials, such as wood for the framework and cloth for the covering, gave way first to partial and total covering in plywood and to monocoque structures, and then to a framework of metal tubing covered with cloth and aluminium. It was the Germans, in

118

1915, who produced the world's first all-metal aeroplane to fly: the Junkers J I. The steel-tube structure was covered with sheet metal. A two-seater monoplane, the CL I, was derived from the J I in the last months of the war. It was one of the best planes employed in the conflict. The monoplane was less popular than the biplane, because it was thought to have a weaker airframe and because of its high landing speed. Hence far more biplanes were constructed. And the biplane's success continued after the end of the conflict. Until the 1930s the usual fighter concept was a biplane with a tractor propeller, an open cockpit, fixed landing gear and synchronized forward-firing machine-guns. Performance and engine power increased year by year, but even as early as 1918 the average fighter plane had a 220-hp engine, a speed of about 125–130 mph (200–210 kph), and a ceiling of over 20,000 feet (6,100 m). They had come a long way from the 'scouts' of 1914, who fired rifles and tried to ram into each other a few hundred feet from the ground.

Four and a half years of war had been an enormous stimulus to the development of aviation. The constant effort to outdo the enemy, a question of life and death, had monopolized the industrial resources of all of Europe. New designs and types of planes were developed one after another, and production figures rose in spectacular fashion. At the outbreak of war about 400 front-line planes were marshalled on both sides (63 British, 24 Belgian, 138 French and about 180 German). By the end of hostilities, there were almost 13,000 fighting planes in service. Between 1914 to 1918 some 177,000 planes of all types were built, almost 18 times the number of all the planes built in the world between 1903 and 1914. In Great Britain, for instance, 55,000 planes were built during the war, and 350,000 men and women were employed in the air industry. The war brought aviation to its first maturity.

Insignia of Austrian and Russian pilots (1914-18)

Red heart, emblem of the Phönix D II piloted by *Feldwebel* Sandor Kaszka of *Flik* 55*j*. Warrior's head painted on the Nieuport 17 of the Russian ace Captain Kruten. The macabre emblem of the Spad flown by Captain Kazakov, the top Russian ace. Another death's head, on a Nieuport of the Russian 1st Fighter Group, Air District XIX.

The Race for Aerial Supremacy 1914 – 1918

The First World War demonstrated the capabilities and importance of the aeroplane as an instrument of war. Theorists and strategists, designers and engineers, all became aware of its immense possibilities. Thus more effective tactics and strategic uses of aircraft were studied, while designers and manufacturers produced better and better combat planes. From early in the war combat planes were considered equally instruments of defence and offence, and all the nations at war were determined not to be outdone by the enemy. The strategic and tactical importance of air power was universally recognized. The fighter plane was a decisive weapon and turned out to be the basic factor in the shifting balance of air power. The chart of the following pages graphically illustrates these developments, as both sides struggled for the upper hand.

Hundreds of different types of planes were turned out during the war, but only a few of them really made history. These aircraft were the result of constant experiment and unflagging effort, the best that the resources of great industries and the talent of designers of genius could produce. Great Britain, France and Germany turned out the best fighters of the war. The Allies' Nieuports, Spads, Sopwith Camels, R.A.F. S.E.5s, and Bristol F.2As and F.2Bs were matched by the equally superb planes produced by the German war industry, including such aircraft as the Fokker E, Dr I, and D VII; the Albatros D II, D III, and D V; and the Halberstadt D II. Genuinely outstanding fighters were not produced by other nations. The other combatants relied, for the most part, on fighting planes produced by these two blocs. The one exception was the Austrian Aviatik-Berg D I, which was used on the Italian front. It stood up well against its adversaries.

The bomber situation was different. Almost all of the combatants produced excellent bombers. In addition to the planes produced by Great Britain, France, and Germany, Italian and Russian bombers were among the most advanced. Italy and Russia were two of the first countries to appreciate the importance of strategic and tactical bombing, and they produced fine machines, like the Sikorsky and Caproni types. The Russians were the first to make strategic bombing in raids on Germany, using squadrons of four-engined *Ilya Muromets* bombers.

The only nation that did not produce outstanding combat planes in the First World War was America, the country where flight began. But only a few years after the end of the war American combat planes set the pace for the rest of the world.

SUPREMACY

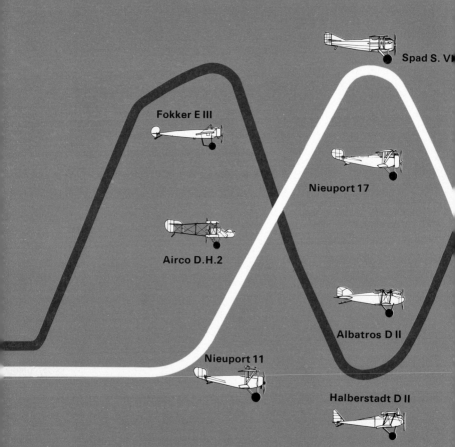

SUMMER 1915

WINTER 1915-16

SPRING 1916

SUMMER 1916

AUTUMN/WINTER 1916-17

Spad S. VII

Fokker E III

Nieuport 17

Airco D.H.2

Albatros D II

Nieuport 11

Halberstadt D II

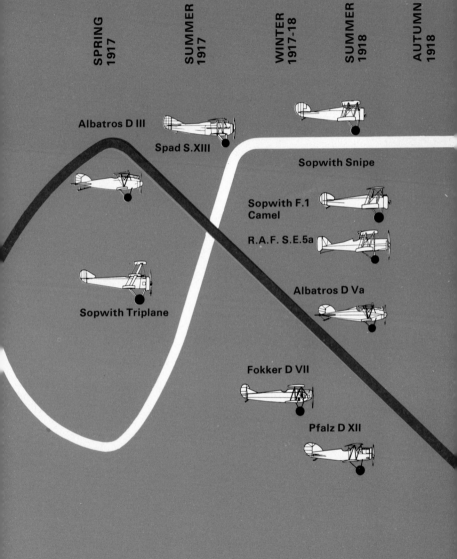

SPRING 1917

SUMMER 1917

WINTER 1917-18

SUMMER 1918

AUTUMN 1918

Albatros D III

Spad S.XIII

Sopwith Snipe

Sopwith F.1 Camel

R.A.F. S.E.5a

Albatros D Va

Sopwith Triplane

Fokker D VII

Pfalz D XII

SCOUTS/FIGHTERS

1914

1915

A great number of scout/fighter types were used in the First World War, the best being produced by Germany, France and Great Britain. In this chart are shown the most interesting types of the war in chronological order.

Bristol Scout D (GB)

Vickers F.B.5 (GB)

R.A.F. F.E.2b (GB)

Nieuport 11 (F)

Fokker E III (G)

1916

1917

1918

Sopwith Pup (GB)

Sopwith F.1 Camel (GB)

Nieuport 17 (F)

Spad S.XIII (F)

R.A.F. S.E.5a (GB)

Halberstadt D II (G)

Sopwith Triplane (GB)

Fokker D VII (G)

Albatros D Va (G)

Spad S.VII (F)

Fokker Dr I (G)

Albatros D II (G)

Hanriot HD.I (F)

BOMBERS

	1914	1915

The development of
good bomber types
was more equally
divided among the
combatant nations than
was the case with
scout and fighter types.

Caudron G.IV (F)

**Sikorsky
Ilya Muromets (R)**

Voisin 5 (F)

Caproni Ca.3 (I)

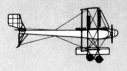

Breguet Br.M. 5 (F)

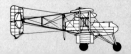

1916

1917

1918

Short 184 (GB)

A.E.G. G IV (G)

Farman F.40 (F)

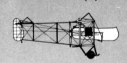

Voisin 8 (F)

Airco D.H.4 (GB)

Friedrichshafen G III (G)

Handley Page O/400 (GB)

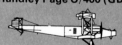

Breguet Br.14 (F)

Gotha G V (G)

Zeppelin (Staaken) R VI (G)

Airco D.H.9 (GB)

Caproni Ca.4 (I)

Caudron R.11 (F)

Caproni Ca.5 (I)

Handley Page V/1500 (GB)

France

France, the cradle of European aviation, provided the backbone of Allied air activity during the First World War. In 1914 the French aviation industry was the most advanced in the world. Early in the war France supplied aircraft and, perhaps more important, engines to the other Allies. And to the end of the war French planes continued to represent the finest in aircraft construction. The planes used by the American Expeditionary Forces and by the Belgian air force were French. Most of Russia's planes were French. And Italy's front-line fighters also included French aircraft. Even Great Britain, with her excellent aviation industry, did not hesitate to use French-designed planes in moments of need.

French military personnel were active in aviation from the very beginning. Captain Ferdinand Ferber, who made such a great contribution to the success of the heavier-than-air machines, is typical. The French War Ministry officially recognized the war potential of the aeroplane on July 12, 1909, when it bought a Wright biplane. In October 1910, France had 30 military planes of various kinds and

had ordered another 61. That same year, military pilots began taking part in racing competition. By 1911 French interest in aviation was so keen that a public subscription of four million francs was made for the purchase of new aircraft. The year 1911 also saw the first Military Aircraft Competition held to select aircraft for the armed forces. Competitors had to meet rigid specifications: the planes had to be two-seaters, with a range of no less than 186 miles (300 km), payload of 661 pounds (300 kg), and a minimum speed of 37 mph (60 kph). The aviation industry's response was massive: some 110 prototypes were entered, and of these, 32 were chosen for the actual competition. The three winners were the Nieuport monoplane, the Breguet biplane, and the Deperdussin monoplane. Orders were placed for ten Nieuports, six Breguets, and four Deperdussins.

These selection competitions, which were introduced in other nations, were a real stimulus to manufacturers. France built 1,350 planes in 1911, 1,425 in 1912, and 1,294 in 1913. The production of engines, a most advanced field, rose from 1,400 in 1911 to

2,217 and 2,440 in the next two years. The Gnome rotary was the outstanding engine of its time and gave France an edge over the rest of the world. The war did not find France unprepared. On August 28, 1912, the French air force (*Aviation Militaire*) was divided into three groups, based in Versailles, Reims, and Lyons. In February 1914, planes and balloons were separated into two distinct and independent services. When war was declared in August, the French air force comprised 25 squadrons. There were 21 squadrons of six two-seaters, and four squadrons of three single-seaters. There was a total of 138 front-line fighting planes, including Blériot, Deperdussin, and Nieuport monoplanes, and Henri Farman, Maurice Farman, Breguet and Voisin biplanes. These various planes were organized in units by function: single-seater fighters, two-seater fighters, daylight bombers, night bombers, and long-range planes.

Apart from its excellent bombers – the real warhorses of the conflict – France also developed some of the best fighter planes: Morane-Saulnier; Nieuport 11, 17, and 28; Spad S.VII and S.XIII; and Hanriot HD.1. These fine planes were flown by French and Allied aces. In France René Paul Fonck downed 75 enemy planes, Georges Marie Guynemer downed 54, and Charles Eugène Nungesser downed 45. Eleven French pilots downed from 20 to 41 enemy planes, and 39 were credited with from 10 to 20 victories. Among the best-known foreign aces who won most of their laurels in French planes were the Italian Francesco Baracca, the Belgian Willy Coppens de Houthulst, and the American Eddie Rickenbacker. René Paul Fonck went down in history as the Allied 'ace of aces', while Georges Marie Guynemer was undoubtedly the most popular. His reputation was greatly enhanced by his physical appearance. He looked frail and delicate and had a melancholy expression. But in the air he showed a determination, courage, and fighting spirit that one who saw him on the ground would never have suspected. He began as a mechanic and after many difficulties managed to get pilot training. His first victory came on July 19, 1915, and earned him the first of many medals he was to receive. He served in the 3rd *Escadrille* of the *Les Cigognes* group, and shot down his last plane, his 54th, on September 6, 1917. He logged a total of 660 hours in the air and more than 600 missions. On September 11, 1917, he was shot down near Poelcapelle by Lieutenant Wissemann.

The macabre insignia of Charles Nungesser, third-ranking French ace of the First World War, with 45 planes downed. He used the insignia for the first time in November 1915, on the side of a Nieuport, when he was first assigned to the 65th *Escadrille*. Nungesser was so pleased with the insignia that he flew the plane to a nearby enemy base and gave a breathtaking performance of aerobatic manoeuvres to impress the Germans.

Morane-Saulnier N
Morane-Saulnier L
Morane-Saulnier LA/P

The first fixed forward-firing machine-gun to be fired in anger from a plane in flight, early in 1915, was installed on a Morane-Saulnier L. The gun, an 8-mm (.315-in) Hotchkiss, was installed just behind the engine cowling, and was fired successfully through the propeller disk with the aid of a simple mechanism: two steel plates fastened to the rear of the blades on the line of fire protected the propeller by deflecting bullets that would have struck its blades. Rudimentary as this deflector plate system may have been, it made the Morane-Saulnier L the first real 'fighter' plane in the history of aviation. The user of this deflector, French pilot Roland Garros, shot down five enemy planes in the first three weeks of April 1915.

The Morane-Saulnier L was the first in a long line of monoplane fighters produced by Robert and Léon Morane and their partner Raymond Saulnier. The design was developed in 1913, and when war broke out, many Type Ls were ordered for reconnaissance work. This high-performance plane was a better aircraft than the contemporary Aviatik and Albatros two-seaters. The crews carried small arms, such as pistols and carbines, to combat enemy planes, and several planes were downed in this primitive system of air combat. One of many pilots who had their baptism of fire in a Type L monoplane was the then Corporal Guynemer, who was to become one of the great aces of the war. He shot down a German two-seater on July 19, 1915, with a machine-gun.

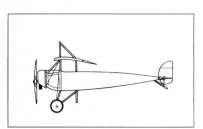

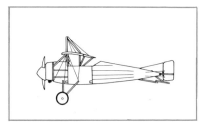

Aircraft: **Morane-Saulnier L**
Type: **Fighter/reconnaissance**
Year: **1913**
Engine: **Gnome rotary, 80 hp**
Wingspan: **36 ft 9 in (11.2 m)**
Length: **22 ft 6.75 in (6.88 m)**
Height: **12 ft 10.5 in (3.93 m)**
Weight: **1,441 lbs (655 kg)**
Maximum speed: **71.5 mph (115 kph) at 6,560 ft (2,000 m)**
Ceiling: **13,123 ft (4,000 m)**
Endurance: **2 hrs 30 mins**
Armament: **1 machine-gun; few bombs**
Crew: **1-2**

Aircraft: **Morane-Saulnier P**
Type: **Reconnaissance**
Year: **1914**
Engine: **Le Rhône 9J rotary, 110 hp**
Wingspan: **36 ft 8.75 in (11.2 m)**
Length: **23 ft 7.5 in (7.2 m)**
Height: **11 ft 4.5 in (3.47 m)**
Weight: **1,610 lbs (730 kg)**
Maximum speed: **97 mph (156 kph) at 6,560 ft (2,000 m)**
Ceiling: **12,000 ft (3,658 m)**
Endurance: **2 hrs 30 mins**
Armament: **1-2 machine-guns**
Crew: **2**

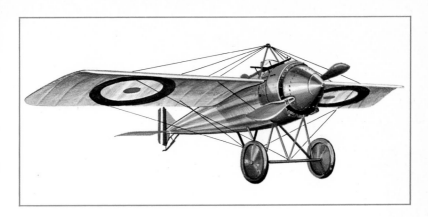

The Morane-Saulnier L, of which about 600 were built, was followed in 1914 by the Types LA and P, larger, more powerful, and better armed. The Type P was the more popular of the two. It did reconnaissance duty in the French air force, and was also used by the British until 1916–17; 595 of them were built.

The Morane-Saulnier N, which also appeared in 1914, was very different from its predecessors. It was a plane of very advanced design, highly streamlined, very fast and extremely manoeuvrable. Nevertheless, it was not as successful as other Morane-Saulnier models, and only 49 were built. One reason for its relative unpopularity was its high landing speed and its delicate handling characteristics. It took a really expert pilot to fly it for the French air force, with another small batch going to the Royal Flying Corps (enough for four squadrons) and an even smaller batch to the Imperial Russian Air Service (enough for just one squadron).

Aircraft: **Morane-Saulnier N**
Manufacturer: **Aéroplanes   Morane-Saulnier**
Type: **Fighter**
Year: **1914**
Engine: **Le Rhône 9C 9-cylinder air-cooled rotary, 80 hp**
Wingspan: **26 ft 8.5 in (8.15 m)**
Length: **19 ft 1.5 in (5.83 m)**
Height: **7 ft 4.5 in (2.25 m)**
Weight: **976 lbs (444 kg)**
Maximum speed: **90 mph (144 kph)**
Ceiling: **13,123 ft (4,000 m)**
Endurance: **1 hr 30 mins**
Armament: **1 machine-gun**
Crew: **1**

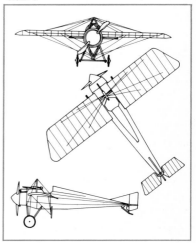

Maurice Farman M.F.7
Maurice Farman M.F.11

The most popular reconnaissance planes of the first years of the war were nicknamed the 'Longhorn' and the 'Shorthorn' by British fliers, because of the relative lengths of their curved landing skids. The Maurice Farman M.F.7 and the Maurice Farman M.F.11 were used in all the reconnaissance units of the French, Belgian, British and Italian air forces from the start of the war until well into 1915. After service on all fronts, they were replaced by newer and more efficient planes, but that was not the end of their career. They became trainers and saw service for several more years.

After the success that followed his 1909 biplane, Henri Farman, the great 'French' pioneer, went into partnership in 1912 with his brother Maurice, another brilliant designer, and between them they set up the *Société Henri et Maurice Farman* in Billancourt. But both brothers continued to develop their own designs. When the war became imminent, they readied their factory for mass production, and in August 1914, the Farman brothers' factory was the only plant that could fill large-scale orders without radically overhauling its whole organization. The brothers' preparedness was responsible for the extensive use of Farman planes throughout the war. Maurice Farman's M.F.7 and M.F.11 were contemporary with the H.F.20 series designed by Henri Farman. The M.F.7, also known as the '1913 type', was clearly inspired by earlier bi-

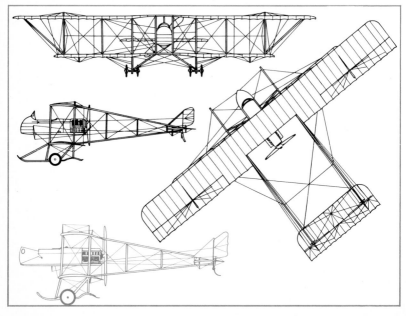

planes. The elevator was well forward, supported by two long curved outriggers that also served as landing skids, hence the nickname 'Longhorn'. Despite its primitive appearance, the plane was extremely functional. Equipped with ever more powerful engines, the plane served for several years. It began operations with French and British forces in 1913 and remained on reconnaissance duty until 1915, when it was replaced by the M.F.11.

The M.F.11, designed in 1914, was a great improvement over its predecessor. Apart from aerodynamic and structural changes, notably the abandonment of the forward elevator in favour of a rear-mounted one, it was also given armament: a machine-gun that could be fired by the observer. It could also carry small bombs. It was an M.F.11 of the Royal Naval Air Service that carried out the first night bombing mission of the war, on December 21, 1914, attacking artillery installations near Ostend. The short-

Aircraft: **Maurice Farman M.F.7**
Manufacturer: **Société Henri et Maurice Farman**
Type: **Reconnaissance**
Year: **1913**
Engine: **Renault 8-cylinder air-cooled in-line V, 70 hp**
Wingspan: **51 ft (15.54 m)**
Length: **37 ft 2.5 in (11.35 m)**
Height: **11 ft 4 in (3.45 m)**
Weight: **1,885 lbs (855 kg)**
Maximum speed: **59 mph (95 kph) at sea level**
Ceiling: **13,123 ft (4,000 m)**
Endurance: **3 hrs 30 mins**
Armament:
Crew: **2**

Aircraft: **Maurice Farman M.F.11**
Manufacturer: **Societé Henri et Maurice Farman**
Type: **Reconnaissance/light bomber**
Year: **1914**
Engine: **Renault 8-cylinder air-cooled in-line V, 100 hp**
Wingspan: **53 ft (16.15 m)**
Length: **30 ft 8 in (9.45 m)**
Height: **10 ft 5 in (3.18 m)**
Weight: **2,045 lbs (928 kg)**
Maximum speed: **66 mph (106 kph) at sea level**
Ceiling: **12,467 ft (3,800 m)**
Endurance: **3 hrs 45 mins**
Armament: **1 machine-gun; 288 lbs (130 kg) of bombs**
Crew: **2**

ening of the outrigger/skids with the abandonment of the forward elevator led to the appellation 'Shorthorn'.

Henri Farman Series 20

Henri Farman's Series 20 planes were just as popular with the Allies as Maurice Farman's M.F.7s, although they were not quite as good. The first four models in the series were underpowered and were only suitable for simple reconnaissance flights. They could carry a machine-gun (Vickers or Lewis) and a load of small bombs, but the extra weight limited their performance considerably. But they were among the few planes readily available when war broke out. So Series 20 Farmans saw combat duty from the first day of the war and were only withdrawn from combat and assigned to training in the summer of 1915, when more powerful planes became available.

The first of the series was the H.F.20, which Henri Farman designed in 1913. The design was based on that of an earlier plane, the H.F.16. Three more models were developed from the H.F.20: the H.F.21, the H.F.22, and the H.F.23. They went into production immediately after the H.F.20. These planes resembled each other in general concept: two-seater pusher biplanes, with the crew in a central nacelle on the lower wing and the tailplane supported by four wooden booms, two stretching back from each set of wings. The main difference between the four versions was the size of wings and fuselage, and the engine. The H.F.21 had a larger wingspan and a shorter fuselage than the H.F.20. The H.F.22 and the H.F.23 had a smaller wingspan than the H.F.20, but the fuselage was longer than that of the H.F.20 and the H.F.21.

When war broke out, Series 20 planes already equipped five French, two Belgian, and seven British squadrons. They also equipped Russian and Romanian units. Production in-

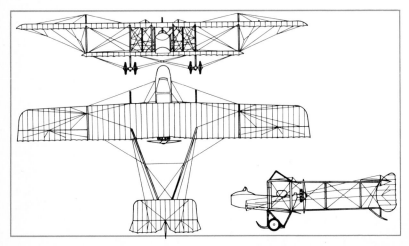

creased as the war went on, and the Farman brothers granted construction rights to various nations, including Belgium, Holland, Great Britain, and Italy. Italy chose the H.F.22, and the Savoia works also built a seaplane version of the plane. Italian Farmans were generally powered by 100-hp Fiat A.10 and 100-hp Colombo engines.

The last plane in the series, the H.F.27, was a considerable improvement over its predecessors. The plane was slightly larger, and its structure (steel tubing) was entirely different. It had a new landing gear (four wheels and no tailskid), and equal-span wings. The fuselage was shorter, and engine power was almost doubled, thanks to the Canton-Unné 140- or 160-hp engine. This model could carry about 551 pounds (250 kg) of bombs, with endurance of four hours. The H.F.27 saw action on almost all fronts: on the Western Front, in the Dardanelles, in East and South-West Africa, and in Mesopotamia, where it

Aircraft: **Henri Farman H.F.20**
Manufacturer: **Farman Frères**
Type: **Reconnaissance**
Year: **1914**
Engine: **Gnome 7A 7-cylinder air-cooled rotary, 80 hp**
Wingspan: **44 ft 10 in (15.54 m)**
Length: **27 ft 9 in (8.79 m)**
Height: **10 ft (3.1 m)**
Weight: **1,565 lbs (710 kg)**
Maximum speed: **65 mph (100 kph) at sea level**
Ceiling: **9,022 ft (2,750 m)**
Endurance: **3 hrs 30 mins**
Armament: **1 machine-gun**
Crew: **2**

took part in the siege of Kut-el-Amara. The British navy bought about 80 H.F.27s, and Romania acquired six British-built H.F.27s.

Nevertheless Series 20 planes were not outstanding in performance. Nor could the Series 40, a joint effort that Henri and Maurice Farman began producing in 1915, be considered totally successful.

There can be no doubt that by the middle of the war, the basic pusher layout employed by the Farman brothers was obsolescent if not actually obsolete.

Voisin 3
Voisin 5

On October 5, 1914, near Reims, an Allied plane shot down an enemy aircraft for the first time, when a German Aviatik was downed by a French Voisin 3. Hundreds of biplanes manufactured by Gabriel Voisin took part in the war. Successive models were more powerful, and the Voisin became the standard bomber of the first years of the war. These planes were extremely sturdy, thanks to their steel-tube structure, and could take a lot of punishment. They were also among the first planes to be used in night bombing raids. Some Voisins were the first planes to be armed with a

cannon instead of a machine-gun. The gun was a 37-mm or even 47-mm Hotchkiss. The weapon was almost useless in air combat but extremely effective against ground targets.

Most of these early Voisin planes were of the Model 3 type. The design of the plane (which was also known as the LA) was prewar, the prototype flying for the first time in February 1914. It was first used in day operations but was soon shifted to night missions. This light bomber saw service with all the Allied air forces. France acquired a total of 800 Voisins, Belgium about 30, and a good number

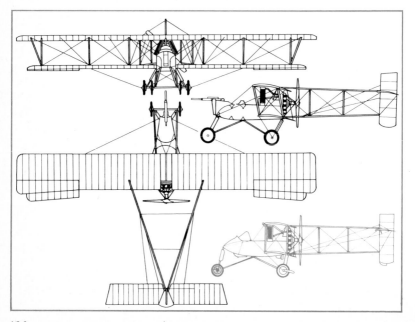

went to Russia. Great Britain bought about 50 French-built Voisin 3s for its two air forces (the R.F.C. or Royal Flying Corps, and the R.N.A.S. or Royal Naval Air Service) and later built another 50 under licence. In Italy 112 Voisins were built by the *Società Italiana Transaerea*. The Canton-Unné engine was replaced by several others in the Italian version, including Fiats, Isotta Fraschinis, and Renaults, all straight or V inlines.

The Voisin 4 and 5 appeared in 1915. They differed slightly in structure from the basic model and were equipped with more powerful engines. They could accommodate a 37-mm or 47-mm forward-firing cannon. Large numbers of these variants were also produced. A total of 200 Voisin 4s was built, in the LB and LB.S series. (The engine of the LB.S was inclined slightly.) And 350 Voisin 5s were manufactured. The last model was the Voisin 6, practically identical with the 5 except for a more powerful engine.

Despite their clumsy and inelegant

Aircraft: **Voisin 3**
Manufacturer: **Compagnie Gabriel Voisin**
Type: **Light bomber**
Year: **1914**
Engine: **Canton-Unné 9-cylinder liquid-cooled radial, 120 hp**
Wingspan: **48 ft 4.75 in (14.75 m)**
Length: **31 ft 2 in (9.5 m)**
Height: **12 ft 6 in (3.8 m)**
Weight: **3,025 lbs (1,370 kg)**
Maximum speed: **74 mph (120 kph) at sea level**
Ceiling: **11,485 ft (3,500 m)**
Endurance: **approx. 310 m (500 km)**
Armament: **1 machine-gun**
Crew: **2**

Aircraft: **Voisin 5**
Manufacturer: **Compagnie Gabriel Voisin**
Type: **Light bomber**
Year: **1915**
Engine: **Salmson (Canton-Unné) 9-cylinder liquid-cooled radial, 150 hp**
Wingspan: **48 ft 4.75 in (14.75 m)**
Length: **31 ft 3.25 in (9.53 m)**
Height: **11 ft 11 in (3.63 m)**
Weight: **2,516 lbs (1,140 kg)**
Maximum speed: **65 mph (105 kph) at sea level**
Ceiling: **11,485 ft (3,500 m)**
Endurance: **3 hrs 30 mins**
Armament: **1 machine-gun or 37-mm cannon; 132 lbs (60 kg) of bombs**
Crew: **2**

appearances, and indifferent performances, Voisin bombers did sterling work for the French right through the war.

Caudron G.4

With two engines instead of one, the Caudron G.4 was an improved and more powerful version of the G.3. Hundreds of G.4s were used by France, Great Britain, Belgium, Italy, and Russia during the first year and a half of the war. The plane appeared early in 1915 and was adopted by the French air force towards the end of the year. It soon made a name for itself for reliability and fast climbing. It was then acquired by Great Britain and Italy. Between 1917 and 1918 the Italian A.E.R. works built 51 Caudrons under licence. The British Caudrons were used from 1916 to early 1917 in day and night bombing missions against German seaplane and Zeppelin bases in Belgium. In 1916, the G.4 was followed by the G.6. This was a transition model to the new Caudron R bombers, which were of completely new and considerably improved design.

Aircraft: **Caudron G.4**
Manufacturer: **Caudron Frères**
Type: **Bomber/reconnaissance**
Year: **1915**
Engines: **80hp Le Rhône 9-cylinder rotaries; or 2 100hp Anzani 10-cylinder radials**
Wingspan: **56 ft 5 in (17.2 m)**
Length: **23 ft 6 in (7.16 m)**
Height: **8 ft 5 in (2.6 m)**
Weight: **2,932 lbs (1,330 kg)**
Maximum speed: **82 mph (132 kph) at 6,560 ft (2,000 m)**
Ceiling: **14,110 ft (4,300 m)**
Endurance: **3 hrs 30 mins**
Armament: **1 machine-gun; 250 lbs (113 kg) of bombs**
Crew: **2**

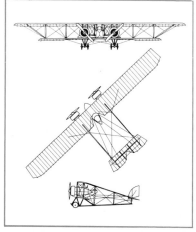

F

F.B.A. Type C

The Type C of the Franco–British Aviation Company (F.B.A.) was the second of a fine series of flying boats, the best of which was to be the Type H. The Type C was so efficient and practical that 982 of them were produced in Italy alone, despite the very strong competition of various types of Macchi flying boats. The F.B.A. Type C already incorporated the basic characteristics that were to be perfected in later models. The Type C had the same lines and general structure as its predecessor, the Type B, but its Clerget engine generated 30 hp more than the Type B's 100-hp Gnome. The F.B.A. Type C was built for the maritime air forces of France, Italy, and Russia, and was used for maritime patrolling and reconnaissance and anti-submarine duty. But it was somewhat underarmed for maximum effect against submarines. The British used their Type Cs for training.

Aircraft: **F.B.A. Type C**
Manufacturer: **Franco-British Aviation**
Type: **Reconnaissance**
Year: **1915**
Engine: **Clerget 9-cylinder air-cooled rotary, 130 hp**
Wingspan: **44 ft 11 in (13.70 m)**
Length: **28 ft 10 in (8.79 m)**
Height: **11 ft 2in (3.4m)**
Weight: **2,072 lbs (940 kg)**
Maximum speed: **68 mph (110 kph) at sea level**
Ceiling: **11,480 ft (3,500 m)**
Endurance: **186 m (300 km)**
Armament: **1 machine-gun**
Crew: **2**

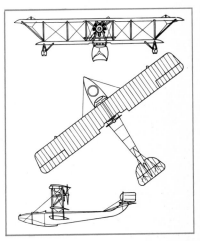

Nieuport 11/16
Nieuport 10/12

One of the most famous fighters of the war, hundreds of which were built, and a plane that served on all fronts and was flown by some of the Allies' most famous aces, was derived from an aeroplane that was originally designed for racing. The '*Bébé*', as the Nieuport 11 was called because of its small size, was designed by Gustave Delage for the 1914 Gordon Bennett Trophy race. The outbreak of war cancelled the meet, but the British and French ordered the plane at once. The *Bébé* entered service in the summer of 1915. Fast and highly manoeuvrable, the *Bébé* was a match for the Fokker monoplanes. During the battle of Verdun (February 1916 onwards), the Nieuport 11 was flown by some of the best French fighter pilots, including Guynemer, de Rose, and Nungesser. The Nieuport inflicted such heavy losses on enemy squadrons that German commanders had to change their fighting tactics. In Italy, where 646 *Bébés* were built under licence by Macchi, the plane remained the standard fighter until the summer of 1917. The basic project that led to the development of the Nieuport 11 was the Type 10, which Gustave Delage designed soon after he started working for the Nieuport company in 1914. The Type 10 was a two-seater tractor biplane and appeared in two versions, the Nie.10*AV* and the Nie.10*AR*. The observer sat in front of the pilot in the

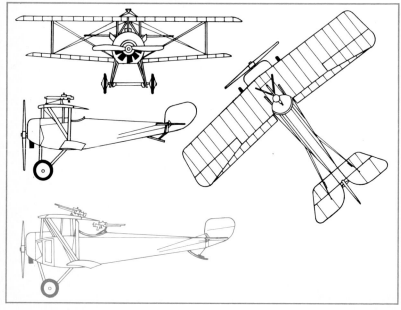

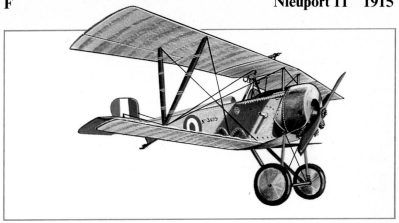

AV model and behind him in the *AR*. The Nieuport 10 entered service in the summer of 1915. It was soon transformed into a single-seater, the observer's position being covered over and a machine-gun installed on the upper wing. The plane was supplied to Great Britain and to Belgium, and it was also built in Italy. It was used as an emergency fighter, alongside the later Type 12, a larger and more powerful aircraft originally designed as a reconnaissance plane. But the single-seater Type 11 was the first 'genuine' fighter designed by Delage.

After brilliant service in the French, British, Italian, Belgian, Dutch, and Russian air forces, and with the first American volunteers, the Nieuport 11 was replaced by the more powerful Type 16, which made its debut in 1916 against the new German fighter planes. The Nieuport 16 had a 110-hp engine and a machine-gun synchronized to shoot through the propeller disk. This new version, which often carried Le Prieur rockets between the

Aircraft: **Nieuport 11**
Manufacturer: **Société Anonyme des Etablissements Nieuport**
Type: **Fighter**
Year: **1915**
Engine: **Le Rhône 9C 9-cylinder air-cooled rotary, 80 hp**
Wingspan: **24 ft 9 in (7.55 m)**
Length: **19 ft 0.33 in (5.8 m)**
Height: **8 ft 0.5 in (2.45 m)**
Weight: **1,060 lbs (480 kg)**
Maximum speed: **97 mph (156 kph) at sea level**
Ceiling: **15,090 ft (4,600 m)**
Endurance: **2 hrs 30 mins**
Armament: **1 machine-gun**
Crew: **1**

Aircraft: **Nieuport 12**
Manufacturer: **Société Anonyme des Etablissements Nieuport**
Type: **Fighter/reconnaissance**
Year: **1915**
Engine: **Clerget 9B 9-cylinder air-cooled rotary, 130 hp**
Wingspan: **29 ft 7.5 in (9.03 m)**
Length: **23 ft 6 in (7.3 m)**
Height: **8 ft 11 in (2.67 m)**
Weight: **2,028 lbs (920 kg)**
Maximum speed: **98 mph (155 kph) at sea level**
Ceiling: **15,420 ft (4,700 m)**
Endurance: **2 hrs 45 mins**
Armament: **1-2 machine-guns**
Crew: **1-2**

wings, saw active duty until 1917 assigned to British, French, and Belgian units.

Breguet Br.M.5

The basic specifications the French government asked for in the summer of 1915 were a bomb capacity of 300 kilograms (about 660 lbs) and a range of 600 kilometres (about 375 miles) for a bomber to attack the German industrial works in the Essen area. The winning design, a pusher biplane with fairly conventional lines and structure, was presented by Louis Breguet in October. The plane was not a new design, but rather an adaptation of the BU3, about 100 of which had been built for the French air force. Changes involved the wingspan, the design of the landing gear, and some structural details. The plane equipped five French bomber squadrons and remained in service with some units until the beginning of 1918. About 10 Br.M.5s, built under licence by the Grahame-White company, equipped units of the British R.N.A.S. Powered by 250-hp. Rolls-Royce engines, these Grahame-White Type 19s were little

more successful than their French counterparts. These and the 25 French-built Breguet-Michelin Br.M.5 bombers bought by the Royal Naval Air Service were soon phased out of active duties.

The Breguet Br.M.5 was produced in two versions, with the military designations 4B.2 and 5Ca.2. The main difference between them was their armament. The 4B.2 was intended mainly for bombing; the 5Ca.2 was a bomber escort. The Breguet 4B.2 was armed with a Lewis or Hotchkiss machine-gun fired by the forward observer and a Michelin bomb-rack under each lower wing outside the landing gear. It could carry a maximum of 40 16-lb (7-kg) bombs. The Breguet 5Ca.2 bomber escort originally had a 37-mm Hotchkiss cannon installed at the nose and a rear machine-gun mounted on the upper wing. The cannon was totally ineffective in combat (as the cannons

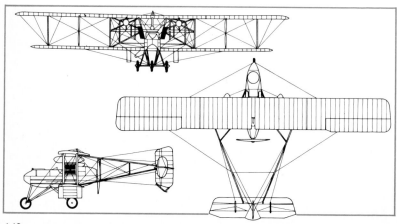

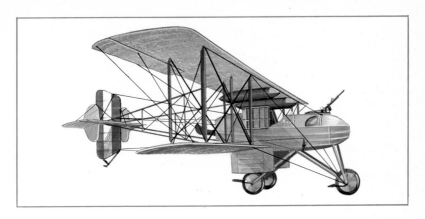

mounted on the Voisin 4 and 5 had been) and was replaced by another machine-gun. The major problem of the heavier weapon was that accurate fire could not be maintained.

At first the Breguet bomber was used on day missions. But the weaknesses of its rather outdated design were soon felt. It could carry a satisfactory bombload, and it had good range, but it was too slow and vulnerable for day bombing. When it had a full load, a very long airstrip was needed for take-off, and landing was also fraught with difficulties. After a disastrous raid on Oberndorf in October 1916, the Breguets were taken off day missions. But there were still problems. The pilots complained about lack of visibility on night missions. The pilot sat behind the gunner/observer, and often the observer had to guide the pilot and direct his manoeuvres. It was almost like blind flying! Nevertheless the plane carried out a great many successful long-range bombing missions.

Aircraft: **Breguet Br. M.5**
Manufacturer: **S.A. des Ateliers d'Aviation Louis Breguet**
Type: **Bomber**
Year: **1915**
Engine: **Renault liquid-cooled inline V, 220 hp**
Wingspan: **57 ft 9 in (17.6 m)**
Length: **32 ft 6 in (9.9 m)**
Height: **12 ft 9 in (3.89 m)**
Weight: **4,235 lbs (1,921 kg)**
Maximum speed: **88 mph (142 kph) at sea level**
Ceiling: **14,110 ft (4,300 m)**
Endurance: **435 m (700 km) or 5 hrs**
Armament: **1-2 machine-guns; 661 lbs (300 kg) of bombs**
Crew: **2**

The Michelin in the designation of the Br.M.5 was André Michelin, the tyre and industrial magnate. It was one of Michelin's companies which designed and produced the Michelin bomb-racks used in the Br.M.5 and Br.14. Michelin had also paid for 100 BU-3 bombers for the French air force.

143

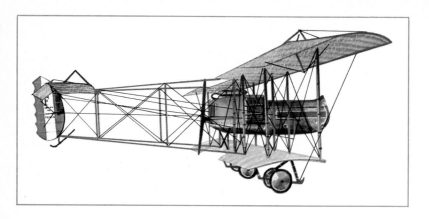

Farman F.40

Although the Farman Series 40 bombers were outdated from the time they entered service, they were used on day missions for a year before they were transferred to night bombing. Only in the last year of the war were they withdrawn from the front altogether and assigned to training. They were the first planes to be designed jointly by Henri and Maurice Farman. Although the planes combined the best features of the aircraft designed by the two brothers separately, they were under-armed. They carried one Lewis machine-gun in the nose and had a small bomb capacity. The basic F.40 model was developed in five later models: the F.41, F.46, F.56, F.60 and F.61. They differed in engine and in wing size, but kept the basic configuration of the F.40: a pusher biplane with a central nacelle. Various models in the series served as reconnaissance planes and light bombers in the French and Belgian air forces.

Aircraft: **Farman F.40**
Manufacturer: **Société Henri et Maurice Farman**
Type: **Reconnaissance/light bomber**
Year: **1915**
Engine: **Renault liquid-cooled inline V, 160 hp**
Wingspan: **57 ft 10 in (17.62 m)**
Length: **30 ft 4 in (9.24 m)**
Weight: **2,475 lbs (1,120 m)**
Maximum speed: **84 mph (135 kph) at 6,560 ft (2,000 m)**
Ceiling: **16,076 ft (4,900 m)**
Endurance: **2 hrs 20 mins**
Armament: **1 machine-gun; 110 lbs (50 kg) of bombs**
Crew: **2**

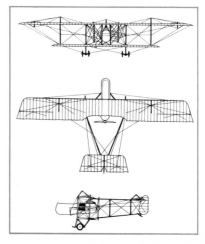

Voisin 8

Gabriel Voisin hoped his 1916 Type 8 would be as successful as the planes he produced in 1914 and 1915. Although about 1,100 Type 8s were produced – better armed, faster, and higher-powered than the earlier planes – they were not really outstanding. The Voisin 8 entered service towards the end of 1916 as a night bomber, but its operational use was limited by the behaviour of the engine. The Peugeot engine was erratic, and the trouble was never completely eliminated. Eventually it was replaced by a 300-hp Renault. A Renault engine also powered the Type 10, which had a better performance and could carry almost double the load of bombs. One version of the Voisin 8 had a cannon mounted at the front of the nacelle. This was a feature copied from the Breguet planes and Voisin's own Types 4 and 5. This version was used only for ground attack.

Aircraft: **Voisin Type 8**
Manufacturer: **Compagnie Gabriel Voisin**
Type: **Bomber**
Year: **1916**
Engine: **Peugeot 8-cylinder liquid-cooled inline, 220 hp**
Wingspan: **61 ft 8 in (18.2 m)**
Length: **36 ft 2 in (11.02 m)**
Height: **11 ft 5.75 in (3.5 m)**
Weight: **4,100 lbs (1,860 kg)**
Maximum speed: **82 mph (132 kph)**
Ceiling: **14,110 ft (4,300 m)**
Endurance: **4 hrs**
Armament: **1-2 machine-guns; 397 lbs (180 kg) of bombs**
Crew: **2**

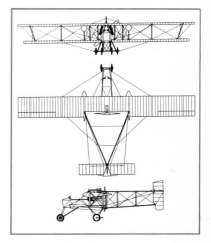

Spad S. VII

The Spads represented the best in aero technology half way through the First World War. The S.VII and S.XIII models are considered by some to have been the best fighter planes of the war, and were flown by such aces as Baracca, Ruffo, Fonck, Guynemer, and Rickenbacker. The Spad owed its success equally to designer, Louis Béchéreau (who had designed the fast 1912–13 Deperdussin monoplanes) and to the Swiss engineer Marc Birkigt, of the Hispano-Suiza company, who created the fighter's 'heart', an 8-cylinder inline V engine. Engine power increased with each new model, and these engines generated far more power than the rotary engines then in production. The new Hispano-Suiza engine was also very reliable and sturdy. From this time onwards the rotary engine, which had contributed so much to the development of aviation, gradually began to fade from the scene.

Louis Béchéreau designed his new fighter around the Hispano-Suiza 'V-8'. The engine was housed in a metal cowling with a round frontal radiator. The plane itself was of the standard wooden construction, covered with canvas, with the exception of the forward part of the fuselage, which was covered with aluminium panels. The armament consisted of a Vickers machine-gun with Birkigt synchronization. The Spad S.VII made its maiden flight at Villacoublay in April 1916. The test pilot, Bequet, flew it superbly, and the plane's performance was impressive. Although the 140-hp engine did not have a very high compression ratio the plane reached 122 mph (196 kph) at sea level and climbed to an altitude of 9,840 feet (3,000 m) in 15 minutes. The French military authorities ordered 268 S.VIIs at once. Orders from abroad and requests for construction licences soon followed.

Deliveries began on September 2,

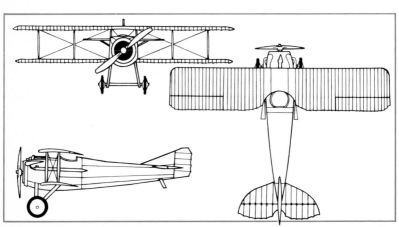

1916, and the plane was soon being produced by the thousand (5,600 in France alone). Spads soon equipped fighter squadrons of all the Allied powers. Great Gritain, France, Belgium, Russia, and the U.S.A. used Spads against German planes.

French squadrons (including the famous '*Les Cigognes*') flew the plane in action until the middle of 1917, when the first S.XIIIs began to arrive. The new aircraft was better armed and generally more powerful. But the career of the Spad S.VII was far from finished. The first S.VIIs reached Italy in March 1917 and was kept in service even after the appearance of the S.XIII in early 1918. Italy acquired a total of 214 Spads, and the first squadrons to receive them were the 77th and the 91st. Francesco Baracca, the Italian ace, was a member of the 91st, and flying a Spad S.VII when he downed his first German plane, a Brandenburg. A few days later, on May 21, Baracca shot down another Brandenburg, his twelfth victory. The Spad S.VII was Baracca's favourite plane,

Aircraft: **Spad S.VII**
Manufacturer: **S.P.A.D. (Société Anonyme Pour l'Aviation et ses Dérivés)**
Type: **Fighter**
Year: **1916**
Engine: **Hispano-Suiza 8 Ac 8-cylinder liquid-cooled inline V, 175 hp**
Wingspan: **25 ft 6 in (7.77 m)**
Length: **20 ft 1 in (6.13 m)**
Height: **7 ft 8.5 in (2.33 m)**
Weight: **1,550 lbs (703 kg)**
Maximum speed: **119 mph (191.5 kph) at 6,560 ft (2,000 m)**
Ceiling: **18,000 ft (5,485 m)**
Endurance: **2 hrs 15 mins**
Armament: **1 machine-gun**
Crew: **1**

and he went on using it even after the arrival of the more powerful S.XIII. The 91st Squadron achieved excellent results with the French fighter. During the first phase of the Austrian offensive in October 1917, 14 enemy planes were shot down in seven days, between the 20th and the 26th. Baracca engaged in five dog-fights on October 25, and by December 7 he had chalked up a total of 30 planes. On the whole, the Spad S.VII was a better plane than the Brandenburg D I and the CC, although its limitations became apparent when it faced the first Albatros D IIIs.

Nieuport 17

The 1916 Nieuport 17, probably Gustave Delage's most famous plane, was developed from the 1915 Nieuport 11 'Bébé'. Larger, stronger, and better armed, the Nieuport 17 was one of the finest combat planes of its time. It was one of the best Allied fighters until the appearance of the Spad S.VII. Delage designed the 17 keeping fairly close to the general formula of the *Bébé*, but eliminated the older plane's defects and improved on its performance. The new plane's fuselage was larger and had better lines. The small lower wing of the *Bébé* had been found wanting in strength during combat manoeuvres, and had shown an unfortunate tendency to break up in flight. Delage strengthened the structure a great deal to keep the lower wing from twisting. The Nieuport 17 was also more heavily armed than its predecessor. Initially a Lewis machine-gun was mounted on the upper wing, but this

was later added to or replaced by a synchronized Vickers machine-gun. There were variations in combat units: some pilots kept the Lewis on the wing, and others mounted twin synchonized machine-guns, although this limited the plane's performance.

The Nieuport 17 reached the front in March 1916, and gradually replaced older planes in French units. The first squadron to fly the new fighter operationally was N.57, on May 2. Five other units followed, including the famous 3rd Squadron of '*Les Cigognes*'. The plane was also adopted by the two British air forces. By the spring of 1917 five R.F.C. squadrons and eight R.N.A.S. squadrons had the 17. Other Nieuport 17s served with the Dutch, Belgian, Russian, and Italian air forces. In Italy 150 were built under licence by Macchi, and the first Italian-built 17s were delivered in October 1916. This fighter was so pop-

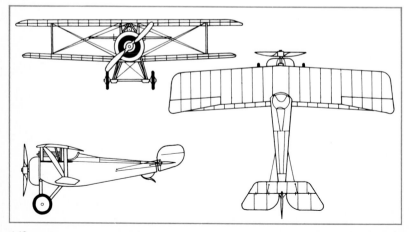

ular with the Allies that in August 1917, 317 of them were still in front-line service.

The Nieuport 17 soon became the favourite plane of the leading aces of the time, from the British Ball and Canadian Bishop to the French Nungesser, Guynemer, Fonck and Navarre. This fighter proved its worth during the battles of the Somme and the Isonzo, and stood up well against the Fokker E monoplanes, Halberstadt D IIs and even Albatros D Is. The Nieuport 17 proved such a threat that the Germans decided to build it themselves, copying Nieuport 17s that had been forced down behind the lines and captured. The German version of the 17 was manufactured by Siemens-Schuckert but never went into action, because more powerful models of the Albatros began reaching their units.

H. A. Jones, the British official historian of the First World War in the air, says the following of the Nieuport 17: 'While our pushers with skill and determination were subduing the Fok-

Aircraft: **Nieuport 17**
Manufacturer: **Société Anonyme des Etablissements Nieuport**
Type: **Fighter**
Year: **1916**
Engine: **Le Rhône 9J 9-cylinder air-cooled rotary, 110 hp**
Wingspan: **26 ft 10 in (8.17 m)**
Length: **18 ft 11 in (5.77 m)**
Height: **8 ft (2.44 m)**
Weight: **1,246 lbs (565 kg)**
Maximum speed: **110 mph (177 kph) at 6,560 ft (2,000 m)**
Ceiling: **17,390 ft (5,300 m)**
Endurance: **2 hrs**
Armament: **1 machine-gun**
Crew: **1**

kers the French produced a very effective fighting scout. This was the small single-seater Nieuport Scout (110 horse-power Le Rhône engine) armed with a Lewis gun fired over the top of the plane by means of a Bowden cable. Its performance was superior to that of any contemporary fighting aeroplane. It could reach 10,000 ft. in 10 and a half minutes and was 10 miles an hour faster than the best aeroplane of the R.F.C.'

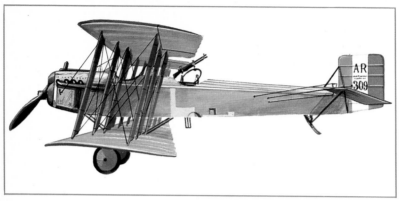

Dorand AR.1

This reconnaissance plane was used extensively in the last months of the war. It was in service with 18 squadrons on the French and Italian fronts. In 1916 the French government was looking for a tractor biplane to replace its Farman reconnaissance planes, but none of the manufacturers the government approached seemed anxious to develop such a plane. Colonel Dorand, then head of the *Section Technique de l'Aéronautique* at Chalais-Meudon, presented a design based on his own 1914 biplane, the DO.1. The new aircraft resembled the earlier one, with a long fuselage and backward-staggered wings (the top ones behind the bottom ones). But the new plane had a much more powerful engine. The Dorand AR.1 completed flight tests in September 1916, and was assigned to reconnaissance units in April 1917. An improved version, the AR.2A2, had a 200-hp Renault engine and radiators in the wings.

Aircraft: **Dorand AR.1**
Manufacturer: **STA**
Type: **Reconnaissance/trainer**
Year: **1917**
Engine: **Renault inline V, 190 hp**
Wingspan: **43 ft 7 in (13.29 m)**
Length: **30 ft (9.14 m)**
Height: **10 ft 10 in (3.30 m)**
Weight: **2,750 lbs (1,247 kg)**
Maximum speed: **94.5 mph (152 kph) at 6,560 ft (2,000 m)**
Ceiling: **18,045 ft (5,500 m)**
Endurance: **3 hrs**
Armament: **2-3 machine-guns; 181 lbs (82 kg) of bombs**
Crew: **2**

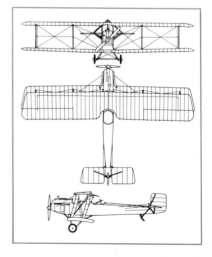

Morane-Saulnier AI

Continuing with their series of fighter planes, Robert and Léon Morane and Raymond Saulnier designed the AI in 1917. It was a streamlined parasol-winged monoplane with a rounded fuselage. Although 1,210 AIs were built, the plane had a short and not altogether successful career. It did, however, provide the basic model for another line of fighter planes the company manufactured until 1930. Three versions of the AI were produced: the MoS.27C.1, with a single machine-gun; the MoS.29C.1, with two guns; and the MoS.30E.1, a training model powered by a 120-hp engine. The first AIs were delivered in December 1917, and the plane first saw combat in January 1918. But barely two months later it was withdrawn from combat duty and assigned to training. The official explanation was that the plane was underpowered, though it was rumoured that the plane had some structural weakness.

Aircraft: **Morane-Saulnier AI (MoS.29C.1)**
Manufacturer: **Morane-Saulnier**
Type: **Fighter**
Year: **1917**
Engine: **Gnome Monosoupape 9N 9-cylinder air-cooled rotary, 150 hp**
Wingspan: **27 ft 11 in (8.51 m)**
Length: **18 ft 6.5 in (5.65 m)**
Height: **7 ft 10.25 in (2.4 m)**
Weight: **1,483 lbs (673.9 kg)**
Maximum speed: **138 mph (220.6 kph)**
Ceiling: **22,965 ft (7,000 m)**
Endurance: **2 hrs 30 mins**
Armament: **2 machine-guns**
Crew: **1**
(Illustration shows MoS.30E.1)

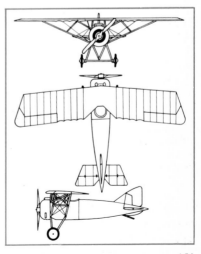

Hanriot HD.1

The Hanriot HD.1, designed by Pierre Dupont in 1916, had the misfortune to come out in France at the same time as such fine fighters as the various Nieuport and Spad models. With such excellent planes already in the air, French authorities did not buy the Hanriot, but Italy and Belgium did. The small fighter plane gave high-performance service on various fronts.

The HD.1 design had smooth lines and a mixed structure. The wings were well staggered, and there was dihedral only on the upper surfaces. The fuselage was rectangular in section, rounded on top, and faired into the metal cowling of the rotary engine. The first engine was a 110-hp Le Rhône 9J, but this was later replaced by more powerful engines in an effort to improve the plane's performance. The final engine was the 170-hp Le Rhône 9R. The standard model, however, had between 110 and 130 hp engines.

The HD.1 was highly manoeuvrable, and the Italian authorities purchased the plane late in 1916 for combat duty against the new German and Austrian fighters. An initial order for 100 planes was placed with the Macchi company, which built the aircraft under licence. The first HD.1s were delivered early the following year, and by summer the planes had reached front-line squadrons. In action the plane proved to be very tough and extremely manoeuvrable, but it was a bit slower than the Brandenburg D I and the various Albatros models the enemy was operating. But the HD.1's overall superiority was demonstrated on several occasions, including the air battle over Istrana on December 26, 1917, when 6th Group Hanriots shot down 11 German reconnaissance planes without a single loss. The plane was the standard fighter in Italy, and the Macchi company

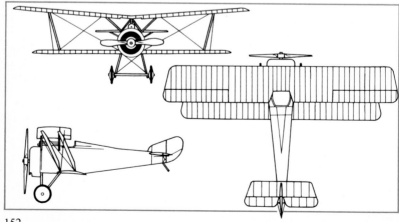

manufactured 831 during the war. At its peak, the HD.1 equipped 16 of the 18 front-line Italian fighter squadrons.

The Hanriot HD.1 also served in a new air unit of the Italian navy, the 241st Squadron. Formed early in 1918, with mixed army-navy crews, the squadron's task was the defence of the great base of Venice from ever more frequent Austrian air attacks. The 12 Hanriots assigned to this squadron also carried out many naval escort missions. This was one of the earliest co-ordinated air-sea operations in history. In the last period of the war, the planes of the 241st Squadron also carried out patrol missions in the Piave area.

In Belgium the Hanriot HD.1 entered action in August 1917. It also saw peacetime service in Belgium until 1926. Belgian pilots were enthusiastic about the plane and preferred it to another famous fighter, the British Sopwith Camel. The Belgians had been offered the Camel early in 1918 but turned it down. The outstanding

Aircraft: **Hanriot HD.1**
Manufacturer: **Société Anonyme des Appareils d'Aviation Hanriot**
Type: **Fighter**
Year: **1917**
Engine: **Le Rhône 9Jb 9-cylinder air-cooled rotary, 120 hp**
Wingspan: **28 ft 6.5 in (8.7 m)**
Length: **19 ft 2.25 in (5.85 m)**
Height: **9 ft 7.75 in (2.94 m)**
Weight: **1,334 lbs (605 kg)**
Maximum speed: **115 mph (184 kph) at sea level**
Ceiling: **20,670 ft (6,000 m)**
Endurance: **2 hrs 30 mins**
Armament: **1 machine-gun**
Crew: **1**

Belgian ace Willy Coppens de Houthulst downed most of his 37 victories at the controls of a Hanriot.

Although the plane was officially turned down by the government, a few Hanriots saw service in France as ship-borne fighters with French naval units.

Final development of the type was the HD.2, a twin-float fighter, some 10 of these were ordered by the US Navy for base defence in 1918, but were soon converted to land planes.

153

Breguet Br.14

One of the finest products of Louis Breguet's talent was the Model 14, which appeared early in 1917. Almost 5,500 Model 14s were built in the last two years of the war. By 1926, when production at last ceased, over 8,000 had been built. The long lifespan of this plane was due not only to the high quality of its basic design, but also to many technological and structural innovations, including the extensive use of Duralumin in the construction. These planes made a great contribution to the Allied effort in the last years of the conflict, chiefly because of their great versatility. Variant models of the two basic versions – the Br.14A.2 reconnaissance plane and the Br.14B.2 bomber – were developed, including a night bomber model and one for ambulance duty. There was also a seaplane version. The Br.14s were such hardy planes that they could fly even in very bad weather.

The prototype of the Breguet 14 first took to the air at Villacoublay on November 21, 1916, only six months after the start of the project. It was piloted by Breguet himself, with the assistant designer, Vuillerme, in the observer's seat. The plane was first produced in a reconnaissance model, and 508 were ordered at the start of 1917. The Br.14B.2 bomber prototype appeared soon after this. By the end of the year, 2,000 bombers had been ordered, to be built by six manufacturers.

The two models were not very dissimilar. The bomber model had lower wings of greater span, transparent side panels in the observer's section, air brakes, and Michelin bomb-racks. The armament for both models was the same: a fixed Vickers machine-gun for the pilot and one or two Lewis machine-guns on a ring-mounting in the observer's cockpit. The bomber could carry as much as 661 pounds (300 kg) of bombs, but the standard load was 32 bombs of 17.63 pounds (8 kg) each.

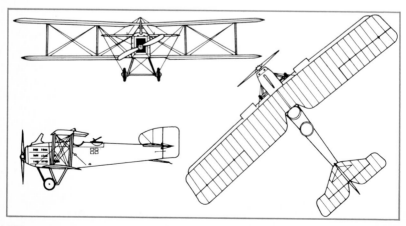

Both versions of the Breguet Br.14 went into action in summer 1917. By the end of the year, three French reconnaissance squadrons and six bomber squadrons had Br.14s. Within a year 93 units were equipped with Br.14s, 71 on the Western Front and the rest in Serbia, Greece, Morocco, and Macedonia. The plane was also adopted by Belgian aviation forces, which equipped two squadrons with it, and by the American Expeditionary Forces (A.E.F.), which acquired 376 Breguet 14s in 1918.

In its long career the Breguet Br.14 was powered by different engines, but the 300-hp Renault remained standard. Other engines included the Renault 12K (400 hp), the Fiat A.12 and A.12*bis* (300 and 400 hp), the Liberty 12 (400 hp) and the Lorraine-Dietrich (370 hp). One of the most important engines used was a special 320-hp Renault with a multistage centrifugal blower, allowing maximum power up to an altitude of 18,045 feet (5,500 m). A plane tested at the end of the war with this engine reached 112 mph

Aircraft: **Breguet Br.14 B2**
Manufacturer: **S.A. des Ateliers d'Aviation Louis Breguet**
Type: **Bomber**
Year: **1917**
Engine: **Renault 12 Fcx 12-cylinder liquid-cooled inline V, 300 hp**
Wingspan: **47 ft 1.25 in (14.36 m)**
Length: **23 ft 1.25 in (8.87 m)**
Height: **10 ft 10 in (3.3 m)**
Weight: **3,892 lbs (1,765 kg)**
Maximum speed: **110 mph (177 kph) at 6,560 ft (2,000 m)**
Ceiling: **19,030 ft (5,800 m)**
Endurance: **2 hrs 45 mins**
Armament: **2-3 machine guns; 661 lbs (300 kg) of bombs**
Crew: **2**

(180 kph) at an altitude of about 22,965 feet (7,000 m). After the war the Breguet 14 continued its brilliant career in France and a dozen non-European countries. It also made an important contribution to the development of commercial aviation. The Br.14 made the first European postal flights, served on the first passenger lines, and made some spectacular long-distance flights. In 1919 it made a return crossing of the Mediterranean (994 miles, or 1,600 km) and a 1,180-mile (1,900-km) flight from Paris to Kenitra, Morocco.

155

Spad S.XIII
Spad S.XI

With the Spad S.XIII Louis Béch-éreau outdid the success of his own S.VII. The new plane was designed late in 1916. More powerful versions of the Hispano-Suiza engine, which had powered the earlier fighter, accounted for much of the S.XIII's superb performance. The S.XIII followed the general lines of its predecessor, but was larger, had better ailerons and empennage, and was more heavily armed, with two synchronized Vickers machine-guns. Above all, it had a 235-hp engine.

The prototype flew for the first time on April 4, 1917, and the plane was immediately accepted as the replacement for the Spad S.VII and for the latest Nieuports serving in French fighter units. The first consignment reached these units about the end of May, and in a short time more than 80 squadrons had S.XIIIs. The plane was flown by such famous aces as Fonck, Nungesser, and Guynemer (who was killed in combat while flying a Spad S.XIII). The S.XIII helped tip the balance of air power in the Allies' favour. This fighter was also used by 16 American squadrons, by a Belgian

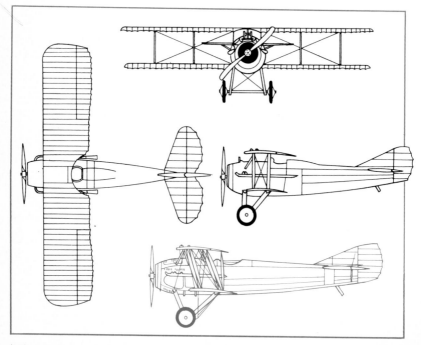

squadron, and by a British one. Italy, too, ordered the new plane, and S.XIIIs reached Italian units about the middle of 1918. Eleven squadrons were equipped with the fighter, but Italian pilots preferred the more agile Hanriot HD.1 to the heavier S.XIII. The French fighter offered an excellent gun platform, and was strong and powerful, but it was also less manoeuvrable and more difficult to handle at low speeds. The Italian ace Francesco Baracca preferred the lighter Spad S.VII to its successor. A total of 8,472 S.XIIIs was built.

Apart from the S.VII and the S.XIII, Louis Béchéreau also designed a two-seater light bomber, the S.XI, which appeared in September 1916. It resembled the S.VII in its general lines. But the wings were radically different, with a slight sweep and a stagger to compensate for the longer fuselage. The Spad S.XI entered action in 1917, but its new Hispano-Suiza engine (still not completely perfected) was unreliable. The plane was extremely sensitive to load distribution and soon

Aircraft: **Spad S.XIII**
Manufacturer: **S.P.A.D. (Société Anonyme Pour l'Aviation et ses Derivés)**
Type: **Fighter**
Year: **1917**
Engine: **Hispano-Suiza 8 BEc 8-cylinder liquid-cooled inline V, 235 hp**
Wingspan: **26 ft 11 in (8.2 m)**
Length: **20 ft 8 in (6.3 m)**
Height: **7 ft 11 in (2.42 m)**
Weight: **1,807 lbs (820 kg)**
Maximum speed: **138 mph (222 kph) at 6,560 ft (2,000 m)**
Ceiling: **21,820 ft (6,650 m)**
Endurance: **2 hrs**
Armament: **2 machine-guns**
Crew: **1**

Aircraft: **Spad S.XI**
Manufacturer: **S.P.A.D.(Société Anonyme Pour l'Aviation et ses Derivés)**
Type: **Reconnaissance-light bomber**
Year: **1916**
Engine: **Hispano-Suiza 8BE 8-cylinder liquid-cooled inline, 235 hp**
Wingspan: **36 ft 10 in (11.23 m)**
Length: **25 ft 5 in (7.75 m)**
Height: **8 ft 6 in (2.59 m)**
Weight: **2,310 lbs (1,048 kg)**
Maximum speed: **109 mph (176 kph) at 6,560 ft (2,000 m)**
Ceiling: **22,965 ft (7,000 m)**
Endurance: **2 hrs 15 mins**
Armament: **2-3 machine-guns; 154 lbs (70 kg) of bombs**
Crew: **2**

earned a reputation for being difficult to fly. It was withdrawn from front-line service in June 1918.

Nieuport 28
Nieuport 27
Nieuport-Delage 29

Gustave Delage's Nieuport 28 represented a radical break with the formula he had so successfully followed in developing his famous Models 11 and 17. The basic differences lay in the wing layout (no longer sesquiplane) and in the very elegant and streamlined fuselage (with a circular section). But this new design was not up to the level of his earlier planes. The Nieuport 28 was underpowered and structurally weak. Production models were ordered, but very few aircraft went into service with the French forces. By accident, however, the plane was not a total failure. Late in 1917 the American Expeditionary Forces were looking desperately for fighters for their first squadrons, but none of the many excellent planes in production was available in large numbers: none except the Nieuport 28, which had gone into production even without customers. The Americans bought 297 planes and put them in action during the last months of the war.

The Nieuport 28 had been preceded by two other Delage designs, the Model 24 and Model 27. These two similar aircraft were developments of the earlier Models 11 and 17, but could not match the performance of the first distinguished Spads, which were already being delivered to Allied

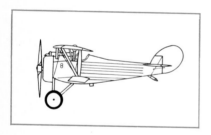

Aircraft: **Nieuport 27**
Manufacturer: **Société Anonyme des Etablissements Nieuport**
Type: **Fighter**
Year: **1917**
Engine: **Le Rhône 9Jb 9-cylinder air-cooled rotary, 120 hp**
Wingspan: **26 ft 11 in (8.18 m)**
Length: **19 ft 2.25 in (5.85 m)**
Height: **8 ft (2.43 m)**
Weight: **1,289 lbs (585 kg)**
Maximum speed: **116 mph (187 kph)**
Ceiling: **18,210 ft (5,550 m)**
Endurance: **1 hr 30 mins**
Armament: **2 machine-guns**
Crew: **1**

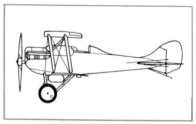

Aircraft: **Nieuport-Delage 29**
Manufacturer: **Société Anonyme des Etablissements Nieuport**
Type: **Fighter.**
Year: **1918**
Engine: **Hispano-Suiza 8Fb 8-cylinder liquid-cooled inline V, 300 hp**
Wingspan: **32 ft 1.25 in (9.79 m)**
Length: **21 ft 5 in (6.5 m)**
Height: **9 ft 1.5 in (2.77 m)**
Weight: **2,420 lbs (1,096 kg)**
Maximum speed: **147.5 mph (237 kph)**
Ceiling: **26,900 ft (8,200 m)**
Range: **360 miles (480 km)**
Armament: **2 machine-guns**
Crew: **1**

squadrons. Like the Nieuport 28, the 24 and 27 found a market with the Americans, who bought about 400 planes for use as trainers.

The Nieuport-Delage 29 was something completely different, even though it did not appear in time to take part in the war. This fighter, which many experts consider Gustave Delage's finest, was wholly unlike his earlier designs. It had a very powerful stationary engine (a 300-hp Hispano-Suiza) instead of the traditional rotary, which made it possible to design a very slim streamlined fus-

Aircraft: **Nieuport 28**
Manufacturer: **Société Anonyme des Etablissements Nieuport**
Type: **Fighter**
Year: **1917**
Engine: **Gnome Monosoupape 9N 9-cylinder air-cooled rotary, 160 hp**
Wingspan: **26 ft 9 in (8.15 m)**
Length: **21 ft (6.40 m)**
Height: **8 ft 1.75 in (2.5 m)**
Weight: **1,627 lbs (737 kg)**
Maximum speed: **122 mph (196 kph)**
Ceiling: **16,995 ft (5,180 m)**
Endurance: **1 hr 30 mins**
Armament: **2 machine-guns**
Crew: **1**

elage. This fast and manoeuvrable plane was one of the best fighters of the 1920s, used by France, Belgium, Italy, Switzerland, and Japan.

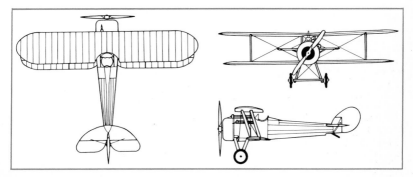

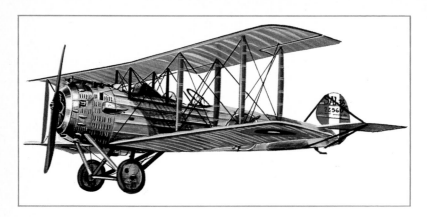

Salmson 2

The tough, versatile, and well-armed Salmson 2 was one of the most widely used French reconnaissance planes in the last year of the war. It was designed in 1917 by the *Société des Moteurs* Salmson for the new Canton-Unné radial engine, for which Salmson had acquired the production rights. The plane had a conventional look, with rounded lines and a metal cowling for the engine. The Salmson 2 passed evaluation tests along with the Breguet 14 and the Spad S.XI, and went into action early in 1918. The French used it in 24 squadrons, the Americans in 11. In all, 3,200 Salmson 2s were built, 705 of which were bought by the Americans. The plane was excellent at reconnaissance and versatile enough for day bombing and ground attack. On one mission, Lieutenant W. P. Erwin of the 1st Squadron of the American Expeditionary Forces shot down eight enemy planes.

Aircraft: **Salmson 2**
Manufacturer: **Société Salmson**
Type: **Reconnaissance**
Year: **1918**
Engine: **Salmson   (Canton-Unné)   9-cylinder liquid-cooled radial, 260 hp**
Wingspan: **38 ft 8.5 in (11.8 m)**
Length: **27 ft 10.75 in (8.5 m)**
Height: **9 ft 6.25 in (2.9 m)**
Weight: **2,954 lbs (1,340 kg)**
Maximum speed: **115 mph (185 kph)**
Ceiling: **20,505 ft (6,250 m)**
Endurance: **3 hrs**
Armament: **2-3 machine-guns**
Crew: **2**

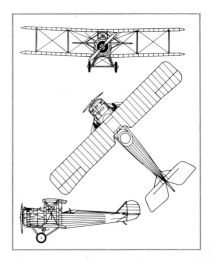

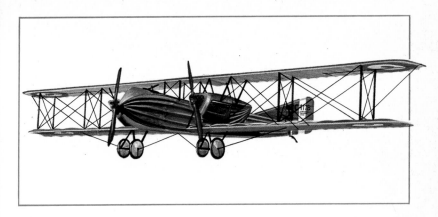

Caudron R.11

This was the last model of the R series bombers that René Caudron had begun building in 1915. The R.11 was designed to replace the R.4, a solid and modern plane for its time, but low in combat performance and bomb capacity. The Caudron R.11 was smaller and lighter than the R.4 and was powered by two larger engines. It was built expressly for night bombing and went into action in April 1918. Although superior to the R.4, the new bomber was not up to the demands of the last phase of the war, and was reassigned to bomber escort missions. In this new role, the plane was armed with a fifth machine-gun. The Caudron R.11 saw service in eight squadrons until the end of the war and took part in the final campaigns of the conflict. From the summer of 1918 to the time of the armistice, Caudron R.11s accompanied all Breguet 14s on bombing missions.

Aircraft: **Caudron R.11**
Manufacturer: **Caudron Frères**
Type: **Bomber/escort**
Year: **1918**
Engines: **Two Hispano-Suiza 8B liquid-cooled inline Vs, 220 hp each**
Wingspan: **58 ft 9 in (11.8 m)**
Length: **36 ft 11 in (8.5 m)**
Height: **9 ft 10 in (2.9 m)**
Weight: **4,775 lbs (2,165 kg)**
Maximum speed: **114 mph (183 kph)**
Ceiling: **19,520 ft (5,950 m)**
Endurance: **3 hrs**
Armament: **5 machine-guns; 265 lbs (120 kg) of bombs**
Crew: **3**

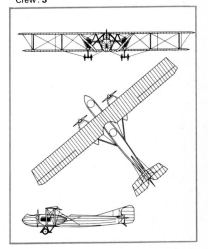

Minor types

1914 Blériot XI – Wingspan: 33 ft 11 in. (10.35 m) – Length: 27 ft 5 in (8.35 m) – Maximum speed: 66 mph (106 kph) – Engine: Gnome 7A rotary, 70 hp. One of the world's first warplanes, the Blériot XI was derived from the monoplane Louis Blériot flew across the English Channel. In the first year of the war, it was one of the most widely used observation planes and served with 21 French, British, and Italian squadrons. Five models were developed, and 132 planes were built.

1914 Breguet 1914 – Wingspan: 44 ft 3.5 in (13.51 m) – Length: 28 ft (8.53 m) – Maximum speed: 68 mph (109 kph) – Engine: Canton–Unné radial, 130 hp. This aircraft was developed from Breguet's 1912 biplane. At the beginning of the war, it served with the *Escadrille* BR.17 on the Alsatian front. Some of the planes were armed with a Hotchkiss machine-gun, but they were not fit for combat. The aircraft was withdrawn in October 1914.

1914 Deperdussin TT – Wingspan: 36 ft (10.97 m) – Length: 26 ft (7.92 m) – Maximum speed: 71 mph (114 kph) – Engine: Gnome rotary, 80 hp. The TT was the military version of one of the monoplanes Deperdussin designed before the war (and before the company went bankrupt in 1913). It was used by the French *Escadrilles*

D.4 and D.6 just after war broke out. It was soon replaced because there were no available spare parts.

1914 REP Type N – Wingspan: 36 ft (10.97 m) – Length: 26 ft (7.92) – Maximum speed: 72 mph (116 kph) – Engine: Gnome rotary, 80 hp. This plane was a military version of the famous monoplane Robert Esnault–Pelterie built in 1909. It served with two French air squadrons until early 1915. On March 2, 1915, a REP Type N attacked an Aviatik near Lanevin. The observer opened fire with a rifle and the German plane caught fire.

1915 Morane Saulnier BB – Wingspan: 28 ft 5 in (8.66 m) – Length: 23 ft (7.01 m) – Maximum speed: 91 mph (146 kph) – Engine: Le Rhône rotary, 80 hp. This reconnaissance biplane was supplied only to Great Britain. It never equipped a whole unit, but a few were assigned to one R.N.A.S. and four R.F.C. squadrons.

1915 Spad A.2 – Wingspan: 31 ft 4 in (9.55 m) – Length: 23 ft 11 in. (7.29 m) – Maximum speed: 81 mph (130 kph) – Engine: Le Rhône rotary, 110 hp. Various attempts were made in 1915 to mount forward-firing machine-guns without a synchronizer. The Spad A.2, a tractor biplane, carried a 'pulpit' for the gunner in front of the engine. Although this solution was not very practical, 100 planes were constructed.

1916 Morane Saulnier T – Wingspan: 57 ft 11 in (17.65 m) – Length: 34 ft 6 in (10.51 m) – Maximum speed: 86 mph (137 kph) – Engines: Two Le Rhône rotaries, 80 hp each. Morane–Saulnier's first two-engined plane was designed in 1914. But it was not put into production until 1916, by which time other more advanced planes had appeared. About one hundred Type Ts were manufactured.

1916 Nieuport 14 – Wingspan: 39 ft 8 in (12.09 m) – Length: 25 ft 10 in (7.87 m) – Maximum speed: 68 mph (109 kph) – Engine: Hispano-Suiza inline, 150 hp. A two-seater biplane bomber, the Nieuport 14 appeared in summer 1916. It was supplied in small numbers to units that were flying Voisins, which had turned out to be too slow for day bombing. The Nieuport 14 was in service for a very short time. It was replaced as soon as the first British Sopwith 1½-Strutters appeared.

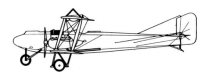

1917 Letord 4 – Wingspan: 58 ft (17.68 m) – Length: 37 ft 1.25 in (11.3 m) – Maximum speed: 82 mph (132 kph) – Engines: Two Lorraine-Dietrich inlines, 160 hp each. Designed by Colonel Dorand as the successor to the Caudron R.4, the Letord 4 went into production in 1916 and was delivered to bombing units in April of the following year. Various models were developed with different engines. Production ended in 1918.

1917 Salmson-Moineau S.M.1 – Wingspan: 57 ft 3.75 in (17.47 m) – Length: 34 ft 5 in. (10.49 m) – Maximum speed: 81 mph (130 kph) – Engine: Salmson (Canton-Unné) radial, 160 hp. Designed by Lieutenant René Moineau and produced by Salmson, this reconnaissance plane was unusual. A radial engine with two transmission shafts drove two propellers set between the wings. Ten planes in all were built, and four of them were in operation for a short time late in 1917.

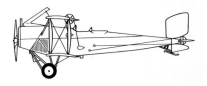

1917 Paul Schmitt 7 – Wingspan: 57 ft 11 in (17.65 m) – Length: 31 ft 6 in (9.6 m) – Maximum speed: 84 mph (135 kph) – Engine: Renault inline, 265 hp. Winner of a 1915 military competition, this large biplane bomber did not reach front-line units until early 1917. The plane was a disappointment. It was slow, vulnerable to attack from below and had small bomb capacity. All the Paul Schmitt 7s were withdrawn from service after a few months.

1918 Farman F.50 – Wingspan: 75 ft (22.86 m) – Length: 39 ft 5 in (12.01 m) – Maximum speed: 94 mph (151 kph) – Engines: Two Lorraine-Dietrich inlines, 250 hp each. The Farman F.50 was the only French heavy bomber developed in the last year of the war to see action before the armistice. The aircraft, which carried a payload of 1,102 lbs (500 kg), was supplied to two units to replace Voisin night bombers.

Great Britain

On August 9, 1914, five days after war was declared, Great Britain sent most of its air force to France: 63 planes (B.E.2 and B.E.2a, Blériot XI, Henri Farman H.F.20, B.E.8 and Avro 504), 105 pilots, and 755 ground crew. This small, heterogeneous group eventually became one of the most important military air forces in the world, with a first-class aviation industry behind it. Almost 55,000 planes of all types were built in Britain during the four years of the war, and at the peak of production 3,500 planes per month were being manufactured. It was thanks to the skills of designers such as Herbert Smith, Geoffrey de Havilland and Frank Barnwell, that Great Britain produced some of its finest combat planes, including the D.H.2, the S.E.5, the Bristol Fighter, the Sopwith Camel and Triplane, and the Handley Page and Short bombers. These aircraft marked important steps in the development of aviation technique and made a decisive contribution to

winning the war.

The idea of the aeroplane as a war machine had been accepted in Great Britain from the very first years of flying. Three artillery officers – Lieutenant L. D. L. Gibbs and Captains J. D. B. Fulton and Bertram Dickson – can be considered the pioneers of British military aviation. But when Dickson first tried to convince the army of the utility of heavier-than-air machines, he was told that the aeroplane would certainly frighten the horses! Nevertheless the first flying school was set up at Larkhill in 1910, and Captain Fulton was made instructor. On February 28, 1911, the Air Battalion of the Royal Engineers was established, the army's first 'air' unit. The battalion comprised one balloon company and a company of five aircraft. The battalion's missions were purely reconnaissance.

On April 13, 1912, the army formed the Royal Flying Corps. It had a naval section (Naval Wing), a military section (Military Wing) and a flying school (Central Flying School). Two years later, on June 23, 1914, another independent service formation, the Royal Naval Air Service, was established. On April 1, 1918, the Royal Air Force (R.A.F.) was set up. This new service absorbed the R.F.C. and the R.N.A.S. (Eight months earlier, on August 17, 1917, General Jan Christian Smuts had recommended the establishment of an independent air force, and royal approval had been granted on November 29.)

British aviation took part in the war on all fronts, including Italy, Macedonia, the Aegean, and the Middle East. Wartime experience led to considerable changes in combat tactics. In 1914 and 1915 British 'scouts', singly or in pairs, flew escort usually for reconnaissance flights. But soon fighter squadrons were flying formation missions all day long. The first all-fighter unit in aviation history was British, the R.F.C. No. 11 Squadron. The squadron began operations on the French front on July 25, 1915, flying Vickers F.B.5 'Gunbus' pusher biplanes.

The progress of the war was reflected by the shifting balance of air supremacy. British aviation was not always able to match enemy forces, and sometimes had to use foreign-made planes. Thus British pilots flew the Nieuport 11 and 17 during the heyday of the Fokker monoplane. The British also flew Spads until they produced top fighter planes of their own. Britain's finest fighters appeared in 1917, the Sopwith Triplanes and Camels, and the S.E.5s. Some of Britain's leading aces made their names at the controls of the Camel and the S.E.5. Curiously enough, the Sopwith Triplane and the Sopwith Camel, both landplanes, were pioneered in service by the R.N.A.S., which also introduced two other fine Sopwith fighters, the Pup and the $1\frac{1}{2}$-Strutter.

By the end of the war Great Britain could boast 532 air aces. The top ace was Edward Mannock, with 73 enemy planes downed, followed by William Bishop with 72. The Canadian Raymond Collishaw became a legend with his Sopwith Triplane and his 60 victories. James McCudden shot down 57 planes. And Albert Ball, one of the most colorful pilots in the war, went down in his S.E.5 near Lens on May 7, 1917, after having shot down a total of 44 enemy planes. Nine other pilots downed more than 40 enemy planes. Eleven had 30 or more to their credit. Forty pilots logged between 20 and 30 victories. And one hundred and thirty were in the 10–20 plane range.

Badge of the Royal Air Force

Avro 504A
Avro 504K

In a long and successful career, the Avro 504 saw duty as a day- and night-fighter, a trainer, a bomber, and a reconnaissance plane. It was one of the most famous planes of the First World War. The plane was designed in 1913, saw service throughout the war, and was used as a civilian training plane until the 1930s. Some 10,000 Avro 504s were built, and some of them were still flying when the Second World War broke out.

Designed by Alliot Verdon Roe early in 1913, the Avro 504 showed its high qualities at once. It could fly at more than 80 mph (128.75 kph), and set a British altitude record of 15,000 feet (4,572 m). The first production models were already in service with the Royal Flying Corps (R.F.C.) and the Royal Naval Air Service (R.N.A.S.) when the war started. The R.F.C. used the 504 as a recon-naissance plane, while the R.N.A.S. used it as a light bomber. An Avro 504 was the first British plane shot down in action, on August 22, 1914. The German Zeppelin threat was met by two new versions, the 504C and 504D. These were fighters. The observer's cockpit was eliminated to make room for another fuel tank.

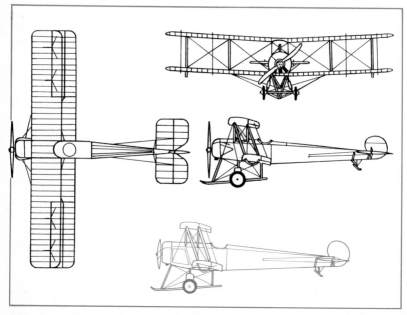

A number of other models were produced until it became clear that the Avro 504 was obsolete as a fighting plane. But production continued. The 504J was developed as a trainer. This model appeared in 1916 and was used at the R.F.C. flying schools. Prince Albert, the future King George VI, learned to fly in a 504. The 504J was enormously popular. Another model, the 504K, was developed with a universal engine-mount to accommodate the various rotary engines then being produced.

The Avro 504K was later adapted for combat. The two-seater trainer was turned into a single-seater night fighter for home defence service against Zeppelin raids. Again the forward cockpit was covered over, and the plane was armed with a Lewis machine-gun on the upper wing. This version of the Avro 504K equipped six home defence squadrons in the northern sector of London in 1918. It was still in use in five units at the end of the war.

Aircraft: **Avro 504A**
Manufacturer: **A.V. Roe & Co. Ltd**
Type: **Reconnaissance/light bomber**
Year: **1914**
Engine: **Gnome 7-cylinder air-cooled rotary, 80 hp**
Wingspan: **36 ft (10.97 m)**
Length: **29 ft 5 in (8.97 m)**
Height: **10 ft 5 in (3.18 m)**
Weight: **1,574 lbs (714 kg)**
Maximum speed: **82 mph (132 kph) at sea level**
Ceiling: **12,000 ft (3,658 m)**
Endurance: **4 hrs 30 mins**
Armament: **1 machine-gun; 80 lbs (36.3 kg) of bombs**
Crew: **2**

Aircraft: **Avro 504K**
Manufacturer: **A.V. Roe & Co. Ltd.**
Type: **Night fighter**
Year: **1918**
Engine: **Le Rhône 9-cylinder air-cooled rotary, 110 hp**
Wingspan: **36 ft (10.97 m)**
Length: **29 ft 5 in (8.97 m)**
Height: **10 ft 5 in (3.18 m)**
Weight: **1,829 lbs (830 kg)**
Maximum speed: **95 mph (153 kph) at sea level**
Ceiling: **16,000 ft (4,877 m)**
Endurance: **3 hrs.**
Armament: **1 machine-gun**
Crew: **1**

The great virtue of the Avro 504 as a trainer lay in the fact that it had good agility and performance, but was entirely without vices in the air.

R.A.F. B.E.2a
R.A.F. B.E.2c

The B.E. biplanes that the Royal Aircraft Factory began producing in 1912 were slow, under-armed, and not very agile. But they bore the brunt of the first years of the air war on all fronts. They often had to face much more advanced enemy aircraft. The first Victoria Cross for air service was awarded to a B.E. pilot, Lieutenant W. B. Rhodes-Moorhouse. Seriously injured on April 26, 1915, during a bombing raid on Courtrai, he managed to get his plane back to base. A B.E.2a of the same squadron, No. 2, was the first British plane to land in France, on August 13, 1914, after war broke out.

The first plane in the series was the B.E.1, designed by Geoffrey de Havilland and F. M. Green. It flew for the first time on January 1, 1912. An improved model, the B.E.2, appeared a month later. The new machine differed from its predecessor in having a larger tailplane and dihedral on the wings, and was clearly superior to the other planes then being evaluated by military authorities. It also set a British one-passenger altitude record of 10,560 feet (3,912 m). When the war started three R.F.C. squadrons had already been equipped with the B.E.2a for some months. It was widely used on reconnaissance and bombing duty.

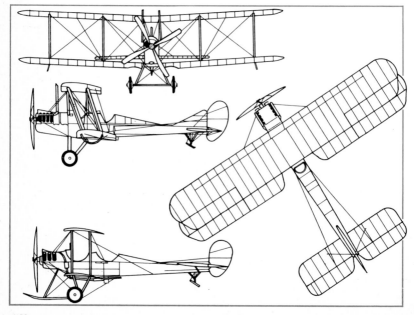

The plane could carry one 100-pound (45.36-kg) bomb or three smaller bombs. The B.E. was not otherwise armed, and was an easy prey for the more agile and powerful German fighters. Moreover the B.E. had a low rate of climb and was too stable in flight for the combat manoeuvres becoming increasingly necessary.

The next version, the B.E.2c, came out in 1914. It was a more manoeuvrable plane, though only slightly faster than its predecessor. But it was better armed and carried a larger bomb load. The B.E.2c had an engine, developed by the Royal Aircraft Factory, that was more powerful than its predecessor's Renault. The airframe was completely redesigned, and ailerons replaced the earlier wing-warping for lateral control. The B.E.2c began to reach the French front late in 1914. The following year it equipped a wing of the R.N.A.S. and 12 R.F.C. squadrons. The Germans soon produced better planes, but the British kept the

Aircraft: **R.A.F. B.E.2a**
Manufacturer: **Royal Aircraft Factory**
Type: **Reconnaissance/light bomber**
Year: **1913**
Engine: **Renault 8-cylinder air-cooled in-line V, 70 hp**
Wingspan: **35 ft 0.5 in (10.68 m)**
Length: **29 ft 6.5 in (9 m)**
Height: **10 ft 2 in (3.1 m)**
Weight: **1,600 lbs (725.75 kg)**
Maximum speed: **70 mph (112.6 kph) at sea level**
Ceiling: **10,000 ft (3,048 m)**
Endurance: **3 hrs**
Armament: **100 lbs (45.35 kg) of bombs**
Crew: **2**

Aircraft: **R.A.F. B.E.2c**
Manufacturer: **Royal Aircraft Factory**
Type: **Reconnaissance/light bomber**
Year: **1914**
Engine: **R.A.F. 1a 8-cylinder air-cooled inline V, 90 hp**
Wingspan: **37 ft (11.28 m)**
Length: **27 ft 3 in (8.31 m)**
Height: **11 ft 1.5 in (3.4 m)**
Weight: **2,142 lbs (971.6 kg)**
Maximum speed: **72 mph (116 kph) at 6,500 ft (1,981 m)**
Ceiling: **10,000 ft (3,048 m)**
Endurance: **3 hrs 15 mins**
Armament: **1 machine-gun; 224 lbs (101.6 kg) of bombs**
Crew: **2**

B.E.2c in service until 1917, when it was reassigned to training and home defence.

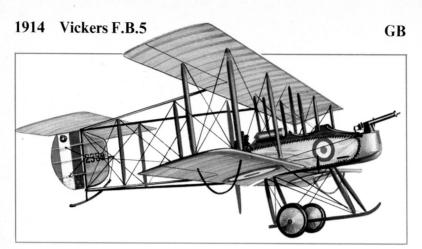

Vickers F.B.5

Aircraft: **Vickers F.B.5**
Manufacturer: **Vickers Ltd.**
Type: **Fighter**
Year: **1914**
Engine: **Gnome Monosoupape 9-cylinder air-cooled rotary, 100 hp**
Wingspan: **36 ft 6 in (11.13 m)**
Length: **27 ft 2 in (8.28 m)**
Height: **11 ft 6 in (3.51 m)**
Weight: **2,050 lbs (930 kg)**
Maximum speed: **70 mph (113 kph) at 5,000 ft (1,524 m)**
Ceiling: **9,000 ft (2,743 m)**
Endurance: **4 hrs 30 mins**
Armament: **1-2 machine-guns**
Crew: **2**

The Vickers F.B.5 'Gunbus' was the only British plane in 1914 designed to mount a machine-gun, and later formed the equipment of the first British all-fighter squadron. The formula of this pusher biplane, with its engine in the rear of the nacelle and the machine-gun in the nose for the best field of fire, had been developed by Vickers in 1913 in the model 18 biplane, which was presented at the Olympia Aero Show. That plane had gradually been perfected through two experimental models before the 1914 F.B.5 was produced. The first Gunbuses were delivered to military units late in 1914, and they served on the Western Front in summer 1915. The F.B.5 remained in service for only a few months as it was no match for the agile, faster, and better-armed Fokkers that appeared late in 1915. It was then used for spotting and reconnaissance work.

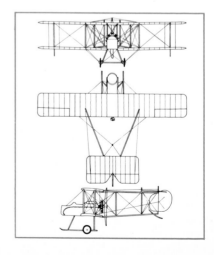

R.A.F. R.E.5

Aircraft: **R.A.F. R.E.5**
Manufacturer: **Royal Aircraft Factory**
Type: **Reconnaissance/light bomber**
Year: **1914**
Engine: **Beardmore 6-cylinder liquid-cooled inline, 120 hp**
Wingspan: **44 ft 6 in (13.56 m)**
Length: **26 ft 2 in (7.98 m)**
Height: **9 ft 8 in (2.95 m)**
Weight:
Maximum speed: **78 mph (126 kph) at sea level**
Ceiling:
Endurance:
Armament: **60 lbs (27.2 kg) of bombs**
Crew: **2**

This was the first specifically reconnaissance biplane produced by the Royal Aircraft Factory. It appeared in 1914 and began its operational career in France, in two squadrons of the Royal Flying Corps. It had a very brief career, because it was not highly manoeuvrable and had no armament. The observer had only personal weapons for defence. The plane carried about 60 pounds (27.2 kg) of small bombs. Because of its toughness and stability, the plane was used for altitude and bombing tests. One R.E.5 was turned into a single-seater with an increased wingspan. This plane reached an altitude of 17,000 feet (5,182 m) in tests in July 1914. Another R.E.5, similarly modified, was used to try out the Royal Aircraft Factory's new 336-pound (154.4-kg) bomb and test the new release mechanism. Captain J. A. Liddell was awarded the V.C. while flying R.E.5s.

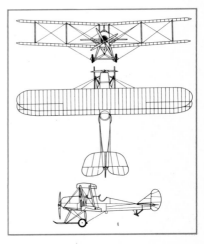

Bristol Scout D

The Scout biplanes, which Frank Barnwell began designing for the Bristol company in 1914, were generally excellent planes. And properly armed they could have been fine combat planes. The first British plane with a synchronized forward-firing machine-gun to see action was a Scout D, on March 25, 1916. But this armament arrived too late. The Scout was already obsolete as an aeroplane. Nevertheless Scouts were kept in service until the autumn of 1916, and almost all British squadrons had a few Bristol Scouts. The plane was also used for experimental purposes, including the first operational take-offs from the deck of an aircraft-carrier. The Bristol Scout also took part in the first attempts to launch one plane from another in flight.

Frank Barnwell began designing the Scout late 1913. He set out to create a fast single-seater biplane, and he succeeded. On February 23, 1914,

Harry Busteed flew the plane at almost 95 mph (153 kph). The plane was very simple in design, and its lines were quite elegant for its time. Lord Carbery, an enthusiastic sports pilot, bought the prototype and flew it in the London–Paris–London roundtrip channel crossing of July 11, 1914. On the return lap the plane ran out of fuel and was forced down in the Channel and sank. This prototype, the Scout A, was soon followed by another two planes (the Scout B). They were delivered to the military authorities at Farnborough in August. After evaluation tests, these two planes were sent to France and assigned to Nos. 3 and 5 Squadrons to be tested on operations.

Both the Royal Flying Corps and the Royal Naval Air Service placed large orders for the plane. This production model was the Scout C. It was practically identical to the earlier models, but it had a different rotary

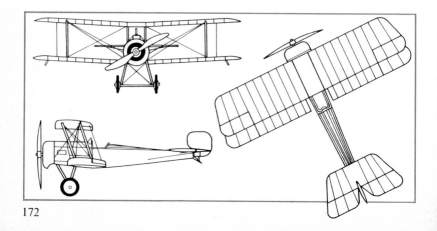

engine. In November 1915, Barnwell produced a new version, the Scout D. There were structural changes, and the empennage was larger. Different engines were installed in the Scout D: the 80-hp Gnome, the 80- and 110-hp Le Rhône, the 80- and 110-hp Clerget, and the 100-hp Gnome Monosoupape. Armament was not standardized, and most of the Scouts were delivered without armament. The first planes flew with personal weapons, anti-Zeppelin rockets, and four small bombs hung on the fuselage next to the pilot. Later Scouts were armed with an unsynchronized Lewis machine-gun and finally with a synchronized Vickers. Small numbers of the plane were allocated to almost all units, and they served on all battle fronts.

As the threat of German Zeppelins increased, the British authorities tried to develop new tactics. Experiments with carrier-launched Scouts were carried out aboard the carrier *Vindex*. Although this experiment did not have much operational success, it laid the

Aircraft: **Bristol Scout D**
Manufacturer: **British & Colonial Aeroplane Co. Ltd.**
Type: **Fighter**
Year: **1915**
Engine: **Le Rhône 9-cylinder air-cooled rotary, 80 hp**
Wingspan: **24 ft 7 in (7.49 m)**
Length: **20 ft 8 in (6.3 m)**
Height: **8 ft 6 in (2.6 m)**
Weight (empty): **760 lbs (345 kg)**
Weight (loaded): **1,250 lbs (567 kg)**
Max speed: **100 mph (161 kph) at sea level**
Ceiling: **16,000 ft (4,877 m)**
Endurance: **2 hrs**
Armament: **1 machine-gun**
Crew: **1**

basis for the aircraft-carrier system, and established early deck take-off and landing techniques. Attempts were also made to launch Bristols from a flying boat in flight. The flying boat was the Porte 'Baby' and the Scout was carried piggy-back on its upper wing. Successful tests were made in May 1916. The fighter 'took off' from the seaplane at an altitude of 1,000 feet (305 m). But this experiment had no practical results.

R.A.F. F.E.2a
R.A.F. F.E.2b
R.A.F. F.E.2c
R.A.F. F.E.2d

The F.E.2 series began its career as a fighter in the second year of the war. By the end of its career it had been turned into a night fighter and night bomber. The F.E.2 series of planes, designed and built by the Royal Aircraft Factory, saw service on various fronts throughout the conflict. The various models were hard-working and reliable planes. It was an F.E.2b, with Lieutenant McCubbin and Corporal Waller of No. 25 Squadron aboard, that shot down the German ace Max Immelmann (15 victories), in his Fokker monoplane, near Annay on June 18, 1916.

All the F.E.s were pusher biplanes. The 100-hp Green engine that pow-

ered the F.E.2a was rather disappointing. The next model, the F.E.2b, was designed to accommodate a better engine, the 120- or 160-hp Beardmore. This became the standard F.E. engine. The F.E.2b was the first model to achieve a broad success. It went into service in the summer of 1915 and saw extensive service both as a fighter and as an escort plane for the next year, until it was outclassed by the new Albatros biplanes introduced by the Germans. At that point, the F.E.2bs were withdrawn from fighter squadrons and reassigned to night bombing. And the Royal Aircraft Factory then developed a new model for night fighter service with home defence units. This was the F.E.2c. The pilot's cockpit was moved ahead of the observer's for better visibility, but this model never went into production.

The last production model was the F.E.2d. It was powered by a 250-hp Rolls-Royce Mk. III (Eagle) engine,

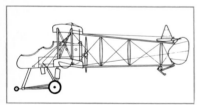

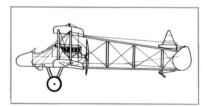

Aircraft: **R.A.F. F.E.2a**
Manufacturer: **Royal Aircraft Factory**
Type: **Reconnaissance/fighter**
Year: **1915**
Engine: **Green 6-cylinder liquid-cooled inline, 100 hp**
Wingspan: **47 ft 9 in (14.55 m)**
Length: **32 ft 3 in (9.83 m)**
Height: **12 ft 7.5 in (3.85 m)**
Weight: **2,680 lbs (1,216 kg)**
Maximum speed: **75 mph (121 kph) at sea level**
Ceiling: **6,000 ft (1,829 m)**
Armament: **1 machine-gun**
Crew: **2**

Aircraft: **R.A.F. F.E.2c**
Manufacturer: **Royal Aircraft Factory**
Type: **Reconnaissance/fighter**
Year: **1916**
Engine: **Beardmore inline, 120 hp**
Wingspan: **47 ft 9 in (14.55 m)**
Length: **32 ft 3 in (9.83 m)**
Height: **12 ft 7.5 in (3.85 m)**
Weight: **2,695 lbs (1,222 kg)**
Maximum speed: **80 mph (129 kph) at sea level**
Ceiling:
Endurance:
Armament: **3 machine-guns**
Crew: **2**

which greatly increased speed and load capacity. This model appeared in July 1916 and remained in service until spring 1917, when it was replaced by the new de Havilland and Bristol fighters and reassigned to home defence units. More than 2,000 F.E.2bs and 2ds were manufactured during the war.

Aircraft: **R.A.F. F.E.2b**
Manufacturer: **Royal Aircraft Factory**
Type: **Reconnaissance/fighter**
Year: **1915**
Engine: **Beardmore inline, 160 hp**
Wingspan: **47 ft 9 in (14.55 m)**
Length: **32 ft 3 in (9.83 m)**
Height: **12 ft 7.5 in (3.85 m)**
Weight: **3,037 lbs (1,378 kg)**
Maximum speed: **91.5 mph (147 kph)**
Ceiling: **11,000 ft (3,353 m)**
Endurance: **2 hrs 30 mins**
Armament: **2 machine-guns**
Crew: **2**

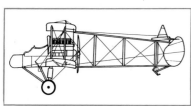

Aircraft: **R.A.F. F.E.2d**
Manufacturer: **Royal Aircraft Factory**
Type: **Reconnaissance/fighter**
Year: **1916**
Engine: **Rolls-Royce Mk. III 12-cylinder liquid-cooled inline V, 250 hp**
Wingspan: **47 ft 9 in (14.55 m)**
Length: **32 ft 3 in (9.83 m)**
Height: **12 ft 7.5 in (3.85 m)**
Weight: **3,470 lbs (1,574 kg)**
Maximum speed: **94 mph (151 kph)**
Ceiling: **17,500 ft (5,334 m)**
Endurance:
Armament: **2 machine-guns; 155 lbs (70.3 kg) of bombs**
Crew: **2**

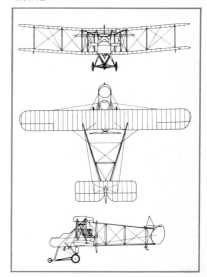

R.A.F. R.E.7

The R.E.7 was a development of the R.A.F. R.E.5. Some R.E.5s had been used to test the Royal Aircraft Factory's new 336-pound (152.4-kg) bomb and its dropping mechanism. But the R.E.7 was expressly designed to accommodate the new bomb. There were structural differences between the aircraft, principally the larger wings of the R.E.7. Delivery began about the middle of 1915, and the first unit to be completely equipped with the new bomber went into action in France early the following year. Bombing missions began only six months later, because the plane was needed for reconnaissance. In late summer, the R.E.7 was replaced by the B.E.12 and withdrawn from front-line service. A total of 250 had been built by this time. In an effort to improve the performance of the R.E.7, various engines were tried out, including the 250-hp Rolls-Royce III.

176

Aircraft: **R.A.F. R.E.7**
Manufacturer: **Royal Aircraft Factory**
Type: **Bomber**
Year: **1915**
Engine: **R.A.F. 4a 12-cylinder air-cooled inline V, 150 hp**
Wingspan: **57 ft (17.37 m)**
Length: **31 ft. 10.5 in (3.72 m)**
Height: **12 ft 7 in (3.84 m)**
Weight: **3,449 lbs (1,564 kg)**
Maximum speed: **85 mph (137 kph) at sea level**
Ceiling: **6,500 ft (1,981 m)**
Endurance: **6 hrs**
Armament: **1 machine-gun; 336 lbs (152.4 kg) of bombs**
Crew: **2**

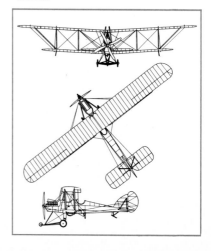

R.A.F. F.E.8

This J. Kenworth design for the Royal Aircraft Factory represented an attempt to create a single-seater fighter in the absence of a suitable synchronization gear for the necessary forward-firing machine-gun. Making full use of experience with the F.E.2, Kenworth built a pusher biplane with a Lewis machine-gun installed in the nose. The F.E.8 made its first flight in October 1915, and production began early the following year. At first the new machine acquired an unenviable notoriety after some spinning accidents, but this was soon cleared up. The F.E.8 only reached the French front in August 1916, when the new German Albatros D I and D II fighters had already gone into action. And the latest British fighting planes, such as the Sopwith Pup and the Sopwith Triplane, showed clearly that the pusher biplane formula was by now outdated. But the plane remained at the front until the middle of 1917.

Aircraft: **R.A.F. F.E.8**
Manufacturer: **Royal Aircraft Factory**
Type: **Fighter**
Year: **1916**
Engine: **Gnome Monosoupape 9-cylinder air-cooled rotary, 100 hp**
Wingspan: **31 ft 6 in (9.6 m)**
Length: **23 ft 8 in (7.21 m)**
Height: **9 ft 2 in (2.79 m)**
Weight: **1,346 lbs (610.5 kg)**
Maximum speed: **94 mph (151 kph) at sea level**
Ceiling: **14,500 ft (4,420 m)**
Endurance: **2 hrs 30 mins**
Armament: **1 machine-gun**
Crew: **1**

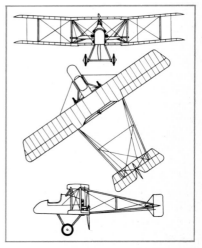

R.A.F. R.E.8

A total of 4,077 R.E.8s was built, making it the most widely-used British two-seater on the Western Front. It was not an outstanding plane, chiefly because of its limited manoeuvrability, and it made an easy target for the more agile enemy fighters, but its toughness and armament kept it in service in almost all theatres of operation until the Armistice. Originally designed for reconnaissance, the R.E.8 was later used as a day and night bomber, and for army co-operation and ground attack.

The R.E.8 was developed late in 1915 to replace the B.E.2c, which had proved too stable and under-armed. The first of the two R.E.8 prototypes took of the air on June 17, 1916. The second was tested a few weeks later, production began in August, and deliveries began in the autumn. The plane's basic weakness was apparent from the start: it was too stable, despite the designer's efforts to make it easier to handle than earlier models. To some extent, the fine armament made up for this deficiency. The first R.E.8s had one Lewis and one Vickers machine-gun: the 'flexible' Lewis gun was installed in the observer's cockpit and the other gun fired through the propeller disk, with the aid of a Vickers, later replaced by a Constantinesco, synchronization gear, The observer/gunner was later provided with a pair of Lewis machine-guns.

The plane had several accidents during its first months in action, and several aircraft were lost. The problem was instability, and the designers solved the problem by increasing the size of the vertical tail surfaces. The plane was soon in action again with 16 Royal Flying Corps and, later, Royal Air Force squadrons. (The R.A.F.

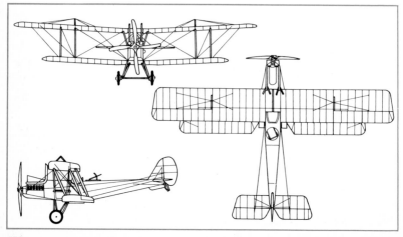

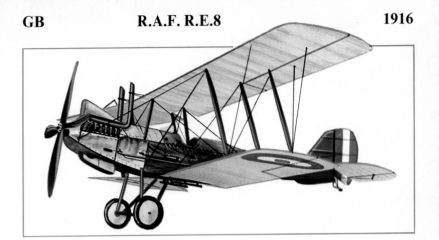

was established on April 1, 1918, and absorbed both the R.F.C. and the R.N.A.S.). Twenty-two planes, with 150- or 180-hp Hispano–Suiza engines, were supplied to the 6th Squadron of the Belgian air force. In addition to service on the Western Front, this reconnaissance plane was also used by two British squadrons in Italy, two in Mesopotamia, two in Palestine and three home defence units.

After serving initially as a reconnaissance plane, the R.E.8 was soon given several other tasks. It was employed for artillery observation, army co-operation, bombing (usually carrying two 112-pound/50.8-kg bombs) and ground attack (carrying four 65-pound/29.5-kg bombs). When the war ended, the plane was still in service with 15 squadrons.

Some improved variant models of the R.E.8 were produced. The first, the R.E.8a, had a 200-hp Hispano–Suiza engine. The others, the R.E.9 and R.T.1, used many components from the R.E.8 but differed from it in wing

Aircraft: **R.A.F. R.E.8**
Manufacturer: **Royal Aircraft Factory**
Type: **Reconnaissance/bomber**
Year: **1916**
Engine: **R.A.F. 4a 12-cylinder air-cooled inline V, 150 hp**
Wingspan: **42 ft 7 in (12.98 m)**
Length: **27 ft 10.5 in (8.5 m)**
Height: **11 ft 4.5 in (3.47 m)**
Weight: **2,678 lbs (1,215 kg)**
Maximum speed: **103 mph (166 kph) at 5,000 ft (1,524 m)**
Ceiling: **13,500 ft (4,115 m)**
Endurance: **4 hrs 15 mins**
Armament: **2-3 machine-guns; 260 lbs (112.8 kg) of bombs**
Crew: **2**

size, in structure and in the nature of their control surfaces. They were powered by new engines as well. These variant models were not outstanding advances over the earlier model. But tests were carried out with an enclosed cockpit and with an adjustable-pitch propeller. The last R.E.8s remained in service in Russia and Ireland until the end of 1919.

In R.A.F. service the R.E.8s were frequently nicknamed 'Harry Tates' after a celebrated music-comedian of the time.

Airco D.H.2

This was the second plane designed by Geoffrey de Havilland for the Aircraft Manufacturing Company. The prototype appeared in July 1915. Because there was no synchronization gear for a forward-firing machine-gun available, de Havilland adopted the current solution to the problem: a pusher biplane with the machine-gun installed in the nose. In February 1916 the plane was delivered to No. 24 Squadron in France, the first squadron to be equipped entirely with single-seater fighters. The pilots soon mastered their new biplanes and won their first air battle on April 2, 1916. On April 25 the first Fokker was shot down, and this did much to raise the squadron's morale. The D.H.2 was soon outclassed by new German fighters but remained in service until the summer of 1917. Some 400 D.H.2 fighters were built before production ceased.

Aircraft: **Airco D.H.2**
Manufacturer: **Aircraft Manufacturing Co. Ltd.**
Type: **Fighter**
Year: **1916**
Engine: **Gnome Monosoupape 9-cylinder air-cooled rotary, 100 hp**
Wingspan: **28 ft 3 in (8.61 m)**
Length: **25 ft 2.5 in (7.68 m)**
Height: **9 ft 6.5 in (2.91 m)**
Weight: **1,441 lbs (653.6 kg)**
Maximum speed: **93 mph (150 kph)**
Ceiling: **14,000 ft (4,267 m)**
Endurance: **2 hrs 45 mins**
Armament: **1 machine-gun**

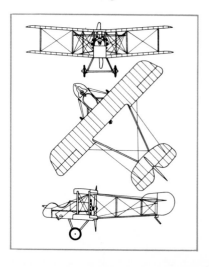

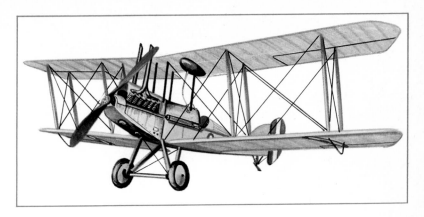

R.A.F. B.E.12

Aircraft: **R.A.F. B.E.12**
Manufacturer: **Royal Aircraft Factory**
Type: **Fighter/bomber**
Year: **1916**
Engine: **R.A.F. 4a 12-cylinder air-cooled inline V, 150 hp**
Wingspan: **37 ft (11.28 m)**
Length: **27 ft 3 in (8.31 m)**
Height: **11 ft 1.5 in (3.39 m)**
Weight: **2,352 lbs (1,067 kg)**
Maximum speed: **102 mph (164 kph) at sea level**
Ceiling: **12,500 ft (3,810 m)**
Endurance: **3 hrs**
Armament: **1-2 machine-guns**

The B.E.12 was designed by the Royal Aircraft Factory to combat the dominant Fokker monoplane. But the new aircraft was a disappointment. It was merely an adaptation of the B.E.2c two-seater, which was already in service with reconnaissance and bombing squadrons of the R.F.C. The only changes consisted of transforming the two-seater into a single-seater and installing a more powerful engine. The flight performance was not much better than that of the original plane. Indeed, the B.E.12 inherited its predecessor's greatest weakness. It was too stable and was thus an easy prey to the more manoeuvrable enemy fighters.

The plane saw fighter service for only a few weeks and was quickly reassigned to light bombing duty in September 1916. At a later date two variants of the B.E.12 were built, the B.E.12a and the B.E.12b.

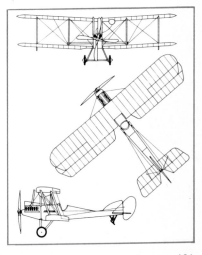

Sopwith 1½-Strutter

Aircraft: **Sopwith 1½-Strutter**
Manufacturer: **Sopwith Aviation Co. Ltd.**
Type: **Fighter/bomber**
Year: **1916**
Engine: **Clerget 9Z, 110 hp**
Wingspan: **33 ft 6 in (10.21 m)**
Length: **25 ft 3 in (7.7 m)**
Height: **10 ft 3 in (3.12 m)**
Weight: **2,149 lbs/975 kg (two-seater);
2,362 lbs/1,071 kg (single-seater)**
Maximum speed: **106 mph (171 kph)**
Ceiling: **13,000 ft (3,962.5 m)**
Endurance: **4 hrs 15 mins**
Armament: **2 machine-guns**

The Sopwith 'Two-Seater' or 'Type 9400' (as the 1½-Strutter was designated by the Royal Flying Corps and the Royal Naval Air Service respectively) was a sort of all-round plane and saw service on all fronts until early 1918. A total of at least 1,513 were built in Great Britain, and 4,500 were manufactured in France. Designed in 1915, the plane incorporated some structural innovations, such as air brakes on the trailing edge of the lower wing and a tailplane whose incidence could be adjusted in flight. The plane went into service early in 1916. It was the first British plane to have an absolutely reliable synchronized forward-firing gun. And it equipped the first strategic bombing air unit in history towards the middle of 1916. The bomber version of the 1½-Strutter was a single-seater.

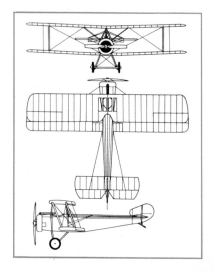

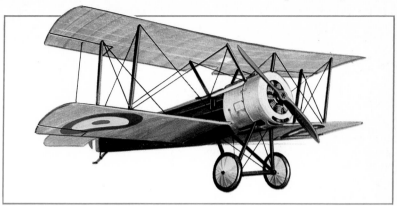

Sopwith Pup

'Simple' and 'impeccable' were just two of the adjectives applied to Sopwith's small fighter plane, It was nicknamed 'Pup' because of its family resemblance to the larger 1½-Strutter. The Pup was developed from the personal plane of the Sopwith Aviation Company's test pilot, Harry Hawker, and appeared in February 1916. A plane with clean, classic lines, it was fast and easy to handle. The Admiralty ordered it for the Royal Naval Air Service. It reached the Western Front in September 1916 and was soon operating with numerous squadrons, including those of the Royal Flying Corps. Its extreme manoeuvrability made it more than a match for many German fighters, including the formidable Albatros D III. The Pup remained in service until late 1917. Then it began to be withdrawn from combat units.

Aircraft: **Sopwith Pup**
Manufacturer: **Sopwith Aviation Co. Ltd.**
Type: **Fighter**
Year: **1916**
Engine: **Le Rhône 9C 9-cylinder air-cooled rotary, 80 hp**
Wingspan: **26 ft 6 in (8.08 m)**
Length: **19 ft 3.75 in (5.89 m)**
Height: **9 ft 5 in (2.87 m)**
Weight: **1,225 lbs (555.7 kg)**
Maximum speed: **111.5 mph (179.5 kph)**
Ceiling: **17,500 ft (5,334 m)**
Endurance: **3 hrs**
Armament: **1 machine-gun**

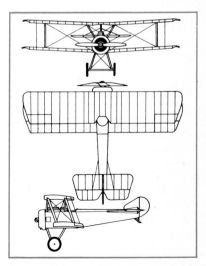

Handley Page O/100
Handley Page O/400

The first heavy bomber to be used for night attacks was ordered, designed, and built expressly for raids on Germany. The Handley Page O/100 filled the British Admiralty's specifications so well that 40 such planes were ordered even before the prototype made its first flight. The O/100 was followed by an improved variant, the O/400, of which 507 were built during the war. Both planes were used extensively in systematic bombing of military objectives in the German-occupied zones. In the last year of the war, the O/400 also bombed the industrial zones of the Saar and the Ruhr, in the heart of Germany.

The O/100 arrived for service on the Western Front in November 1916, the O/400 variant in the spring of 1917. The two planes differed only in engine power (the O/400 was more powerful) and in the location of the fuel tanks, which in the O/400 were transferred from the rear of the engine nacelles to the fuselage. The planes had a very complex structure, and the wings could be folded back, outboard of the nacelles, so that the plane would fit in a normal-sized hangar.

The first O/100s were used on daylight maritime patrol missions for a few months. In the spring of 1917 they began large-scale night bombing raids

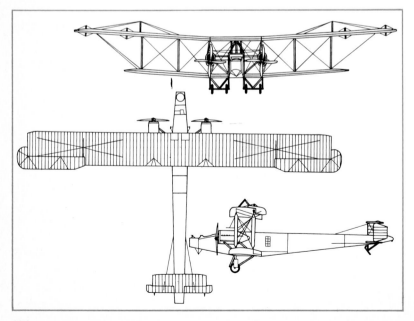

on enemy military installations, submarine bases, and strategically important cities. The Handley Page O/400 was first used as a day bomber, replacing the O/100, which had been reassigned to night missions. In the last months of the war, the O/400 carried the new 'giant' 1,650-pound (748.4-kg) bomb and was flown by seven bomber squadrons. At the end of the war, the R.A.F. had 258 Handley Page O/400s in operation.

The career of the O/400 bombers did not end with the close of hostilities, the Royal Air Force keeping the type in service until 1920. Some were modified for passenger transport, of senior officers 'commuting' to the various peace conferences for the most part. Four O/400s opened up the first intercontinental air routes, routes that were later to be served by the civilian planes of Imperial Airways. A civilian transport version of the O/400, the O/7, was developed. Not many were built, and they were sold to China and South Africa.

Aircraft: **Handley Page O/100**
Manufacturer: **Handley Page Ltd.**
Type: **Heavy bomber**
Year: **1916**
Engines: **Two Rolls-Royce Eagle II 12-cylinder liquid-cooled inline Vs, 250 hp each**
Wingspan: **100 ft (30.48 m)**
Length: **62 ft 10.25 in (19.16 m)**
Height: **22 ft (6.71 m)**
Weight: **14,020 lbs (6,359.4 kg)**
Maximum speed: **85 mph (137 kph) at sea level**
Ceiling: **7,000 ft (2,134 m)**
Endurance: **8 hrs**
Armament: **4.5 machine-guns; 1,792 lbs (812.8 kg) of bombs**
Crew: **4**

Aircraft: **Handley Page O/400**
Manufacturer: **Handley Page Ltd.**
Type: **Heavy bomber**
Year: **1917**
Engines: **Two Rolls-Royce Eagle VIII 12-cylinder liquid-cooled inline Vs, 360 hp each**
Wingspan: **100 ft (30.48 m)**
Length: **62 ft 10.25 in (19.16 m)**
Height: **22 ft (6.71 m)**
Weight: **13,360 lbs (6,060 kg)**
Maximum speed: **97.5 mph (157 kph) at sea level**
Ceiling: **8,500 ft (2,591 m)**
Endurance: **8 hrs**
Armament: **4-5 machine-guns; 2,000 lbs (907.2 kg) of bombs**
Crew: **4**

Short Bomber
Short 184

The 'Bomber' built by Short Brothers in 1915 was not widely used in military operations. It was a transitional type and served operationally only as a stop-gap measure until the specially-designed Handley Page heavy bombers were ready. The Short Bomber was developed from an illustrious predecessor, the Short 184 seaplane. The 184 was designed for the Admiralty as a torpedo-bomber and was in fact the first aircraft to sink a ship with a torpedo. The pilot was Commander C. H. K. Edmonds, and the operation took place in the Dardanelles on August 12, 1915, when a Turkish merchant ship fell victim to this first successful plane-launched torpedo.

About 900 Short 184s were built, but after its initial success, the type was reassigned to reconnaissance, bombing, and anti-submarine patrol duty. It served all through the war, and was assigned to coastal bases in Great Britain and to naval seaplane-carriers in the Mediterranean, the Far East, and the North Sea.

Variant models of the seaplane were developed. They differed in engine type and power, and payload. The Type B, built by Mann, Egerton, also differed in size and structure.

In 1915, in answer to a request for bombers, Short Brothers produced a

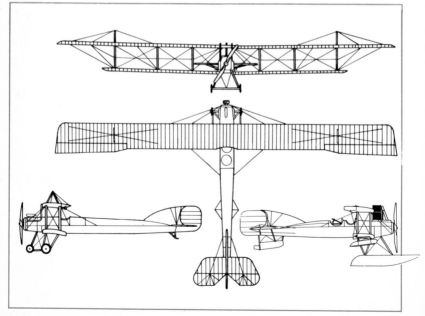

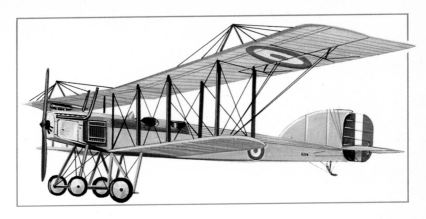

landplane based on their 184 seaplane. The early bombers closely resembled the seaplane, but later ones were significantly different, and the rear of the fuselage was lengthened. The standard bomb load consisted of four 230-pound (104.3-kg) bombs or eight 112-pound (50.8-kg) bombs carried under the lower wings. A Lewis machine-gun on a Scarff ring mount was installed in the rear cockpit. A total of 83 Short Bombers (the plane was never given an official designation) were manufactured by Short Brothers and by four subcontractors. The first bombers were delivered in late 1916, to No. 7 Squadron, Royal Naval Air Service. The Short Bomber was also supplied to No. 3 Wing, R.N.A.S., the first British 'strategic' bomber force, in spring 1916. But operations did not start until October as No. 3 Wing had had to lend some of its machines to the R.F.C., which was desperately short of aircraft for the battle of the Somme. The Short Bomber had its baptism of fire as a night bomber on the night of

Aircraft: **Short Bomber**
Manufacturer: **Short Brothers**
Type: **Heavy bomber**
Year: **1916**
Engine: **Rolls-Royce Eagle III 12-cylinder liquid-cooled inline V, 250 hp**
Wingspan: **85 ft (25.91 m)**
Length: **45 ft (13.72 m)**
Height: **15 ft (4.57 m)**
Weight: **6,800 lbs (3,084.5 kg)**
Maximum speed: **77.5 mph (125 kph) at 6,500 ft (1,981 m)**
Ceiling: **9,500 ft (2,896 m)**
Endurance: **6 hrs**
Armament: **1 machine-gun; 920 lbs (417.3 kg) of bombs**
Crew: **2**

Aircraft: **Short 184**
Manufacturer: **Short Brothers**
Type: **Reconnaissance/torpedo-bomber**
Year: **1915**
Engine: **Sunbeam 12-cylinder liquid-cooled inline V, 240 hp**
Wingspan: **63 ft 6.25 in (19.36 m)**
Length: **40 ft 7.5 in (12.38 m)**
Height: **13 ft 6 in (4.11 m)**
Weight: **5,100 lbs (2,313.3 kg)**
Maximum speed: **80 mph (129 kph) at 2,000 ft (610 m)**
Ceiling: **5,500 ft (1.676 m)**
Endurance: **4 hrs**
Armament: **1 machine-gun; 520 lbs (235.9 kg) of bombs or 1 14-in (35.56-cm) torpedo**
Crew: **2**

November 15, 1916, during a raid over Ostend. It remained in service until April 1917.

Martinsyde G.100

The Martinsyde G.100 was very large for a single-seater, hence the nickname applied to its development, the G.102. The G.100 was designed as a long-range escort fighter by A. A. Fletcher in 1915. It was not a success in this role because of its size: it was too large and too hard to handle to enter combat against fast and agile German fighters, and the pilot's field of vision was limited by the broad-chord wings. The plane redeemed itself, however, when it was reassigned to bombing and ground attack duty. The Martinsyde G.100 could carry two 112-pound (50.8-kg) bombs under its wings. The payload was increased in the later G.102, nicknamed the 'Elephant', which was powered by a 160-hp Beardmore engine. A total of 100 Martinsyde G.100s and 171 G.102s was built, and the types did a lot of very useful but unglorious work as long-range escorts.

Aircraft: **Martinsyde G.100**
Manufacturer: **Martin and Handasyde Ltd.**
Type: **Fighter/bomber**
Year: **1916**
Engine: **Beardmore 6-cylinder liquid-cooled inline, 120 hp**
Wingspan: **38 ft (11.58 m)**
Length: **26 ft 6 in (8.08 m)**
Height: **9 ft 8 in (2.95 m)**
Weight: **2,424 lbs (1,100 kg)**
Maximum speed: **95 mph (153 kph) at 6,500 ft (1,981 m)**
Ceiling: **14,000 ft (4,267 m)**
Endurance: **5 hrs 30 mins**
Armament: **1-2 machine-guns; 230 lbs (104.3 kg) of bombs**
Crew: **1**

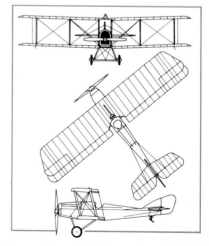

Bristol M.1C

It was only prejudice that kept the Bristol M.1C, one of the finest planes of its day, from being fully appreciated and used as an excellent combat aeroplane. Its one 'defect' was that it was a monoplane in an era in which official opinion considered biplanes safer and more efficient. A commission set up in 1912 to find out why of late monoplanes had suffered so many accidents did not reject the monoplane formula outright, but the impression remained that monoplanes were untrustworthy. F. S. Barnwell, the designer of the Bristol M.1C, was firmly convinced of the monoplane's superiority to the biplane formula, however. The performance of his M.1 proved him right. The prototype (M.1A) reached 132 mph (212 kph) with only a 110-hp rotary engine. Although 129 of the final model (the M.1C) were ordered, the type saw service only in Macedonia, Palestine, and Mesopotamia.

Aircraft: **Bristol M.1C**
Manufacturer: **British & Colonial Aeroplane Co. Ltd.**
Type: **Fighter**
Year: **1917**
Engine: **Le Rhône 9J 9-cylinder air-cooled rotary, 110 hp**
Wingspan: **30 ft 9 in (9.37 m)**
Length: **20 ft 5.5 in (6.24 m)**
Height: **7 ft 9.5 in (2.37 m)**
Weight: **1,348 lbs (611.5 kg)**
Maximum speed: **130 mph (209 kph) at sea level**
Ceiling: **20,000 ft (6,096 m)**
Endurance: **1 hr 45 mins**
Armament: **1 machine-gun**
Crew: **1**

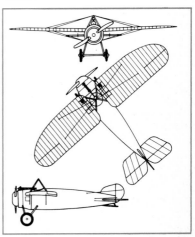

Bristol F.2A
Bristol F.2B

Designed as reconnaissance planes, the F.2A and F.2B ended up as two of the most successful fighter planes of the war. They were not immediately successful, but this was a question of tactics. During the type's first operational mission, on April 5, 1917, near Douai in France, six Bristol F.2As of No. 48 Squadron, R.F.C,. were attacked by five Albatros D IIIs of *Jagdstaffel* II, commanded by Manfred von Richthofen, the legendary 'Red Baron'. Only two of the British planes got back to their base at Bellevue after the dog fight. At first imaginary structural weaknesses were blamed, but it soon became clear that the problem was tactical: the pilots handled the fighter as if it were a traditional two-seater, relying on the 'flexible' rear machine-gun, and ignoring the synchronized forward gun. It was some time before the pilots completely mastered the necessary new tactics, based on the notion of using

the machine as a single-seater with a 'sting in the tail'. But in the end the Bristol became one of the most famous fighters of its day.

The design that resulted in the F.2A and F.2B was developed by Frank S. Barnwell of the British & Colonial Aeroplane Company, in March 1916. Barnwell's original intention was to produce a two-seater reconnaissance plane that could take over from the obsolete R.A.F. B.E.2 series. The two original designs (R.2A and R.2B) were to have been powered by 120-hp Beardmore and 150-hp Hispano-Suiza engines respectively. When the new 190-hp Rolls-Royce Falcon I appeared, however, Barnwell realized it was an ideal fighter engine. He abandoned the R.2A and R2B designs and developed a wholly different plane. The F.2A prototype (F for Fighter) made its first flight on September 9, 1916, and was followed by a second, Hispano-Suiza powered, plane on October 25. After minor alterations, the planes had their evaluation tests, and a first consignment of 50 planes, Rolls-Royce powered, was ordered. No. 48 Squadron, R.F.C.,

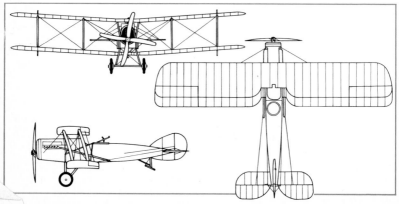

began receiving the new aircraft in December 1916. The unit reached the French front in March 1917.

The F.2A version was followed by an improved model, the F.2B. The new plane had structural changes in its wings and empennage, longer range, and a better field of vision for the pilot. And, most important, it had a more powerful Rolls-Royce engine. The first 150 F.2Bs were powered by the Falcon I. The next 50 had 220-hp Falcon IIs. Others had the 275-hp Falcon III, considered to be the acme of aero engine design at the time. But F.2B production exceeded Falcon III deliveries, and so an alternative had to be found: the 200-hp Sunbeam Arab was chosen. Several hundred F.2Bs were equipped with Sunbeams. These planes were used chiefly for reconnaissance, because their performance was generally inferior to that of the model equipped with the Falcon III. The Bristol Fighter went into front-line service in the summer of 1917, and 3,101 of them were built during the

Aircraft: **Bristol F.2A**
Manufacturer: **British & Colonial Aeroplane Co. Ltd.**
Type: **Fighter**
Year: **1916**
Engine: **Rolls-Royce Falcon I 12-cylinder liquid-cooled inline V, 190 hp**
Wingspan: **39 ft 3 in (11.96 m)**
Length: **25 ft 9 in (7.85 m)**
Height: **9 ft 4 in (2.84 m)**
Weight: **2,667 lbs (1,210 kg)**
Maximum speed: **110 mph (177 kph) at sea level**
Ceiling: **18,000 ft (5,486 m)**
Endurance: **3 hrs 15 mins**
Armament: **2 machine-guns**
Crew: **2**

Aircraft: **Bristol F.2B**
Manufacturer: **British & Colonial Aeroplane Co. Ltd.**
Type: **Fighter**
Year: **1917**
Engine: **Rolls-Royce Falcon III 12-cylinder liquid-cooled inline V, 275 hp**
Wingspan: **39 ft 3 in (11.96 m)**
Length: **25 ft 10 in (7.87 m)**
Height: **9 ft 9 in (2.97 m)**
Weight: **2,779 lbs (1,261 kg)**
Maximum speed: **123 mph (198 kph) at 5,000 ft (1,524 m)**
Ceiling: **21,500 ft (6,553 m)**
Endurance: **3 hrs**
Armament: **3 machine-guns; 240 lbs (108.9 kg) of bombs**
Crew: **2**

war. The plane was used by the R.A.F. until 1932, and total production reached 5,500.

R.A.F. S.E.5
R.A.F. S.E.5a

With the Sopwith Camel, the Royal Aircraft Factory's S.E.5 and S.E.5a share the honour of having been the best British fighter planes of the First World War. They were extremely tough, fast and manoeuvrable, and proved to be superior to their most famous German adversaries, including the Albatros D III and D V, the Pfalz D III, and the Fokker Dr I. Aces like Mannock, Bishop and McCudden won most of their victories in the S.E.5a. The prototype took to the air on November 22, 1916. By the end of the war, 5,205 had been built for service in 24 British, one Australian, and two American squadrons.

The S.E.5 project was initiated in the summer of 1916 by H. P. Folland, J. Kenworthy and Major F. W. Goodden. They designed the plane around the new 150-hp Hispano-Suiza engine, which Britain had ordered the preceding August. After the prototype's test flights, a second plane was sent to France for operational tests, which began just before Christmas 1916. The plane proved to be very fast and tough. It carried two fixed machine-guns: one, a Vickers, was synchronized and the other, a Lewis, was installed on the upper wing to fire over the propeller disk. The S.E.5 was tested extensively against two of the best fighter planes then in service, the Nieuport 17 and Spad S.VII. Test results proved the S.E.5's general superiority, although it was slightly less manoeuvrable than the Nieuport 17. A tragic accident delayed the start of production: the chief test pilot, Frank Goodden, was flying the plane at Farnborough on January 28, 1917 when the wings collapsed, Goodden being killed in the resultant crash. An inquiry discovered a structural weakness. The connections between the spars and struts were strengthened, and the production model incorporated other improvements as well.

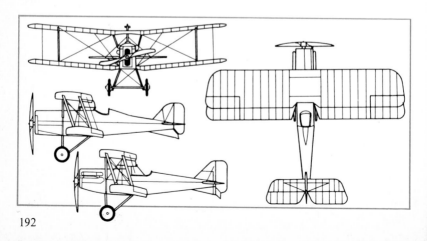

A total of 58 S.E.5s were built and they served for only three months on combat duty. The next model, the S.E.5a, was built around the uprated 200-hp Hispano-Suiza engine. It reached combat units in June 1917. Production of the new fighter was delayed while mechanical defects in the reduction gears of the engine were rectified. Airframe production also outstripped the supply of engines. In the meantime, other equally powerful engines were tried out. The Wolsely Viper, a redesigned Hispano-Suiza without reduction gears, was settled on. It was installed in most of the new planes and accounted for the plane's square nose.

The S.E.5a was an outstanding fighter and did much to help the Allies retain air supremacy in the last year of the war. When the conflict ended, the Royal Air Force had about 2,700 S.E.5as in service. They were retired a short time later. Many of these aircraft were sold abroad, to Australia (which took 50), Canada, South Africa, Poland, and the United States. Amer-

Aircraft: **R.A.F. S.E.5**
Manufacturer: **Royal Aircraft Factory**
Type: **Fighter**
Year: **1917**
Engine: **Hispano-Suiza 8A 8-cylinder liquid-cooled inline V, 150 hp**
Wingspan: **26 ft 7.5 in (8.12 m)**
Length: **21 ft 4 in (6.5 m)**
Height: **9 ft 5 in (2.87 m)**
Weight: **1,940 lbs (880 kg)**
Maximum speed: **132.5 mph (213 kph) at 10,000 ft (3,048 m)**
Ceiling: **22,000 ft (6,706 m)**
Endurance: **2 hrs 30 mins**
Armament: **2 machine-guns**
Crew: **1**

Aircraft: **R.A.F. S.E.5a**
Manufacturer: **Royal Aircraft Factory**
Type: **Fighter**
Year: **1917**
Engine: **Wolseley W.4 Viper 8-cylinder liquid-cooled inline V, 200 hp**
Wingspan: **26 ft 7.5 in (8.12 m)**
Length: **20 ft 11 in (6.38 m)**
Height: **9 ft 6 in (2.9 m)**
Weight: **1,940 lbs (880 kg)**
Maximum speed: **138 mph (222 kph) at sea level**
Ceiling: **19,500 ft (5,944 m)**
Endurance: **2 hrs 30 mins**
Armament: **2 machine-guns**
Crew: **1**

ica had already considered manufacturing at least 1,000 S.E.5as under licence before the war came to an end.

Sopwith Triplane

When the Sopwith Triplane was first put in combat, its clear superiority over contemporary German fighters greatly alarmed the enemy. About 14 German aircraft constructors all set out to design triplanes to match the Sopwith. The plane's outstanding qualities were a high rate of climb combined with great manoeuvrability. Nevertheless, the Sopwith Triplane had a relatively short combat career, and its fame was soon overshadowed by that of its most illustrious successor, the Sopwith Camel. Only 144 were built. The appearance of the Camel brought Triplane production to an immediate halt, and the planes began to be withdrawn from front-line service in July 1917.

The Sopwith Triplane was designed by Herbert Smith, who was also responsible for the Camel. Smith chose the unusual triplane formula in order to create a plane that would be more manoeuvrable than the Pup biplane and could provide good visibility for the pilot. The prototype made its first flight on May 28, 1916, with Sopwith's test pilot, Harry Hawker, at the controls. The compact new aircraft was so impressive that a couple of weeks later the plane was sent to France for operational testing. Orders then followed from both the Royal Flying Corps and the Royal Naval Air Service, for a total of more than 400 planes. But the Sopwith Triplane saw service only with naval units, because the Royal Flying Corps agreed to trade the Triplanes it had ordered for a badly-needed batch of R.N.A.S. Spad S.VIIs. And the original order was reduced.

The first R.N.A.S. units equipped with the new fighter went into action in April 1917. Performance was excellent, and the naval squadrons' successes enhanced the Triplane's reputation, especially during the battle of Arras. The Sopwith fighter was also

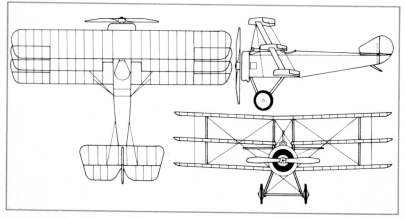

associated with the fame of the Canadian ace Raymond Collishaw, who shot down seven enemy planes and damaged another 17 in May and June 1917. The Triplane's effect on the enemy was clearly summed up by an historian of the period who remarked that 'The sight of a Sopwith Triplane formation, in particular, induced the enemy pilots to dive out of range.'

But the Triplane's career soon ended, the Sopwith Camel gradually taking its place in R.N.A.S. units. By October, only one squadron still had Triplanes. Pilots were reluctant at first to give up their elegant and manageable planes for the more unpredictable Camels.

Very few Sopwith Triplanes saw action outside the European theatre. Early in 1917, one was attached to No. 2 Wing of the Royal Naval Air Service, operating from Mudros, in the Aegean. Four planes were sent to the French government, one was delivered to the United States Navy, and another went to Russia. The Russian

Aircraft: **Sopwith Triplane**
Manufacturer: **Sopwith Aviation Company Limited**
Type: **Fighter**
Year: **1917**
Engine: **Clerget 9B 9-cylinder air-cooled rotary, 130 hp**
Wingspan: **26 ft 6 in (8.08 m)**
Length: **18 ft 10 in (5.74 m)**
Height: **10 ft 6 in (3.2 m)**
Weight: **1,541 lbs (699 kg)**
Maximum speed: **117 mph (188 kph) at 5,000 ft (1,524 m)**
Ceiling: **20,500 ft (6,248 m)**
Endurance: **2 hrs 45 mins**
Armament: **1 machine-gun**
Crew: **1**

plane was altered during the winter of 1917–18, and given a ski landing gear. Only a few Triplanes were left by the time of the Armistice. As they were withdrawn from combat units, they were reassigned to flying schools or used experimentally.

Sopwith continued to experiment with the triplane formula. Two more triplanes were designed around the new 150- and 200-hp Hispano-Suiza engines. They seem to have been based on the structure of the 1½-Strutter, but never got beyond the prototype stage.

Sopwith F.1 Camel
Sopwith 2F.1 Camel

This superb fighting plane was nick-named 'Camel' because of the hump-shaped fairing over its two synchronized forward-firing machine-guns. It became famous for its manoeuvrability and outstanding performance in combat: the Camel shot down 1,294 enemy planes during the war. In handling characteristics this small Sopwith fighter differed radically from its predecessors, the Sopwith Pup and the Sopwith Triplane, which were as docile and manageable as the Camel was jumpy and highstrung. In skilled hands, though, the Camel was surprisingly manoeuvrable and ideal for close combat. It was more agile than any other contemporary plane, with the possible exception of the Fokker Dr I triplane.

The Camel was developed by Herbert Smith towards the end of 1916. The prototype flew on December 22, and a few more planes were built for evaluation tests and trials with the different engines specified by the Royal Naval Air Service and the Royal Flying Corps. For the first time on a British plane the armament was standardized: two forward-firing Vickers machine-guns. These were fixed and synchronized, like their German counterparts. Delivery of Camels began in May 1917, and the Camels went into action in July. Pilots were not enthusiastic about the new plane at first. The fighter was very sensitive to the torque effect of the large rotary engine, especially in turns. It took an experienced pilot to control the plane. There were many accidents, especially at take-off, and a two-seater training version had to be built. What made the plane tricky in the hands of inexperienced pilots were the same qualities that made the Camel such an outstanding plane in the hands of experts.

The Camels were also used as ground attack planes. During the battles of Ypres and Cambrai, Camels carried four 20-pound (9-kg.) bombs under the fuselage, and made raids on enemy trenches, rear-area facilities,

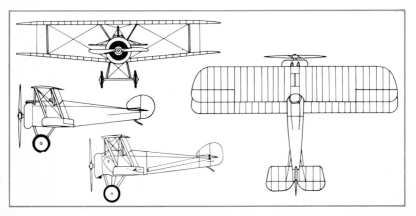

and road junctions. Many Camels were shot down on these missions, and a 'trench' version, the T.F.1, was developed. Its cockpit was armour-plated and its armament comprised two machine-guns firing obliquely downwards and forwards. This model did not go into production but served as the basis for the Sopwith T.F.2 Salamander.

A carrier-based version of the Camel was also built, in the form of the 2F.1. This began official evaluation trials in March 1917, and went into operation in the early months of 1918. It had slightly smaller wings than the land fighter and carried a Lewis machine-gun tilted up to fire through an opening in the centre section of the upper wing. Some 2F.1s were used as dive-bombers, after a rack for two 50-pound (22.68-kg) bombs had been installed under the fuselage. During the war, the naval Camels served on four carriers, 10 battleships and battle-cruisers, and 17 cruisers. Three hundred and forty of

Aircraft: **Sopwith F.1 Camel**
Manufacturer: **Sopwith Aviation Company Limited**
Type: **Fighter**
Year: **1917**
Engine: **Clerget 9B 9-cylinder air-cooled rotary, 130 hp**
Wingspan: **28 ft (8.53 m)**
Length: **18 ft 9 in (5.72 m)**
Height: **8 ft 6 in (2.59 m)**
Weight: **1,453 lbs (659 kg)**
Maximum speed: **115 mph (185 kph) at 6,500 ft (1,981 m)**
Ceiling: **19,000 ft (5,774 m)**
Endurance: **2 hrs 30 mins**
Armament: **2 machine-guns**
Crew: **1**

Aircraft: **Sopwith 2F.1 Camel**
Manufacturer: **Sopwith Aviation Company Limited**
Type: **Fighter**
Year: **1918**
Engine: **Admiralty (Bentley) B.R.1 9-cylinder air-cooled rotary, 150 hp**
Wingspan: **26 ft 11 in (8.2 m)**
Length: **18 ft 8 in (5.69 m)**
Height: **9 ft 1 in (2.77 m)**
Weight: **1,530 lbs (694 kg)**
Maximum speed: **124 mph (200 kph) at 6,500 ft (1,981 m)**
Ceiling: **17,300 ft (5,273 m)**
Endurance: **2 hrs 30 mins**
Armament: **2 machine-guns**
Crew: **1**

them were built. More than 5,450 Camels were built by Sopwith and eight subcontractors.

Armstrong Whitworth F.K.8

The Armstrong Whitworth F.K.8 'Big Ack' was one of the most widely used reconnaissance planes of the last two years of the war. It was designed by Frederick Koolhoven as a larger and more powerful successor to his 1916 F.K.3 'Little Ack'. The F.K.8 soon made a name for itself because of its strength and armament. It was generally considered better than the Royal Aircraft Factory's R.E.8. During an action on March 27, 1918, in France, an F.K.8 was attacked by eight Fokker Dr Is. Both of the crew were wounded, and the plane was badly damaged. But it still managed to shoot down four enemy planes before crash-landing. The Armstrong Whitworth F.K.8 entered service in January 1917 with No. 35 Squadron, R.F.C., and in a short time it equipped eight other units. About 1,500 planes were built.

Aircraft: **Armstrong Whitworth F.K.8**
Manufacturer: **Armstrong, Whitworth & Co. Ltd.**
Type: **Reconnaissance/bomber**
Year: **1917**
Engine: **Beardmore 6-cylinder liquid-cooled inline, 160 hp**
Wingspan: **43 ft 6 in (13.26 m)**
Length: **31 ft (9.45 m)**
Height: **11 ft (3.35 m)**
Weight: **2,811 lbs (1,275 kg)**
Maximum speed: **98.4 mph (158 kph)**
Ceiling: **13,000 ft (3,962 m)**
Endurance: **3 hrs**
Armament: **2 machine-guns; 160 lbs (72.6 kg) of bombs**
Crew: **2**

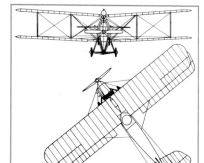

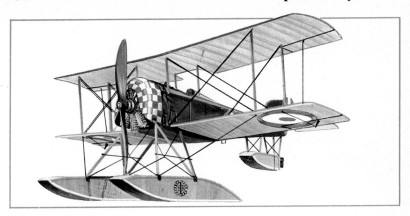

Sopwith Baby

The Royal Naval Air Service ordered 136 Sopwith Tabloids equipped with floats, the type being known as the Sopwith Schneider, and used them for observation and maritime patrol in the first two years of the war. (The Tabloid won the Schneider Trophy in 1914, with Howard Pixton at the controls.) In 1916, a new version of this seaplane was developed, with a more powerful engine half enclosed in a horse-shoe shaped cowling. This model was called the Baby, and 286 were built by Sopwith and by three other firms. It served for most of 1917–18 at British coastal bases and aboard seaplane carriers. It saw service in the Channel and in the North Sea, as well as in the Mediterranean, Egypt, Palestine, and Italy. In these areas the Baby was used as an anti-submarine patrol plane and as a reconnaissance–observation aircraft. In Italy, the Sopwith Baby was built under licence by Ansaldo.

Aircraft: **Sopwith Baby**
Manufacturer: **Sopwith Aviation Company Limited**
Type: **Reconnaissance/light bomber**
Year: **1917**
Engine: **Clerget 9-cylinder air-cooled rotary, 130 hp**
Wingspan: **25 ft 8 in (7.82 m)**
Length: **23 ft (7.01 m)**
Height: **10 ft (3.05 m)**
Weight: **1,715 lbs (778 kg)**
Maximum speed: **100 mph (161 kph)**
Ceiling: **7,600 ft (3,217 m)**
Endurance: **2 hrs 15 mins**
Armament: **1 machine-gun; 130 lbs (59 kg) of bombs**
Crew: **1**

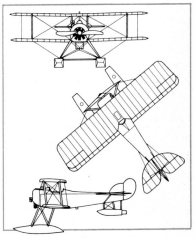

Airco D.H.4

The D.H.4 is considered the best single-engined bomber of the war. It was the only American-built British plane to take part in hostilities. More than two-thirds (4,846 planes) of the 6,295 built were made in the U.S.A. The Americans called the D.H.4A the 'Liberty Plane' for the 400-hp. Liberty engine that powered it. The D.H.4 saw service in 13 squadrons of the American Expeditionary Forces during the last months of the war.

Geoffrey de Havilland designed the plane in 1916, around the B.H.P. engine (160 hp), as a fast day bomber. The first prototype took to the air in August, but there then followed difficulties with the production of the engine. A second prototype was built with a 250-hp Rolls-Royce Eagle engine. This plane was fast, tough, and easy to handle, and it went into immediate production. Because only relatively few Rolls-Royces were available, other engines were installed, including the 230-hp Siddeley Puma, the 200-hp R.A.F. 3a, and the 260-hp Fiat

A.12. The best production model, however, was powered by the 375-hp Rolls-Royce Eagle VIII, which gave this highly manoeuvrable bomber an excellent performance.

Delivery began early in 1917, and in March the D.H.4 went into action in France with No. 55 Squadron. It was soon in service with nine other bomber units. The standard payload was two 230-pound (104.3-kg) or four 112-pound (50.8-kg) bombs. Defensive armament consisted of one or two Vickers forward-firing machine-guns, fixed and synchronized, and one or two Lewis guns installed on a Scarff ring mount in the observer's cockpit. The D.H.4 was not limited to day bombing. Naval units in particular used it extensively for photographic reconnaissance missions, on anti-submarine patrol and for artillery-spotting. The D.H.4 was in service up to the end of the war, and saw duty on other fronts, including the Middle East, the Mediterranean, and the Adriatic.

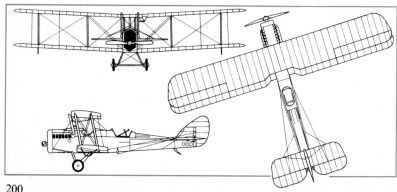

The plane began its American career in July 1917, when a D.H.4 was sent to the United States for comparative testing with American planes. On October 29, 1917, it made its first flight with a 400-hp Liberty engine (12-cylinder liquid-cooled inline V). The installation of this engine entailed a revision of the original design, and months went by before planes started coming off the assembly line. The D.H.4s of the American Expeditionary Forces went into action in August 1918. An improved version, the D.H.4B, appeared in October, but did not reach the front in time to take part in the fighting. Production of other models continued for some time, and the plane remained in service with the American air force until 1932.

The D.H.4 had a long career in other countries as well. After the Armistice, the R.A.F. sold D.H.4s to Belgium, Canada, New Zealand, South Africa, Spain, Chile, and Greece, where they were used until 1930. And private citizens bought D.H.4s for pleasure and racing.

Aircraft: **Airco D.H.4**
Manufacturer: **Aircraft Manufacturing Co. Ltd.**
Type: **Bomber**
Year: **1917**
Engine: **Rolls-Royce Eagle VIII 12-cylinder liquid-cooled inline V, 375 hp**
Wingspan: **42 ft 4.5 in (12.92 m)**
Length: **30 ft 8 in (9.35 m)**
Height: **11 ft (3.35 m)**
Weight: **3,472 lbs (1,575 kg)**
Maximum speed: **143 mph (230 kph) at sea level**
Ceiling: **23,500 ft (7,163 m)**
Endurance: **6 hrs 45 mins (maximum)**
Armament: **2-4 machine-guns; 460 lbs (208.7 kg) of bombs**
Crew: **2**

Aircraft: **Airco D.H.4**
Manufacturer: **Dayton-Wright Airplane Co.**
Type: **Bomber**
Year: **1918**
Engine: **Liberty 12 12-cylinder liquid-cooled inline V, 400 hp**
Wingspan: **42 ft 5.75 in (12.95 m)**
Length: **30 ft 6 in (9.3 m)**
Height: **10 ft 3.5 in (3.13 m)**
Weight: **4,297 lbs (1,949 kg)**
Maximum speed: **124.7 mph (201 kph) at sea level**
Ceiling: **19,500 ft (5,944 m)**
Endurance: **3 hrs**
Armament: **4 machine-guns; 908 lbs (412 kg) of bombs**
Crew: **2**

Airco D.H.5

This Geoffrey de Havilland design was not a particular success. The D.H.5 served at the front for only eight months, the period from May 1917 to January 1918. Originally designed as a fighter, it was then relegated to training duty. The plane performed poorly above 10,000 feet (3,048 m), and it tended to lose altitude easily in combat. De Havilland had tried to produce a plane that combined the exceptional visibility of the D.H.2 with the advantages of the biplane formula: for maximum visibility, he staggered the wings back, and the pilot's cockpit was located in front of the upper wing. Although the plane was a failure as a fighter, however, its strength and high speed at low altitudes made it a good machine for ground attack missions.

The odd arrangement of the wings led to some unusual handling problems, but experienced pilots were well able to cope with these. Not so trainees, however.

Aircraft: **Airco D.H.5**
Manufacturer: **Aircraft Manufacturing Co. Ltd.**
Type: **Fighter**
Year: **1917**
Engine: **Le Rhône 9J rotary, 110 hp**
Wingspan: **25 ft 8 in (7.82 m)**
Length: **22 ft (6.71 m)**
Height: **9 ft 1.5 in (2.78 m)**
Weight: **1,492 lbs (677 kg)**
Maximum speed: **102 mph (164 kph)**
Ceiling: **16,000 ft (4,877 m)**
Endurance: **2 hrs 45 mins**
Armament: **1 machine-gun**

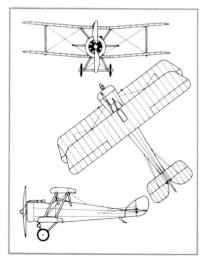

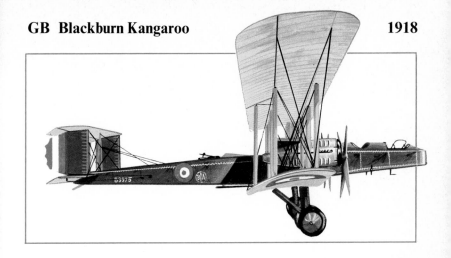

Blackburn Kangaroo

The Kangaroo, one of the least-known planes of the First World War, was developed from the S.P. seaplane bomber and maritime patrol aircraft as a landplane bomber. The Kangaroo was designed in 1918 and only 11 had been delivered to the R.A.F. before the Armistice. But this bomber distinguished itself in the newly-formed R.A.F.'s No. 246 Squadron. In August the squadron's Kangaroos were instrumental in sinking a German submarine during a patrol action in the North Sea. The plane also damaged four more submarines in the last months of the war. The plane's career lasted well beyond 1918: Kangaroos bought back by the Blackburn company were used for many years for passenger, training, and cargo flights.

To ease the problems of 'hangaring' so large a machine, the wings were designed to fold. The long nose gave a good field of vision.

Aircraft: **Blackburn Kangaroo**
Manufacturer: **Blackburn Aeroplane & Motor Co. Ltd.**
Type: **Bomber**
Year: **1918**
Engines: **Two Rolls-Royce Falcon II 12-cylinder liquid-cooled inline Vs, 255 hp each**
Wingspan: **74 ft 10.25 in (22.82 m)**
Length: **46 ft (14.02 m)**
Height: **16 ft 10 in (5.13 m)**
Weight: **8,017 lbs (3,636 kg)**
Maximum speed: **100 mph (161 kph)**
Ceiling: **10,500 ft (3,200 m)**
Endurance: **8 hrs**
Armament: **2 machine-guns; 929 + lbs (417.3 + kg) of bombs**
Crew: **4**

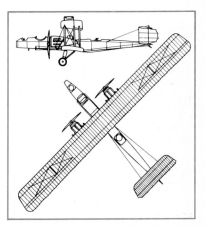

Airco D.H.9
Airco D.H.9A

The increasing number of German air raids on Great Britain in 1917 spurred the British authorities to find a successor to the D.H.4 that could retaliate with similar raids on Germany. The peak of German raids was reached on June 13, 1917, when London was bombed. The D.H.9 appeared in the late summer of 1917 and was basically similar to the D.H.4. The wings and empennage were identical, but the engine installation and the arrangement of the cockpits was altered. The pilot and his observer were now closer together and could therefore communicate. But the new plane was plagued with engine trouble, and at first the D.H.9 was decidedly inferior to the model it was supposed to replace. Only when a new and thoroughly reliable engine was installed, the American-built 400-hp Liberty, did the plane become a success. This model, the D.H.9A, had a first-rate performance. When the war ended production of the D.H.9A slowed down, but the plane's career continued until the 1930s. A total of 2,500 D.H.9As was built, and 4,000 D.H.9s were manufactured.

The first D.H.9s entered service in December 1917, with No. 103 Squadron, and within a few months many other units were supplied with the new

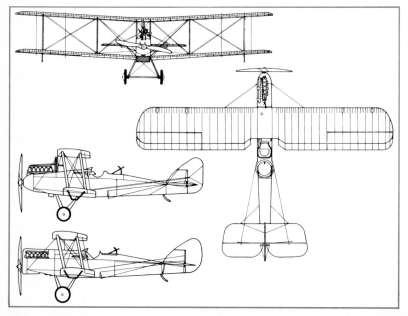

bomber. Its efficiency was limited by the mechanical difficulties with the engine. The plane remained at the front until the D.H.9A appeared. The first D.H.9As went into action in France at the end of August 1918.

Part of this delay was due to the unavailability of Liberty engines. After the plane was tested with the new engine in 1917, Great Britain ordered 3,000 Liberty engines, but only 1,050 were delivered. The D.H.9A had a greater wingspan than its predecessor, and the fuselage was modified in structure and reinforced with internal wire bracing. Although performance was much improved, armament remained unchanged. The bomb load remained the same, and so did the defensive armament: one Vickers fixed, synchronized machine-gun in the nose, and one or two Lewis guns in the observer's cockpit.

Belgium was supplied with 18 D.H.9s, and Russia built some D.H.9As. The United States cancelled orders for 14,000 D.H.9s and 3,991 D.H.9As in 1918.

Aircraft: **Airco D.H.9**
Manufacturer: **Aircraft Manufacturing Co. Ltd.**
Type: **Bomber**
Year: **1918**
Engine: **B.H.P. 6-cylinder liquid-cooled inline, 230 hp**
Wingspan: **42 ft 4.5 in (12.92 m)**
Length: **30 ft 6 in (9.3 m)**
Height: **11 ft 2 in (3.4 m)**
Weight: **3,669 lbs (1,664 kg)**
Maximum speed: **111.5 mph (179 kph) at 10,000 ft (3,048 m)**
Ceiling: **17,500 ft (5,334 m)**
Endurance: **4 hrs 30 mins**
Armament: **2-3 machine-guns; 460 lbs (208.7 kg) of bombs**
Crew: **2**

Aircraft: **Airco D.H.9A**
Manufacturer: **Aircraft Manufacturing Co. Ltd.**
Type: **Bomber**
Year: **1918**
Engine: **Liberty 12-cylinder liquid-cooled inline V, 400 hp**
Wingspan: **45 ft 11.5 in (14 m)**
Length: **30 ft 3 in (9.22 m)**
Height: **11 ft 4 in (3.45 m)**
Weight: **4,645 lbs (2,107 kg)**
Maximum speed: **123 mph (198 kph) at sea level**
Ceiling: **18,000 ft (5,486 m)**
Endurance: **5 hrs 15 mins**
Armament: **2-3 machine-guns; 460-660 lbs (208.7-299.4 kg) of bombs**
Crew: **2**

Handley Page V/1500

Built too late to take part in the war, the Handley Page V/1500 still occupies an important place in the history of aviation. It was the largest British plane of the First World War, the first real strategic bomber expressly designed for that role (the forerunner of the Boeing B-17, Handley Page Halifax, and Avro Lancaster bombers of the Second World War), and the first British four-engined plane. Only three were delivered before the Armistice, and the total production was 35 planes.

British Air Board specifications called for a plane with a range of about 600 miles (966 km), a plane that could reach Berlin from bases in eastern England. The prototype's first flight took place in May 1918. A second prototype was ready in June, after the first one had crashed. The plane's large size and powerful armament were impressive. There were five machine-guns, including the first tail gun on a British plane. The aircraft could carry 30 250-pound (113.4-kg) bombs. Plans were also made for the plane to carry two 'giant' bombs each weighing 3,300 pounds (1,496.9 kg). To improve the plane's aerodynamics, the four engines were mounted in pairs, one tractor and one pusher, in two nacelles. During production, more powerful engines were installed in place of the Rolls-Royce Eagle VIII. These included the 450-hp Napier Lion and the 500-hp Galloway

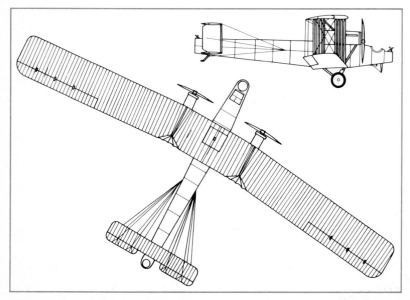

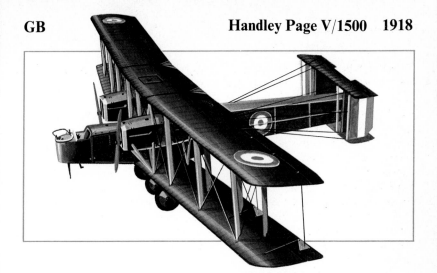

Atlantic.

The Armistice ended the potential career of the Handley Page V/1500, as it was too large and costly a plane for economical commercial flights. The models already produced remained in service for a fairly short time. The bomber's only combat mission was from India in May 1919: a V/1500 bombed Kabul during the 3rd Afghan War.

In 1919 a Handley Page V/1500 was readied for an attempt at the first nonstop crossing of the Atlantic, but test results were unsatisfactory because of problems that developed in the engine cooling system. Another British plane made the crossing – a Vickers Vimy piloted by Alcock and Brown. The Handley Page was sent on a demonstration tour of Canada and the United States, in hopes of finding customers in civil aviation. But only in Great Britain was the plane used commercially. A V/1500 was used by the Handley Page Transport Ltd. in 1919,

Aircraft: **Handley Page V/1500**
Manufacturer: **Handley Page Ltd.**
Type: **Heavy bomber**
Year: **1918**
Engines: **Four Rolls-Royce Eagle VIII 12-cylinder liquid-cooled inline Vs, 375 hp each**
Wingspan: **126 ft (38.41 m)**
Length: **62 ft (18.9 m)**
Height: **23 ft (7.01 m)**
Weight: **24,700 lbs (11,204 kg)**
Maximum speed: **97 mph (156 kph) at 8,750 ft (2,667 m)**
Ceiling: **10,000 ft (3,048 m)**
Endurance: **6 hrs (normal)**
Armament: **4-5 machine-guns; 7,500 lbs (3,402 kg) of bombs**
Crew: **4**

carrying passengers between London and Brussels. As an airliner this converted bomber could carry 40 people.

Sopwith 5F.1 Dolphin
Sopwith TF.2 Salamander
Sopwith 7F.1 Snipe

The last important designs developed by the Sopwith Aviation Company before the war ended were a 'pure' fighter (the Snipe) and two 'fighter-bomber' planes (the Dolphin and the Salamander). All three were excellent planes, but production was curtailed by the end of the war. The Salamander represented an interesting advance in the development of ground attack aircraft, but the most brilliant achievement was the Snipe, which was designed to replace the famous Camel. The Snipe was the best Allied fighter in service when the Armistice came.

The Sopwith 7F.1 Snipe was expressly designed by Herbert Smith for the new 230-hp Bentley B.R.2 rotary engine. In structure and design the Snipe was similar to the camel. The

fuselage had an even more noticeable 'hump', but the empennage was the same. Both sets of wings had dihedral and had more elaborate bracing than on the Camel, and the centre section of the upper wing featured an opening to give the pilot a better field of vision forwards and upwards. The production order for the Snipe came at the start of 1918. The first planes went to France in March, and by the Armistice the 7F.1 Snipe equipped one Australian Flying Corps and two R.A.F. squadrons. The Snipe fighter was extremely manoeuvrable, strong, and had a very high rate of climb, but was not exceptionally fast in horizontal flight. About 1,500 Snipes were built, and they were a standard postwar R.A.F. fighters until 1927.

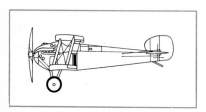

Aircraft: **Sopwith 7F.1 Snipe**
Manufacturer: **Sopwith Aviation Co. Ltd.**
Type: **Fighter**
Year: **1918**
Engine: **Bentley B.R.2 9-cylinder air-cooled rotary, 230 hp**
Wingspan: **30 ft (9.14 m)**
Length: **19 ft 10 in (6.05 m)**
Height: **9 ft 6 in (2.9 m)**
Weight: **2,020 lbs (916 kg)**
Maximum speed: **121 mph (195 kph)**
Ceiling: **19,500 ft (5,944 m)**
Endurance: **3 hrs**
Armament: **2 machine-guns**
Crew: **1**

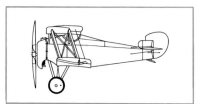

Aircraft: **Sopwith 5F.1 Dolphin**
Manufacturer: **Sopwith Aviation Co. Ltd.**
Type: **Ground attack/fighter**
Year: **1918**
Engine: **Hispano-Suiza 8E 8-cylinder liquid-cooled inline V, 200 hp**
Wingspan: **32 ft 6 in (9.91 m)**
Length: **22 ft 3 in (6.78 m)**
Height: **8 ft 6 in (2.59 m)**
Weight: **2,000 lbs (907 kg)**
Maximum speed: **117 mph (188 kph)**
Ceiling: **19,000 ft (5,791 m)**
Endurance: **1 hr 45 mins**
Armament: **3-4 machine-guns**
Crew: **1**

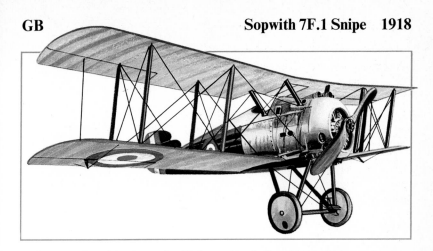

Another Sopwith plane, the Dolphin, reached France shortly before the Snipe but was not as popular with pilots. For improved visibility the wings were staggered backwards, but the pilot was wedged in between the steel tubing of the upper wing's centre section and the breeches of the four machine-guns. The situation was improved when two of the guns were removed. The plane was in service until the war ended, in both escort and ground attack capacities. A total of 1,532 Dolphins was built.

The Sopwith Salamander arrived on the scene too late; only 37 planes were in R.A.F. service by the time the Armistice was signed. The prototype, which made its debut on April 27, 1918, was modelled after the T.F.1, a Camel modified for ground attack. The Salamander performed so well that 1,100 were ordered, but only 102 were finally built. Although this plane saw only a brief period of service, it represented an advance in the development of attack planes, an increasingly important type.

Aircraft: **Sopwith T.F.2 Salamander**
Manufacturer: **Sopwith Aviation Co. Ltd.**
Type: **Ground attack**
Year: **1918**
Engine: **Bentley B.R.2 9-cylinder air-cooled rotary, 230 hp**
Wingspan: **31 ft 2.5 in (9.49 m)**
Length: **19 ft 6 in (5.94 m)**
Height: **9 ft 4 in (2.84 m)**
Weight: **2,512 lbs (1,139 m)**
Maximum speed: **125 mph (201 kph)**
Ceiling: **13,000 ft (3,962 m)**
Endurance: **1 hr 30 mins**
Armament: **2 machine-guns**
Crew: **1**

Vickers Vimy

A contemporary of the Handley Page V/1500, the Vickers Vimy represented the last generation of First World War British heavy bombers. The Vimy, like the V/1500, was designed to reach Berlin, and like the V/1500, only three Vimy bombers reached air units before the Armistice brought its wartime career to an end. But the Vickers Vimy twin-engined biplane had a long postwar career, serving in the Royal Air Force until 1924. It made several endurance flights, including the first nonstop crossing of the Atlantic (June 1919) and the first flight from Great Britain to Australia (November 1919).

The Vimy project got under way in late spring 1917, and three prototypes were ordered in August for pre-production testing. The first prototype took to the air on November 30. Various engines were tried out, and many details were modified. In March 1918, a first order was placed for 150 planes, and total orders reached 1.000 by the end of the war. Like most other large war orders, this one too was cancelled with the Armistice, and only 221 planes were actually built.

After the war the Vimy served with nine Royal Air Force squadrons in the Middle East, as well as at home. It also saw service in some training units. Standard armament was four machine-guns, and the plane carried a maximum bomb load of 2,476 pounds (1,123 kg). In later years, about 80

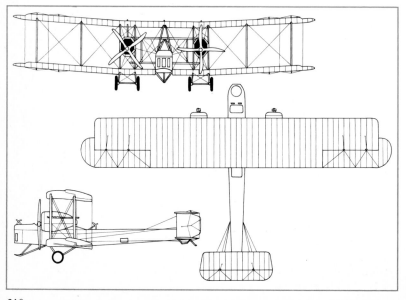

GB   Vickers Vimy

1918

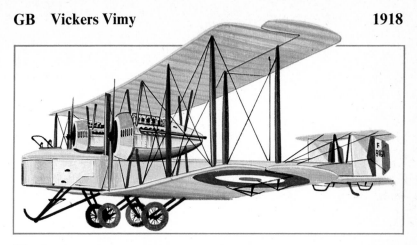

Vimy bombers had their inline engines replaced with radials, including the Bristol Jupiter and the Armstrong–Siddeley Jaguar. But the two standard engines of Vickers Vimy were the Fiat A.12-*bis* and the Rolls-Royce Eagle VIII on the Vimy III and Vimy IV respectively.

The highpoints of the Vimy's career were the 1919 long-distance flights. In June Captain John Alcock and Lieutenant Arthur Whitten Brown flew a specially adapted Vimy nonstop across the Atlantic Ocean. The plane flew from St. Johns, Newfoundland, to Clifden, in western Ireland, a distance of about 1,900 miles (3,058 km). In November another Vickers Vimy, piloted by two Australian brothers, Captain Ross Smith and Lieutenant Keith Smith, flew some 11,000 miles (17,703 km) from Great Britain to Australia in just under 136 hours. This was the first time an Australian crew flew a British plane in this sort of flight.

Other remarkable flights were made in Vimys during the 1920s.

Aircraft: **Vickers Vimy**
Manufacturer: **Vickers Ltd.**
Type: **Heavy bomber**
Year: **1918**
Engines: **Two Rolls-Royce Eagle VIII 12-cylinder liquid-cooled inline Vs, 360 hp each**
Wingspan: **67 ft 2 in (20.47 m)**
Length: **43 ft 6.5 in (13.27 m)**
Height: **15 ft 3 in (4.65 m)**
Weight: **12,500 lbs (5,670 kg)**
Maximum speed: **103 mph (166 kph) at sea level**
Ceiling: **10,500 ft (3,200 m)**
Range: **900 miles (1,448 km)**
Armament: **2-4 machine-guns; 2,476 lbs (1,123 kg) of bombs**
Crew: **3**

Minor types

1914 Martinsyde S.1 – Wingspan: 27 ft 8 in (8.43 m) – Length: 21 ft (6.4 m) – Maximum speed: 87 mph (140 kph) – Engine: Gnome rotary, 80 hp. Similar to the Sopwith Tabloid, the S.1 was used on the Western Front for fast reconnaissance. A few planes were supplied to operational units. It was less stable and generally inferior to the Bristol Scout and the Sopwith Tabloid.

1914 R.A.F. B.E.8 – Wingspan: 39 ft 6 in (12.04 m) – Length: 27 ft 3 in (8.31 m) – Maximum speed: 70 mph (113 kph) – Engine: Gnome rotary, 80 hp. Already in service a few months before the outbreak of war, the B.E.8s were assigned to units in France in summer 1914. They were first used for bombing but soon reassigned to training duty along with a variant model, the B.E.8a, which had modified wings and ailerons. Up to 1915, 22 B.E.8s and 38 B.E.8as had been delivered to the R.F.C.

1914 R.A.F. S.E.2a – Wingspan: 27 ft 6 in. (8.38 m) – Length: 20 ft. 6 in (6.25 m) – Maximum speed: 96 mph (155 kph) – Engine: Gnome rotary, 80 hp. Designed by Geoffrey de Havilland, this plane was exceptional in quality and performance, but it never fully achieved its potential because it had no armament. When it was decided to install a machine-gun, other planes were already in advanced stages of development.

212

1914 Sopwith Tabloid – Wingspan: 25 ft 6 in. (7.77 m) – Length: 20 ft 4 in (6.2 m) – Maximum speed: 92 mph (148 kph) – Engine: Gnome rotary, 80 hp. The plane that won the Schneider Trophy in 1914 was later developed into a military version. It equipped some units early in the war, first as a fast reconnaissance plane and then as a light bomber. Some Tabloids had a fixed machine-gun with deflector plates on the propeller.

1915 Airco D.H.1A – Wingspan: 41 ft (12.5 m) Length: 28 ft 11.25 in (8.82 m) – Maximum speed: 88 mph (129 kph) – Engine: Beardmore, 120 hp. Resembling the 1910 F.E.1 and F.E.2 in configuration, the D.H.1 was a two-seater pusher biplane designed for combat and reconnaissance. The designer, Geoffrey de Havilland, piloted the prototype himself in 1915, and 100 of them were ordered. Seventy-three D.H.1As served in home defence units until 1917.

1915 Armstrong Whitworth F.K.3 – Wingspan: 40 ft 0.5 in (12.2 m) – Length: 29 ft (8.84 kph) – Maximum speed: 87 mph (140 kph) – Engine: R.A.F. 1a, 90 hp. Designed by Frederick Koolhoven and put into production in summer 1915, 500 were built. They were used mainly for training, as the plane turned out to be underpowered. One squadron used the F.K.3 for reconnaissance and patrol missions in Macedonia.

1915 R.A.F. B.E.2e – Wingspan: 40 ft 9 in. (12.42 m) – Length: 27 ft 3 in (8.31 m) – Maximum speed: 90 mph (145 kph) – Engine: R.A.F. 1a, 90 hp. This last model in the B.E.2 series was something of a step backwards in respect to the earlier versions: it was slower and less well armed. Nevertheless, 1,801 of them were built. They were used in all the units that had been equipped with the earlier models. Deliveries began in 1916. Later the plane was reassigned to training duty.

1916 Vickers F.B. 12 – Wingspan: 26 ft (7.93 m) – Length: 21 ft 6 in (6.55 m) – Maximum speed: 93 mph (150 kph) – Engine: Gnome Monosoupape rotary, 100 hp. Produced in June 1916, this was one of the last pusher biplanes. The formula was obsolete, and better-armed tractor biplanes were beginning to appear. The few planes that were sent to the front proved unsatisfactory.

1916 Vickers F.B. 19 Mk.II – Wingspan: 24 ft (7.32 m) – Length: 18 ft 2 in (5.54 m) – Maximum speed: 98 mph (158 kph) – Engine: Le Rhône 9J rotary, 110 hp. Although fast and well-armed, this plane was not considered combat-worthy. It was built in two series, the Mk.I and Mk.II, but only small numbers were produced. After operational tests in France, it was rejected for use on the Western Front and used for training.

1916 Vickers F.B.9 – Wingspan: 33 ft 9 in (10.29 m) – Length: 28 ft 5.5 in (8.67 m) – Maximum speed: 83 mph (134 kph) – Engine: Gnome Monosoupape rotary, 100 hp. This improved model of the famous F.B.5 'Gunbus' came out early in 1916. The improvements consisted mainly of alterations in wing and fuselage structure for better aerodynamics. The fixed machine-gun mounting was replaced by a fully rotatable one.

1917 Airco D.H.6 – Wingspan: 35 ft 11 in. (10.95 m) – Length: 27 ft 3.5 in (8.32 m) – Maximum speed: 66 mph (106 kph) – Engine: R.A.F. 1a, 90 hp. Designed as a trainer, the D.H.6 was used as a maritime reconnaissance plane and anti-submarine bomber in the last year of the war. Production began in January 1917, with orders for 2,850 aircraft. When the Avro 504 became the standard trainer, the D.H.6 was assigned to the R.N.A.S.

1917 Felixstowe F.2A – Wingspan: 95 ft 7.5 in (29.15 m) – Length: 46 ft 3 in (14.1 m) – Maximum speed: 95.5 mph (154 kph) – Engines: Two Rolls-Royce Eagle VIII, 345 hp each. Derived from Curtiss H.12 'Large America' flying boat, this excellent aircraft established the basic formula for British seaplanes until the 1930s. One hundred and seventy F.2As were ordered between November 1917 and March 1918; they were used on patrol missions in the North Sea.

Minor types

1917 Austin Ball A.F.B.1 – Wingspan: 30 ft (9.15 m) – Length: 21 ft 6 in (6.55 m) – Maximum speed: 138 mph (222 kph) – Engine: Hispano-Suiza, 200 hp. This fighter was designed and built in collaboration with the British ace Captain Albert Ball. It turned out to be an excellent plane, superior in performance to the S.E.5a. But the Camel was then in full production and the A.F.B.1 was never mass-produced.

1917 Fairey F.17 Campania – Wingspan: 61 ft 7.5 in (18.78 m) – Length: 43 ft 0.5 in (13.12 m) – Maximum speed: 80.5 mph (130 kph) – Engine: Rolls-Royce Eagle VIII, 345 hp. This was the first plane, a patrol seaplane, designed to operate from an aircraft-carrier: the transatlantic liner *Campania*, adapted for carrier duty. Two prototypes appeared in 1917, and the second took the designation F.17. The plane was used in various models until 1919, both on aircraft-carriers and at British naval bases.

1917 Sopwith T.1 Cuckoo – Wingspan: 46 ft 9 in (14.25 m) – Length: 28 ft 6 in (8.69 m) – Maximum speed: 103.5 mph (167 kph) – Engine: Sunbeam Arab, 200 hp. Developed at the end of 1916 for the Admiralty, this was a landplane that could carry one torpedo. Its endurance was four hours. One hundred and fifty were built, but they reached units too late to take part in combat.

1917 Martinsyde F.3 – Wingspan: 32 ft 10 in (10 m) – Length: 25 ft 6 in (7.77 m) – Maximum speed: 129.5 mph (208 kph) – Engine: Rolls-Royce Falcon III, 275 hp. Designed by G.H. Handasyde and tested in November 1917, this proved to be a fast and manoeuvrable fighter plane. Because of a shortage of Falcon engines, most of which were earmarked for the top-priority Bristol Fighter, production plans were cancelled, and only six planes were built.

1918 Martinsyde F.4 Buzzard – Wingspan: 32 ft 9.5 in (9.99 m) – Length: 25 ft 5.5 in (7.76 m) – Maximum speed: 140 mph (225 kph) – Engine: Hispano-Suiza 8F, 300 hp. This plane was a development of the unfortunate F.3. The F.4 was powered by a more readily available engine than the Rolls-Royce Falcon, and had some minor structural changes. Although it was an excellent fighter, production was curtailed in 1918.

1918 B.A.T. Bantam Mk.I – Wingspan: 25 ft (7.62 m) – Length: 18 ft 5 in (5.61 m) – Maximum speed: 146 mph (235 kph) – Engine: A.B.C. Wasp II radial, 200 hp. Designed by Frederick Koolhoven early in 1918, the Bantam was one of the first products of the newly-formed British Aerial Transport Company. It was a fast and manoeuvrable plane, but the new and still imperfect radial engine made it unreliable. About 15 planes were built.

Russia

The development of Russian aviation was brought to an abrupt halt by the 1917 revolution. Until that time it had relied heavily on other countries (France in particular) for engines and planes. Consequently Russia did not make a major contribution to aviation history in those years. One remarkable plane, however, put Russia briefly in the vanguard. This was Igor Sikorsky's *Ilya Muromets*, the world's first four-engined strategic bomber.

Russia had taken an early interest in aviation and soon appreciated the aeroplane's military possibilities. Two military flying schools were opened in 1910: one at Gatchina, near St Petersburg, the other in Sebastopol. Officers were also sent to France and Great Britain to learn to fly. The first Military Aviation Rally took place at Gatchina in 1911, and was followed by army manoeuvres in which planes took part for the first time. When war broke out, the Imperial Russian Air Service had 224 planes, 12 dirigibles, and 46 balloons. Units at the front had 145 aircraft in all at the beginning of September 1914.

At the start of the war Russian air power was comparable with that of the other belligerents, but there were no real advances as the war progressed. The aeronautical industry did not flourish, and most of the planes it produced were French aircraft built under licence, including Voisin, Nieuport, Farman and Morane planes, built by Dux in Moscow, and the Henri and Maurice Farman biplanes produced by the Russo-Baltic works. Moreover, Russia was almost totally dependent on engines imported from the rest of Europe. Among those built in Russia under licence were Gnome and Hispano engines. And fighting planes were supplied directly by France, Great Britain (B.E.2e, Vickers F.B.19, Sopwith 1½-Strutter), and the United States (chiefly Curtiss seaplanes).

Russia too had its aces, although their scores were lower than those of the other nations at war. The top ace was Captain Alexander Alexandrovich Kazakov, who had a large skull painted on the rudder of his plane. He shot down 17 enemy planes. He was followed by Captain Paul V. d'Argueeff with 15, and Lieutenant Alexander Prokofieff de Seversky with 13 victories.

Sikorsky Ilya Muromets V

The world's first four-engined plane was nicknamed the Russian Knight, *Russkii Vitiaz*. Designed by Igor Sikorsky and G. I. Lavrov, the plane flew for the first time on May 13, 1913. Sikorsky developed an even larger four-engined model from the *Vitiaz*. The new plane, the *Ilya Muromets*, was a remarkably fine plane for its time. On February 12, 1914, it made an astonishing flight: it reached an altitude of about 6,562 feet (2,000 m) in the Moscow sky and flew for five hours at an average speed of more than 60 mph (97 kph), carrying 16 passengers and a dog. This plane, which was named for a legendary Russian hero, was produced in a modified version for military use. Ten aircraft were ordered, and when war broke out the order was increased to

80. The planes were manufactured by the *R.B.V.Z.,* the Russo-Baltic Wagon Works.

This four-engined plane was produced in five models, varying in size, weight and engine type and power. The problem of finding engines was chiefly responsible for the fact that there was no 'standard' model. The Russians were almost totally dependent on imported engines, which were not always readily available. So the plane had to be modified to accommodate the engines that were available. Salmson, Sunbeam, Argus, Renault, and *R.B.V.Z.* engines were all used, and some planes even had two pairs of different engines. The largest and most powerful version of the *Ilya Muromets* was designated E-1. It had four 220-hp Renault engines, weighed

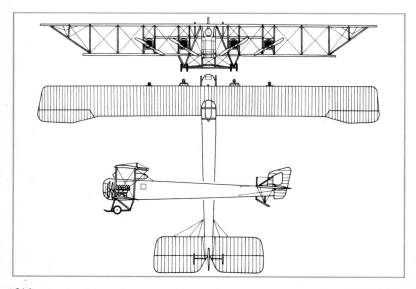

7 tons (7,000 kg) and had a maximum speed of about 85 mph (137 kph).

The operational career of the *Ilya Muromets* did not get off to a good start. The first two planes were disappointing in service, and the chief of the military technical inspection service, General Helgard, ordered the *R.B.V.Z.* to suspend production. The president of the factory, M. V. Shidlovski, succeeded in having the order rescinded. On December 10, 1914, Shidlovski was promoted to the rank of major-general and given the command of the newly-formed *Vozdushnykh Korablei* ('Flying Ships') squadron, operating the *Ilya Muromets*. The unit went into action in February 1915, from a base at Jablonna in Poland. The first bombing mission set off on February 15 to bomb targets in East Prussia. From then until the revolution, *Ilya Muromets* bombers completed more than 400 bombing missions over Germany and Lithuania. Only two planes were lost, for the type was extremely sturdy

Aircraft: **Sikorsky Ilya Muromets V**
Manufacturer: **R.B.V.Z.**
Type: **Heavy bomber**
Year: **1915**
Engines: **Four Sunbeam 8-cylinder liquid-cooled inline Vs, 150 hp each**
Wingspan: **97 ft 9 in (29.8 m)**
Length: **56 ft 1.5 in (17.1 m)**
Height: **15 ft 6 in (4.72 m)**
Weight: **10,117 lbs (4,589 kg)**
Maximum speed: **75 mph (121 kph)**
Ceiling: **9,840 ft (3,000 m)**
Endurance: **5 hrs**
Armament: **3-7 machine-guns; 1,150 lbs (522 kg) of bombs**
Crew: **4-7**

and could absorb a lot of punishment without crippling effect. By 1916 the *Ilya Muromets* was so famous that Great Britain and France asked for construction rights to build the type. Although the Czar granted permission, the planes were never built outside Russia.

The *Ilya Muromets* was in every respect a remarkable machine for its time. Had Russia possessed the manufacturing facilities to mass produce the type and the necessary engines, and had the organization to use the bombers *en masse,* much might have come of the *Ilya Muromets.*

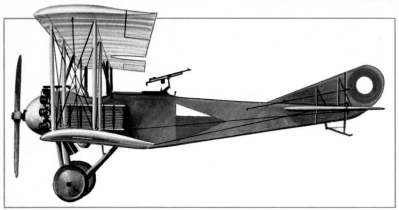

Lebed' 12

The first reconnaissance plane designed and built in Russia was modelled on a German Albatros B II captured in 1915. This Lebed' 11 was built
by one of the pioneers of Russian
aviation, Vladimir A. Lebedev, who
had learned to fly in France in 1910
and then established an aircraft manufacturing company in Russia. The
model 11, which was not a success,
was soon followed by the model 12,
which went into production. The
Lebed' 12 made its first flight on
December 28, 1915, and although the
report of Sleptzov, the pilot, was not
unreservedly enthusiastic, 225 planes
were ordered, to replace the Voisins
used by the Imperial Russian Air
Service. It took a long time to get
Lebed' 12 production going and the
type did not go into service until the
following autumn. This biplane was
not very popular with pilots because
it tended to fail to recover from
dives.

Aircraft: **Lebed' 12**
Manufacturer: **V.A. Lebedev**
Type: **Reconnaissance**
Year: **1916**
Engine: **Salmson 150 hp**
Wingspan: **43 ft 1.75 in (13.15 m)**
Length: **26 ft 1 in (7.95 m)**
Height:
Weight: **2,674 lbs (1,213 kg)**
Maximum speed: **83 mph (134 kph)**
Ceiling: **11,482 ft (3,500 m)**
Endurance: **3 hrs**
Armament: **1   machine-gun;   200 lbs
   (90.7 kg) of bombs**
Crew: **2**

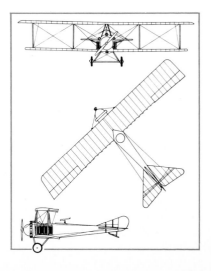

Anatra DS

Aircraft: **Anatra DS**
Manufacturer: **Zavod A.A. Anatra**
Type: **Reconnaissance**
Year: **1917**
Engine: **Salmson 9-cylinder liquid-cooled radial, 150 hp**
Wingspan: **40 ft 7 in (12.37 m)**
Length: **26 ft 6.75 in (8.1 m)**
Height: **10 ft 5.5 in (3.19 m)**
Weight: **2,566 lbs (1,164 kg)**
Maximum speed: **89.5 mph (144 kph)**
Ceiling: **14,110 ft (4,300 m)**
Endurance: **3 hrs 30 mins**
Armament: **2 machine-guns**
Crew: **2**

The company that produced the DS was founded by an Italian banker, A. Anatra, in Odessa. The plane appeared in 1917, but production was curtailed by the revolution. About 70 planes in all were completed. This type was a development of the unsuccessful 1916 model D, which was plagued by structural failures and the indifferent performance given by its 100-hp Gnome Monosoupape rotary engine. The engine problem was solved by equipping the Anatra DS with a 150-hp Salmson (Canton-Unné) radial engine. The plane was nicknamed 'Anasal' (Anatra-Salmson). Like its predecessor, the DS followed the general design of the German Aviatik biplane reconnaissance machine.

Like its predecessor, the Anatra D, the DS had structural problems, and the water-cooled radial engine had a tendency to overheat and then seize up.

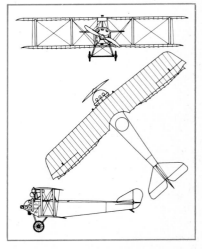

Italy

Italy entered the war in 1915. Its air force was well-trained and ready for action, but it lacked combat experience. Italy put into action a dozen squadrons, equipped with a variety of planes, most of them outdated Blériots, Farmans and Nieuports. They were all French planes, because Italian industry was not as yet on a level with those of other countries. For most of the war, Italian pilots flew foreign planes. Italy relied heavily on France for its fighter planes, and it was 1918 before an Italian-designed fighter went into action.

Naval combat planes and bombers were exceptions to the rule. The excellent Capronis and Macchis here put Italy in the vanguard, and the Caproni bombers were particularly successful. Caproni Ca.3 series planes were among the first strategic bombers to be developed during the war, second

only to the Russian *Ilya Muromets*. Capronis bore the full weight of the first air operations against Austria. Their first war mission, on August 20, 1915, was a bombing raid on the Austrian airfield at Aisovizza.

Prospects looked brighter in 1916, especially for fighters. Italian units received Nieuport 11s and 17s. On April 6 morale was raised when Francesco Baracca shot down the first plane to fall to Italian guns, over Medeuzza. By the end of the year the Italian aviation industry had turned out 1,255 planes and 2,300 engines, and 49 squadrons were in action: 13 bomber, 22 reconnaissance, nine fighter, and five 'strategic defence' fighter, the last for the protection of major rear-area targets. The following year, production figures rose higher, with the designing and construction of 3,861 planes and 6,726 engines.

In 1917 the air force was restructured, and organization was simplified. Each army had its own air unit, with another air unit under the high command's control. Fighter squadrons were increased to 12 and then later to 15 in number, and were equipped with some of the finest fighters of the day, including the Hanriot HD.1 and the first Spad S.VIIs. The arrival of the Spad S.XIII in 1918 improved performance of the Italian air force even further and gave Italy air supremacy.

In the last decisive battles of the war Italian fighters were used in an absolutely new way. The planes attacked the enemy in mass formation, and these huge onslaughts overwhelmed the Austrian air force. By the armistice, the Italian Army Air Force included 84 squadrons, 5 dirigibles, and 4 special sections, while the Naval Air Force, which had played such a decisive role in the Adriatic, comprised 44 seaplane squadrons and 15 dirigibles. Most of the army fighter units were equipped with the Hanriot HD.1, but two squadrons had the latest model of the Spad, the S.XIII. Bomber units used the excellent S.V.A., as did some reconnaissance squadrons. Capronis were used for long-range missions. There were 1,020 reconnaissance planes in service, 135 bombers, and 528 fighters for a total of 1,683 first-line machines. Wartime aircraft production had reached a total of 11,986 which included planes of all types.

Italy had 43 aces, the top one Francesco Baracca with 34 planes downed. Silvio Scaroni had 26 victories, Pier Ruggiero Piccio 24, Flavio Baracchini 21, Fulco Ruffo di Calabria 20, Marziale Cerutti and Ferruccio Ranza both 17, and Luigi Olivari 12. Eighteen aces served in the same unit, Francesco Baracca's famous 91st Squadron. Baracca's exploits became legendary. He shot down his first plane on April 6, 1916, and flew fighters for two more years. His squadron was involved in several dog fights, particularly in late 1917, with the Austrian ace Godwin Brumowski and his squadron. (Brumowski ended the war with 40 victories). Francesco Baracca was shot in the head by ground fire on June 19, 1918, and his plane crashed.

A rearing black pony on a white ground was the emblem of Francesco Baracca, the top Italian ace (34 victories). Eight years after his death, on the occasion of the first Savio automobile race, near Ravenna, Baracca's mother gave her son's emblem to Enzo Ferrari, the automobile designer, for luck. It is still the Ferrari emblem.

Caproni Ca. 3
Caproni Ca. 5

Along with Russia, Italy was the first nation to develop and use heavy bombers. The first such Caproni, the Ca.30, appeared in 1913. It was the only plane of that size at the time and the only bomber, with the sole exception of the Russia's giant four-engined *Ilya Muromets* designed by Sikorsky. These two planes were the first heavy bombers, the ancestors of such famous bombers as the German Gothas and the British Handley Pages.

The first Italian bombing raid of the war was flown by Caproni Ca.32s (military designation Ca.2) on August 20, 1915. The Ca.32, of which 164 were built, was followed by the Ca.33 (military designation Ca.3) early in 1917. The two models were very similar in concept, but the Ca.33 represented a great improvement in engine power, performance, and bomb load. The Ca.33 was powered by three Isotta-Fraschini V.4B engines, of 150 hp each. Two engines with tractor propellers were installed in wing nacelles. The third engine, with a pusher propeller, was installed at the rear of the central fuselage. The unusual location of the rear machine-gun was not completely satisfactory: it was installed at the level of the trailing edge of the upper wing, and the gunner

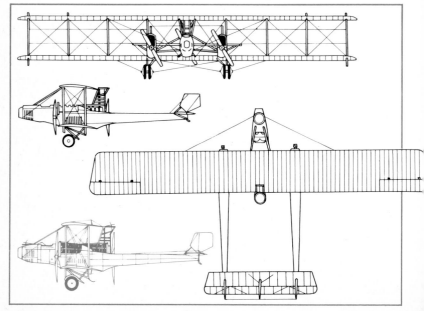

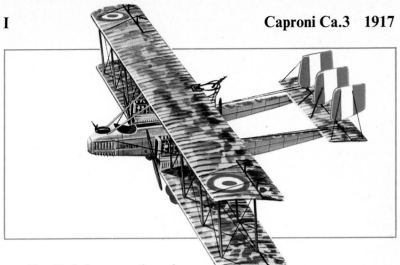

stood in a kind of cage over the pusher engine. The plane's structure was distinctive, with large wings, two booms supporting the tailplane, elevators, and three polygonal rudders.

Two hundred and sixty-nine Ca.33s were built. They saw service with many army squadrons and the 1st Naval Torpedo Plane Squadron. Two French air units were also equipped with Ca.33s built under licence by Esnault-Pelterie. The bomber was in service until the end of the war.

In October 1918, a new model began to reach the front. This was the Ca.46, one of the series designated as Ca.5 by the military. The first biplane model to appear after the Ca.4 (Ca.40–43) triplanes was the Ca.44. It came out early in 1918 and was soon followed by the Ca.45 and the Ca.46, both designed for large-scale production. Much of this series' superiority to the triplanes was due to greater engine power. Before the war ended, 225 series 5 Capronis had been built, and manufacturing rights had

Aircraft: **Caproni Ca.33**
Manufacturer: **Società di Aviazione Ing. Caproni**
Type: **Heavy bomber**
Year: **1917**
Engines: **Three Isotta-Fraschini V.4B, 6-cylinder liquid-cooled inlines, 150 hp each**
Wingspan: **72 ft 10 in (22.2 m)**
Length: **35 ft 9 in (10.9 m)**
Height: **12 ft 2 in (3.7 m)**
Weight: **8,400 lbs (3,810 kg)**
Maximum speed: **85 mph (136.8 kph) at sea level**
Ceiling: **13,451 ft (4,100 m)**
Endurance: **3 hrs 30 mins**
Armament: **2-4 machine-guns; 1,000 lbs (453 kg) of bombs**

Aircraft: **Caproni Ca.46**
Manufacturer: **Società di Aviazione Ing. Caproni**
Type: **Heavy bomber**
Year: **1918**
Engines: **Three Fiat A.12bis 6-cylinder liquid-cooled inlines, 300 hp each**
Wingspan: **76 ft 9.25 in (23.4 m)**
Length: **41 ft 4 in (12.6 m)**
Height: **14 ft 8.5 in (4.48 m)**
Weight: **11,684 lbs (5,300 kg)**
Maximum speed: **94.5 mph (152 kph) at sea level**
Ceiling: **14,760 ft (4,500 m)**
Endurance: **4 hrs**
Armament: **2 machine-guns; 1,984 lbs (900 kg) of bombs**
Crew: **4**

been granted to France, Great Britain, and the United States.

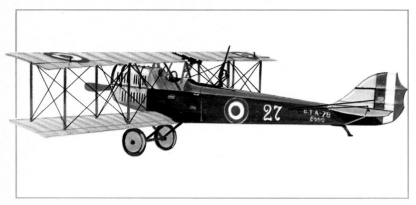

S.I.A.7B.1

Aircraft: **S.I.A. 7B.1**
Manufacturer: **Società Italiana Aviazione**
Type: **Reconnaissance**
Year: **1917**
Engine: **Fiat A.12bis 6-cylinder liquid-cooled inline, 260 hp**
Wingspan: **43 ft 8.5 in (13.32 m)**
Length: **29 ft 8.5 in (9.06 m)**
Height: **9 ft 10 in (3 m)**
Weight: **3,455 lbs (1,567 kg)**
Maximum speed: **116 mph (186.6 kph)**
Ceiling: **22,965 ft (7,000 m)**
Endurance: **4 hrs**
Armament: **2 machine-guns; 132 lbs (60 kg) of bombs**
Crew: **2**

The *S.I.A.* (*Società Italiana Aviazione*) was a subsidiary of the Fiat company and built planes under licence during the first two years of the war. In 1917 the company turned out a two-seater biplane designed by Savoia and Verduzio, the men who designed the Ansaldo-built S.V.A. The new plane was designated the *S.I.A.* 7B.1 and immediately went into production, entering front-line service by the end of the year. It was an elegant aircraft, with a mixed structure of wood and steel tubing, covered with canvas (wings and empennage) and plywood (fuselage). The wings were of equal span, and only the upper one had ailerons. The 7B.1 was a fast plane, easy to handle, and had a good rate of climb. In 1917 Laureati piloted the plane to a record climb-to-altitude of 22,145 feet (6,750 m).

In operation, however, the plane's wings proved to be weak structurally, and it was withdrawn in July 1918.

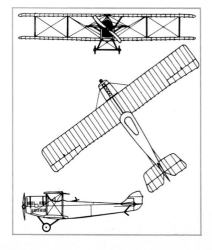

S.A.M.L S.2

S.A.M.L. (*Società Aeronautica Meccanica Lombarda*) was the main Italian builder of the German Aviatik B I biplane up to 1915. In 1916–17 the company developed an original design, the S.1, with a 260-hp Fiat A.12 engine. The next model, the S.2, appeared in 1917. Its wings were smaller, with two bays to the *S.A.M.L.*1's three bays. The S.2 also had a different, rounded rudder, a second machine-gun, and a more powerful engine. Both the S.1 and the S.2 saw much front-line service and were used by 16 reconnaissance squadrons in Italy, Albania, and Macedonia. Total production, including those built under licence by other Italian companies, amounted to 660 aircraft. Some S.2s were equipped with cameras instead of light bombs. Others were given double controls for training. Pilots liked the *S.A.M.L.* planes, and some of the aircraft saw service in Italy's African campaigns after the First World War.

Aircraft: **S.A.M.L. S.2**
Manufacturer: **S.A.M.L.**
Type: **Reconnaissance**
Year: **1917**
Engine: **Fiat A.12bis 6-cylinder liquid-cooled inline, 300 hp**
Wingspan: **39 ft 8.5 in (12.1 m)**
Length: **27 ft 10.75 in (8.5 m)**
Height: **9 ft 9.25 in (2.98 m)**
Weight: **3,075 lbs (1,395 kg)**
Maximum speed: **101 mph (162 kph) at sea level**
Ceiling: **16,405 ft (5,000 m)**
Endurance: **3 hrs 30 mins**
Armament: **2 machine-guns; 88 lbs (40 kg) of bombs**
Crew: **2**

Caproni Ca.4

Between the Ca.3 and the later Ca.5 biplanes, Caproni brought out a series of triplane bombers. The additional wing was intended to increase the plane's effectiveness. The Ca.4 was larger than the Ca.3 and Ca.5, and although its performance was not very good, it could deliver a heavy payload to a long-range target.

The manufacturer designated the first triplane of the Ca.4 series the Ca.40. Apart from its three wings, the plane was based on the earlier biplanes in fuselage structure and empennage. The armament was improved. Instead of the rear machine-gun in its cage above the pusher engine, provision was made for a gun in each of the two tail booms. The Ca.40 had its problems: the three 200-hp Isotta-Fraschini engines were insufficient for a plane of that size. Only three planes were built before an improved model, the Ca.41, appeared. The fuselage structure was altered, and more powerful engines were installed. The final production model was the Ca.42. Some Ca.42s were powered by 270-hp Isotta-Fraschini engines, and others were equipped with more powerful engines including the Fiat and the American 400-hp Liberty. Increased power made it possible to increase the armament. In some planes the number of machine-guns was doubled, by installing pairs of guns in the tail turrets.

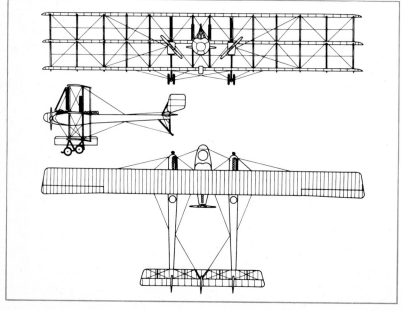

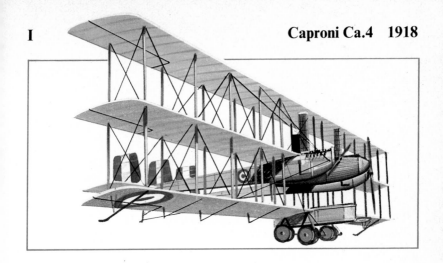

Bombs were carried in a streamlined container between the wheels of the landing gear. The plane could carry a payload of almost 3,200 pounds (1,450 kg) of bombs.

Twenty-three Ca.42s were built, and six were supplied to the British Royal Naval Air Service for the duration of the war. The plane was used chiefly as a night bomber but towards the end of the war it also took part in day missions.

A few other interesting models were developed. The navy's Ca.43 had two floats and carried two torpedoes. The Ca.51 and Ca.52 had a biplane empennage with a machine-gun position. A civilian version, the Ca.48, was also produced. The plane was basically a Ca.42 with a cabin that could accommodate 18–23 passengers. After the war, this variant was further improved in the Ca.58 model. The Ca.58 had a closed, two-level cabin (with inside staircase) that could accommodate 30 people. The plane made several

Aircraft: **Caproni Ca. 42**
Manufacturer: **Società di Aviazione Ing. Caproni**
Type: **Heavy bomber**
Year: **1918**
Engines: **Three Isotta-Fraschini 5 6-cylinder liquid-cooled inlines, 270 hp each**
Wingspan: **98 ft 1 in (29.9 m)**
Length: **42 ft 11.75 in (13.1 m)**
Height: **20 ft 8 in (6.3 m)**
Weight: **14,793 lbs (6,710 kg)**
Maximum speed: **78 mph (126 kph) at sea level**
Ceiling: **9,842 ft (3,000 m)**
Endurance: **7 hrs**
Armament: **4 machine-guns; 3,197 lbs (1,450 kg) of bombs**
Crew: **4**

passenger flights, but efforts to set up regular commercial services were unsuccessful.

Ansaldo A.1 *Balilla*

The first Italian-designed fighter, the Ansaldo A.1 *Balilla* (Hunter), appeared late in the war. A total of 108 *Balillas* was built, but only a few saw combat. The plane was designed by Brezzi of the Ansaldo company in 1917. It was clearly based on the already-famous S.V.A. reconnaissance plane, though the fighter was smaller. The A.1 had speed, strength, and manoeuvrability. The plane was thoroughly tested in November 1917 by three of the most famous pilots of the day, Baracca, Piccio, and Ruffo di Calabria. They were impressed by its speed, but they found it less manoeuvrable than some of the very agile foreign fighters, such as the Nieuports and Hanriots, already serving in Italian squadrons. Some alterations were made, and the *Balilla* went into production. Most of the planes were earmarked for home defence service.

Aircraft: **Ansaldo A.1 Balilla**
Manufacturer: **Società Giovanni Ansaldo**
Type: **Fighter**
Year: **1918**
Engine: **S.P.A. 6A 6-cylinder liquid-cooled inline, 220 hp**
Wingspan: **25 ft 2.25 in (7.68 m)**
Length: **22 ft 5.25 in (6.84 m)**
Height: **8 ft 3.75 in (2.53 m)**
Weight: **1,951 lbs (885 kg)**
Maximum speed: **137 mph (220 kph)**
Ceiling: **16,405 ft (5,000 m)**
Endurance: **1 hr 30 mins**
Armament: **2 machine-guns**
Crew: **1**

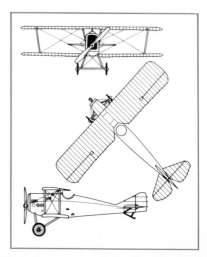

Pomilio PE

Aircraft: **Pomilio PE**
Manufacturer: **Fabbrica Aeroplani Ing. O. Pomilio & Compagnia**
Type: **Reconnaissance**
Year: **1918**
Engine: **Fiat A.12, 260 hp**
Wingspan: **38 ft 8.5 in (11.78 m)**
Length: **29 ft 4 in (8.94 m)**
Height: **11 ft (3.35 m)**
Weight: **3,391 lbs (1,538 kg)**
Maximum speed: **120 mph (194 kph)**
Ceiling: **16,405 ft (5,000 m)**
Endurance: **3 hrs 30 mins**
Armament: **2 machine-guns**
Crew: **2**

The PE was the most successful of a series of two-seater biplanes built by the Pomilio company in Turin during 1917 and 1918. They were the most widely produced Italian-designed planes of the war (1,616 in all). The PE had the same structure as its predecessors (the PC and PD models): wood and metal with canvas covering. The empennage of the PE was modified and had a larger area. The PE was very fast and climbed well, and was widely used for reconnaissance and artillery spotting. Over 100 such planes took part in the battle of Vittorio Veneto, which began on October 20, 1918. Thirty squadrons in all were equipped with various models of the plane. A Pomilio subsidiary manufactured the plane in the United States, with the 400-hp Liberty engine.

After the war the Pomilio brothers sold out to Ansaldo and emigrated to the United States.

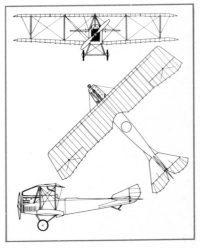

Ansaldo S.V.A. 5
Ansaldo S.V.A. 9

After a flight of 3.5 hours, eight planes of the Italian 87th Squadron appeared in the sky over Vienna at 9.20 am on August 9, 1918. For half an hour the planes flew in close formation over the Austrian capital, dropping leaflets and taking photographs. At 12.40 pm, seven of the eight S.V.A.s returned to their base at San Pelagio. They had flown more than 620 miles (1,000 km), almost 500 (800) of them over enemy territory. The plane flown by Lieutenant Giuseppe Sarti had engine trouble and had to land near Wiener-Neustadt just outside Vienna. This flight was arranged by the poet Gabriele d'Annunzio. One of the S.V.A. 5s had been modified from a single-seater into a two-seater to accommodate d'Annunzio and the pilot, Captain Natale Palli. The other planes were all single-seaters. An extra 66-gallon (300-litre) fuel tank had to be installed for this flight.

Much of the S.V.A.'s renown is linked to that peaceful air raid over Vienna, but the plane was outstanding in its own right. It was generally considered one of the war's best light bomber and reconnaissance planes. It was designed by Umberto Savoia and Rodolfo Verduzio, with the assistance of Celestino Rosatelli, who was later to design many famous planes himself. The prototype made its first flight on March 19, 1917. In military evaluation trials, it proved to be fast and strong, but not sufficiently manoeuvrable to

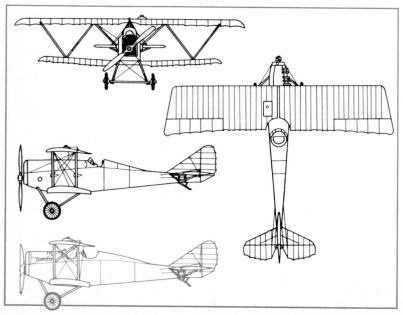

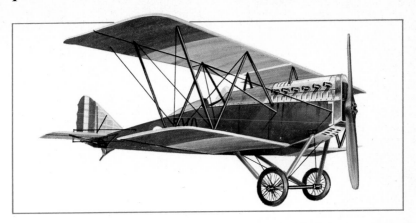

make a fighter plane. As a result, the S.V.A. was assigned to reconnaissance duty.

The first version was the S.V.A.4, which was followed by the S.V.A.5. The main difference between the two models was their fuel capacity (four hours endurance for the S.V.A. 4, six for the S.V.A. 5) and their armament. In service from February 1918, the single-seater S.V.A. equipped six reconnaissance squadrons. Its performance was excellent, and the plane completed many outstanding flights, carrying out such exceptional missions including the reconnaissance flight of Locatelli and Ferrarin over Friedrichshafen on May 21, 1918, a flight of about 435 miles (700 km).

Two new versions of the plane were developed at the same time, both of them two-seaters: the S.V.A.9 and the S.V.A.10. The S.V.A.9, a trainer, was without armament, had double controls, and had a shorter range than the S.V.A.5. The S.V.A.10 was designed for armed reconnaissance and light

Aircraft: **Ansaldo S.V.A.5**
Manufacturer: **Società Giovanni Ansaldo**
Type: **Reconnaissance**
Year: **1918**
Engine: **S.P.A. 6A 6-cylinder liquid-cooled inline, 220 hp**
Wingspan: **29 ft 10.25 in (9.1 m)**
Length: **26 ft 7 in (8.1 m)**
Height; **10 ft 6 in (3.2 m)**
Weight: **2,315 lbs (1,050 kg)**
Maximum speed: **143 mph (230 kph)**
Ceiling: **21,980 ft (6,700 m)**
Endurance: **6 hrs**
Armament: **2 machine-guns**
Crew: **1**

Aircraft: **Ansaldo S.V.A.9**
Manufacturer: **Società Giovanni Ansaldo & Compagnia**
Type: **Reconnaissance**
Year: **1918**
Engine: **S.P.A. 6A 6-cylinder liquid-cooled inline, 220 hp**
Wingspan: **29 ft 10.25 in (9.1 m)**
Length: **26 ft 7 in (8.1 m)**
Height: **9 ft 7 in (2.92 m)**
Weight: **2,293 lbs (1,040 kg)**
Maximum speed: **137 mph (218.8 kph)**
Ceiling: **16,405 ft (5,000 m)**
Endurance: **4 hrs**
Armament:
Crew: **2**

bombing, and went into action during the last months of the war. About 2,000 S.V.A.s were built, and they saw service until the 1930s. In 1920 Ferrarin and Masiero flew an S.V.A. from Rome to Tokyo.

Macchi M.5

One of the best seaplane fighters of the war, the Macchi M.5 was designed by Buzio and Calzavara early in 1917. It was a single-seater seaplane, armed with two forward-firing Revelli machine-guns, and it was so efficient that it could match the performance of some land fighters. The first planes (of a total production of 240) entered service in autumn 1917 and were assigned to reconnaissance and escort duty. Five Italian naval squadrons were supplied with this plane at the beginning of 1918. Later in the year, units were also supplied with the M.5 Mod. (Modified) or Macchi 7, which was somewhat smaller in size and was equipped with a more powerful 250 hp version of the Isotta-Fraschini engine. M.5s remained in front-line service until the end of the war. By the end of the conflict, the squadrons equipped with M.5s had carried out 700 missions and shot down 16 enemy planes.

Aircraft: **Macchi M.5 Mod.**
Manufacturer: **S.A. Nieuport-Macchi**
Type: **Reconnaissance/fighter**
Year: **1918**
Engine: **Isotta-Fraschini V.6B 6-cylinder liquid-cooled inline, 250 hp**
Wingspan: **32 ft 7.75 in (9.95 m)**
Length: **26 ft 7 in (8.1 m)**
Height: **9 ft 8 in (2.95 m)**
Weight: **2,381 lbs (1,080 kg)**
Maximum speed: **130 mph (209 kph) at sea level**
Ceiling: **16,405 ft (5,000 m)**
Endurance: **3 hrs 40 mins**
Armament: **2 machine-guns**
Crew: **1**

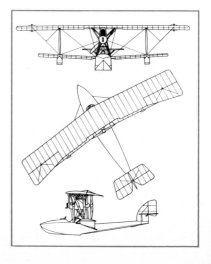

Minor types

1914 Macchi Parasol – Wingspan: 42 ft 8 in (13 m) – Length: 23 ft 7.5 in (7.2 m) – Maximum speed: 78 mph (125 kph) – Engine: Gnome rotary, 80 hp. Designed in 1913, this was the first original plane produced by Macchi. A high-wing reconnaissance monoplane, it established a national altitude record in 1914 with 8,858 feet (2,700 m). It turned out to be hard to handle, and there were several accidents.

1914 Caproni Ca.18 – Wingspan: 35 ft 10 in (10.93 m) – Length: 25 ft 2 in (7.67 m) – Maximum speed: 81 mph (130 kph) – Engine: Gnome rotary, 80 hp. Like the Macchi Parasol, this was designed in 1913 and won the first competition held by the Italian War Ministry. The Ca.18 was followed by other models, including the Ca.24 and Ca.25. Small numbers of these planes were also produced for the military. The Ca.25 had a rotary engine of only 35 hp.

1915 Macchi L.1 – Wingspan: 53 ft 10 in (16.4 m) – Length: 33 ft 8 in (10.25 m) – Maximum speed: 69 mph (110 kph) – Engine: Isotta-Fraschini, 150 hp. In the summer of 1915, Macchi developed an almost identical copy of a captured Austrian Lohner seaplane. This was the L.1. A total of 150 was built. Like the original, this seaplane was a fine performer and saw extensive service in maritime patrol and reconnaissance. It was the first of a series of fine planes.

1916 Macchi L.2 – Wingspan: 52 ft 6 in. (16 m) – Length: 33 ft 8 in (10.25 m) – Maximum speed: 87 mph (140 kph) – Engine: Isotta-Fraschini, 160 hp. Basically an elaboration of the L.1, the Macchi L.2 was a transitional model. It was soon followed by a completely redesigned model. The main changes were structural improvements in the wings, lighter weight, and a more powerful engine. Only 10 planes were built.

1916 Macchi L.3 – Wingspan: 52 ft 4 in (15.95 m) – Length: 32 ft 8.5 in (9.97 m) – Maximum speed: 91 mph (145 kph) – Engine: Isotta-Fraschini, 160 hp. This was the definitive and completely original development of the L.1 seaplane. With the wings completely redesigned and with an improved structure, it proved to be an excellent plane, and 200 of the type were built. It was used throughout the war for fighter, bomber and reconnaissance duty.

1916 S.I.A. S.P.2 – Wingspan: 54 ft 11 in. (16.74 m) – Length: 35 ft 4 in (10.77 m) – Maximum speed: 75 mph (120 kph) – Engine: Fiat A.12, 260 hp. Really an improved version of the basic Farman planes, the S.P.2 was developed by Umberto Savoia and Ottorino Pomilio. The 402 planes that were built equipped observation and reconnaissance units, and flying schools. On April 17, 1917, an S.P.2 set a world altitude record, reaching 21,171 ft (6,453 m).

1917 Macchi M.8 – Wingspan: 52 ft 6 in (16 m) – Length: 32 ft 8 in (9.97 m) – Maximum speed: 101 mph (162 kph) – Engine: Isotta-Fraschini, 170 hp. Continuing the development of its seaplane series, Macchi designed this reconnaissance plane in 1917 and produced 57 production examples of it. The M.8 was used till the end of the war for naval reconnaissance and anti-submarine patrol.

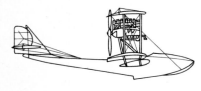

1917 S.I.A.I. S.8 – Wingspan: 41 ft 11 in (12.77 m) – Length: 32 ft (9.75 m) – Maximum speed: 89 mph (142 kph) – Engine: Isotta-Fraschini, 170 hp. The S.8 appeared in 1917, the first original design from *S.I.A.I.*, which had been building F.B.A. seaplanes under licence. Designed for naval reconnaissance and anti-submarine patrol, the plane was so impressive that 900 were ordered. Only 172 were actually delivered.

1918 Macchi M.9 – Wingspan: 50 ft 8 in (15.45 m) – Length: 31 ft. 2 in (9.50 m) – Maximum speed: 116 mph (187 kph) – Engine: Fiat A.12*bis*, 300 hp. One of the last flying boats that Macchi built, the M.9 was developed from the M.8. But it was designed for bombing rather than reconnaissance. Only 16 were delivered in 1918, but they saw combat duty. The M.9 remained in service until 1923.

234

1918 S.V.A. 10 – Wingspan: 31 ft (9.18 m) – Length: 26 ft. 8 in (8.1 m) – Maximum speed: 129 mph (207 kph) – Engine: Isotta-Fraschini, 225 hp. The final model of the famous S.V.A.5, this was a two-seater plane designed for light bombing and reconnaissance duty. It entered service in the last months of the war and was supplied to several units. Its excellent performance kept it in service for many years after hostilities ended.

1918 S.I.A. 9B – Wingspan: 50 ft 11 in (15.5 m) – Length: 31 ft 9 in (9.7 m) – Maximum speed: 128 mph (205 kph) – Engine: Fiat A.14, 700 hp. Developed from the 7B model of 1917, the 9B prototype first took to the air late in 1917 and began to reach units during the last months of the war. It was a fine plane, thanks chiefly to its new 700-hp Fiat engine. Of 500 planes ordered, only 62 were built.

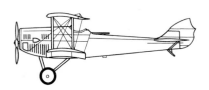

1918 Fiat R.2 – Wingspan: 40 ft 5 in (12.3 m) – Length: 28 ft 8 in (8.8 m) – Maximum speed: 109 mph (175 kph) – Engine: Fiat A.12*bis*, 300 hp. The first plane to bear the Fiat name was designed by Celestino Rosatelli. This two-seater reconnaissance biplane was very strong and well-armed; 500 of them were ordered. The war ended after only 129 had been built.

The United States of America

The early development of military aviation in the U.S.A. was very slow. Until March 1911, when funds were found to buy five planes, the American air force consisted of one aircraft, the famous Wright biplane bought in August 1909. On July 18, 1914, the aviation branch of the army was established as a permanent organization, the Aviation Section of the Signal Corps, with 60 officers and 260 men. In 1915 and 1916 the government initiated a vast reorganization programme. Plans were made for plane production, personnel was increased, and flying schools were set up. Nevertheless, when the U.S.A. entered the war on April 9, 1917, its air potential comprised 131 officers (83 of them pilots), 1,087 men, and less than 250 planes, none of which was up to contemporary fighting standards. At that time the air war in Europe had been going on for almost three years.

Despite massive efforts to catch up, it was only in 1918 that the American Expeditionary Forces managed to organize their air units successfully, under the command of William Mitchell.

Mostly French planes were used: Nieuports and Spads in fighter squadrons, Breguet 14s in bomber squadrons, and Salmsons in reconnaissance units. By the end of the war, on November 11, 1918, General Mitchell commanded 45 fighting squadrons at the front, with a potential of 740 planes, about 800 pilots, and 500 observers.

Nonetheless America made an important contribution to the war in the air. The first unit to distinguish itself was the 94th Squadron. On April 14, 1918, Lieutenants Douglas Campbell and Alan Winslow shot down two German planes. American volunteers had been fighting since 1916, in the famous Lafayette *Escadrille*, flying Nieuport fighters. American air activity in the war could be summed up in the following statistics: 781 enemy planes and 73 balloons shot down, against 289 planes and 48 balloons lost; 150 bombing missions; 308,000 pounds of bombs dropped. There were 88 aces (with five or more downed planes to their credit), including Edward Rickenbacker (26), Frank Luke (21), and Raoul Lufbery (17).

Curtiss JN-4

The 'Jenny', as the entire series of Curtiss JN-4/JN-6 biplanes was nicknamed, was not an exceptional aeroplane. Its 'classic' status in aviation history is due more to good fortune than to the intrinsic qualities of the plane, which were neither better nor worse than many others of its time. The Jenny was a basic trainer, not a combat plane, and as such was used in flying schools in America, Great Britain, and France throughout the war years. After the war, the US Army put thousands of these planes on the civilian market. The plane was used in flying schools all over America until 1928, when safety regulations compelled its retirement.

In 1914 a United States Army specification called for a tractor biplane for training purposes. The Curtiss Aeroplane and Motor Corporation of Hammondsport, New York state, the main supplier of training aircraft for the army, developed two prototypes, both with 90-hp engines. These two planes – the Types J and N – were later assimilated in a single model that combined their best qualities. Thus was born the JN. After evaluation by the US Army and the Navy, a small number was ordered in 1915. There were two intermediate versions (the JN-2, of which 10 were built; and the JN-3, of which 104 were produced) before the main production version appeared in the form of the 1916 JN-4. The Curtiss company manufactured 701 JN-4s, and Canadian Aeroplanes Ltd. of Toronto built another 1,260. The Canadian-built variant was designated JN-4Can, and was popularly known as the 'Canuck'.

A few months later, another variant, the JN-4A, was developed. It had significant improvements: greater wing dihedral, ailerons on all four wings, a new fin and rudder, and an engine with a pronounced downward thrust-line. A total of 781 of this model was built.

The most popular model of the Jenny appeared in June 1917. This was the JN-4D. It was similar to the JN-4A variant, except for its flight controls and the opening in the centre of the

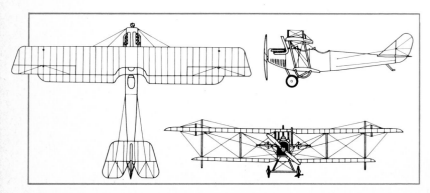

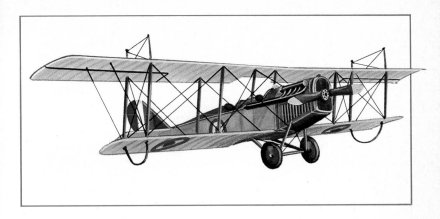

upper wing centre-section for improved visibility. A total of 2,765 JN-4Ds was built. A later model, the JN-4H, was also developed, to train pilots for the faster and more powerful aircraft that were appearing: a JN-4D was modified to accommodate a 150-hp Hispano-Suiza engine. This did not involve a great many changes, since there was little difference in weight and size between the new engine and the older Curtiss. But the radiator area and fuel capacity were increased. A total of 929 JN-4Hs was built. They were assigned to various specialized training groups: bombing, fighter, reconnaissance and aerial gunnery. The last version (1,035 planes) was the JN-6H, with Hispano engines built by Wright.

The Curtiss 'Jenny' is one of those planes, like the Sikorsky *Ilya Maromets,* whose achievements exceed their actual performance in the air. A whole generation of Americans learned to fly on them, and to many Americans 'flying' meant a Jenny.

Aircraft: **Curtiss JN-4D**
Manufacturer: **Curtiss Aeroplane and Motor Corporation**
Type: **Trainer**
Year: **1916**
Engine: **Curtiss OX-5 8-cylinder liquid-cooled inline V, 90 hp**
Wingspan: **43 ft 7 in (13.28 m)**
Length: **27 ft 4 in (8.33 m)**
Height: **9 ft 10.5 in (3 m)**
Weight: **2,130 lbs (966 kg)**
Maximum speed: **75 mph (121 kph) at sea level**
Ceiling: **11,000 ft (3,353 m)**
Endurance: **2 hrs 15 mins**
Armament: **none**
Crew: **1 pilot and 1 student**

Aircraft: **Curtiss JN-4H**
Manufacturer: **Curtiss Aeroplane and Motor Corporation**
Type: **Trainer**
Year: **1917**
Engine: **Wright-built Hispano-Suiza A 8-cylinder liquid-cooled inline V, 150-hp**
Wingspan: **43 ft 7 in (13.28 m)**
Length: **27 ft 4 in (8.33 m)**
Height: **9 ft 10.5 in (3 m)**
Weight: **2,150 lbs (975 kg)**
Maximum speed: **79.2 mph (127.5 kph)**
Ceiling: **8,000 ft (2,438 m)**
Range: **250 miles (402 km)**
Armament: **none**
Crew: **1 pilot and 1 student**

Curtiss N-9

A good seaplane trainer, the Curtiss N-9 was derived from the 'Jenny' trainers. It served in US Army and Navy flying schools until 1927. The N-9 was developed in late 1916. A variant of the JN-4 (the JN-4B) was the basis for the new project. With its large wingspan, the JN-4B was well able to bear the extra weight of floats in place of the landing gear. A more powerful version of the Jenny's engine was used to compensate for the seaplane's extra weight: a 100-hp Curtiss 8-cylinder inline. About 450 Curtiss N-9s were built. Delivery to Army and Navy flying schools began early in 1917. The Armistice curtailed orders for another 1,200 planes. The N-9 was used as a training plane until 1924.

The most distinctive feature of the N-9 was the fact that the upper wing was some 10 feet (3 metres) longer than the lower one, kingpost-braced like the JN-4's upper wing.

Aircraft: **Curtiss N-9**
Manufacturer: **Curtiss Aeroplane and Motor Corporation**
Type: **Trainer**
Year: **1917**
Engine: **Curtiss OX-6 8-cylinder 100hp**
Wingspan: **53 ft 3.75 in (16.25 m)**
Length: **30 ft 10 in (9.4 m)**
Height: **10 ft 8.5 in (3.26 m)**
Weight: **2,765 lbs (1,254 kg)**
Maximum speed: **80 mph (129 kph)**
Ceiling: **9,850 ft (3,002 m)**
Endurance: **2 hrs**
Armament: **none**
Crew: **1 pilot and 1 student**

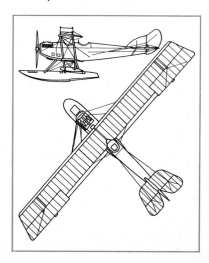

Thomas-Morse S.4

B. D. Thomas, one of the senior designers of the Curtiss 'Jenny', designed the S.4 in early 1917. It made its first flight in June, and after evaluation tests was acquired by the US Army for advanced fighter training. Engine trouble developed and the original 100-hp Gnome Monosoupape rotary engine was replaced by an 80-hp Le Rhône. This variant of the plane was known as the S.4C. A total of 500 planes was ordered, but with the Armistice the last 155 were cancelled. Only 97 were completed. The performance of the S.4 was superior to that of the 'Jenny', and it became a popular civil trainer after the war. The S.4, also known familiarly as the 'Tommy' had an illustrious career after the First World War as a film aircraft, playing British, French and German aircraft with little more than different paint jobs and tail surfaces. It appeared in *Hell's Angels* and *Dawn Patrol*.

Aircraft: **Thomas-Morse S.4C**
Manufacturer: **Thomas-Morse Aircraft Co.**
Type: **Trainer**
Year: **1917**
Engine: **Le Rhône 9C rotary, 80 hp**
Wingspan: **26 ft 6 in (8.08 m)**
Length: **19 ft 10 in (6.05 m)**
Height: **8 ft 1 in (2.46 m)**
Weight: **1,373 lbs (623 kg)**
Maximum speed: **95 mph (153 kph)**
Ceiling: **15,000 ft (4,572 m)**
Endurance: **2 hrs 30 mins**
Armament: **1 machine-gun**
Crew: **1**

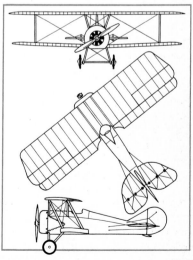

Packard Le Père-Lusac 11

This was the first American-built escort fighter of the war. It was designed in 1918 by Captain G. Le Père of the French air mission to the United States. The prototype began tests in September of that year, and the results were so impressive that immediate mass production was planned. (About 4,500 planes were ordered from the Packard Motor Car Co. of Detroit). Only 27 planes were completed before the Armistice, and only two of these reached the front for operational tests. The Lusac 11 (which stood for Le Père US Army Combat) was strong, fast, manoeuvrable, and had a high rate of climb. The armament was up to the standards of the day: two fixed Marlin machine-guns in the nose and two Lewis guns on a Scarff ring mount in the rear cockpit. Variant models were developed from the Lusac 11, but they never got beyond the prototype stage, unfortunately.

Aircraft: **Packard Le Père-Lusac 11**
Manufacturer: **Packard Motor Car Co.**
Type: **Fighter**
Year: **1918**
Engine: **Liberty 12A 12-cylinder liquid-cooled inline V, 400 hp**
Wingspan: **41 ft 7 in (12.67 m)**
Length: **25 ft 6 in (7.77 m)**
Height: **9 ft 6 in (2.9 m)**
Weight: **3,746 lbs (1,699 kg)**
Maximum speed: **132 mph (212 kph) at 2,000 ft (610 m)**
Ceiling: **20,000 ft (6,096 m)**
Range: **320 miles (515 km)**
Armament: **4 machine-guns**
Crew: **2**

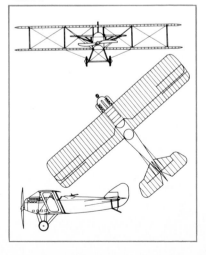

Standard E-1

The Standard E-1 was designed as a fighter plane. The project was started in 1917 at the Standard Aircraft Corporation in Elizabeth, New Jersey, a company that manufactured European planes under licence. Two prototypes were delivered in January 1918, and after evaluation tests, 98 E-1s were ordered. The small plane had smooth lines and resembled the British Sopwith fighters of the time. But it soon became clear that the Standard E-1 was underpowered. Even the installation of a more powerful engine, the 100-hp Gnome 9B rotary, failed to give it the speed and agility needed for front-line service. So the plane was reassigned to advanced training duty. A total of 168 was built before the Armistice, when production was curtailed.

After the war, Sperry converted three E-1s into radio-controlled aerial torpedoes for trials.

Aircraft: **Standard E-1**
Manufacturer: **Standard Aircraft Corp.**
Type: **Trainer**
Year: **1918**
Engine: **Le Rhône 9-cylinder air-cooled rotary, 80 hp**
Wingspan: **24 ft (7.32 m)**
Length: **18 ft 10 in (5.74 m)**
Height: **7 ft 10 in (2.39 m)**
Weight: **1,144 lbs (519 kg)**
Maximum speed: **100 mph (161 kph)**
Ceiling: **14,800 ft (4,511 m)**
Endurance: **2 hrs 30 mins**
Armament: **none**
Crew: **1**

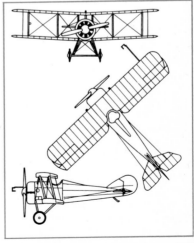

Curtiss H-16

A plane especially designed and built to fly across the Atlantic was the grandfather of a series of planes that played a vital role in the First World War. These were the Curtiss 'America' flying boats, named after the 1914 civil plane. The Americas were flown by the British against German submarines and Zeppelins over the North Sea. A British Curtiss H-12 was the first American-built plane to shoot down an enemy aircraft.

Glenn Curtiss, the American aviation pioneer, began his project for a large flying boat in 1914, in collaboration with a former British naval pilot, John C. Porte, who hoped to fly across the Atlantic. The outbreak of the First World War halted his pro-

ject, and Porte went back to Great Britain. He persuaded the military authorities there to purchase the two America flying boats that had been prepared for the Atlantic crossing. These planes, designated H-4, were delivered late in 1914. They were so impressive in service that first 12 and then 50 of them were ordered. They were high-performance planes, and Great Britain also ordered later models of the H-4, which were bigger, more powerful, better armed, and generally improved. The most popular version was the H-12. The British version was powered by 250-hp Rolls-Royce Eagle I engines, while the American naval model had 200-hp Curtiss V-X-X engines. (In 1918 some

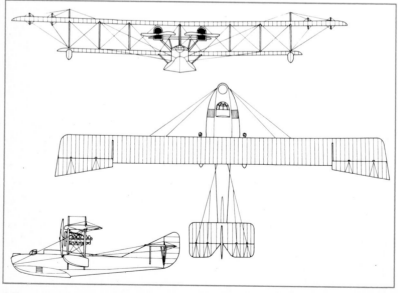

were fitted with 330-hp Liberty motors.) The H-12 had a four-man crew. It was armed with three or four machine-guns and carried a maximum bomb load of 450 pounds (204 kg). This plane was designated 'Large America' to distinguish it from the H-4, the 'Small America'. Fifty H-12s served in British R.N.A.S. units. In May 1917, H-12s downed their first Zeppelin and sank their first German submarine.

A larger and better-armed version of the Curtiss flying boat appeared late in 1917: the H-16. The structure and shape of the hull were improved, and the bomb load was doubled. This model carried six machine-guns. The Naval Aircraft Factory in Philadelphia produced 150 H-16s, 74 of which were assigned to the United States Navy. The others were sent to the British Royal Naval Air Service, which put only 25 planes into service at first. Only 15 of these were combat-ready before the war ended. The British version had 375-hp Rolls-Royce

Aircraft: **Curtiss H.16**
Manufacturer: **Naval Aircraft Factory**
Type: **Naval reconnaissance**
Year: **1918**
Engines: **Two Liberty 12-cylinder liquid-cooled inline Vs, 400 hp each**
Wingspan: **95 ft 0.75 in (28.98 m)**
Length: **46 ft 1.5 in (14.06 m)**
Height: **17 ft 8.5 in (5.4 m)**
Weight: **10,900 lbs (4,944 kg)**
Maximum speed: **95 mph (153 kph) at sea level**
Ceiling: **9,950 ft (3,033 m)**
Range: **378 miles (608 km)**
Armament: **5-6 machine-guns; 920 lbs (417 kg) of bombs**

Eagle VIII engines, instead of the 400-hp American Liberty. The Curtiss H-16 remained in service at naval bases along the British coast until 1921.

Curtiss built an experimental model of the H-16 as a pusher type. As the engines had to be moved rearwards for the propellers to clear the trailing edge, it also became necessary to sweep the wings back a little: this had the effect of shifting the centre of lift back to the right position relative to the centre of gravity, which had been pushed back by the engine move.

Minor types

1916 Curtiss S.3 – Wingspan: 25 ft (7.62 m) – Length: 19 ft 6 in (5.94 m) – Maximum speed: 112 mph (180 kph) – Engine: Curtiss O-X-X-2, 100 hp. This single-seater triplane, designed in 1916 for reconnaissance duty, became the first American fighter plane, when, in March 1917, it was equipped with two machine-guns. The United States Signal Corps took four of them, but they were used only as unarmed trainers.

1918 Orenco B – Wingspan: 26 ft (7.92 m) – Length: 18 ft 10 in (5.74 m) – Maximum speed: 132 mph (212 kph) – Engine: Gnome Monosoupape, 160 hp. Based on the Spad S.VII, this was the first army fighter designed as such. Four 6.5-mm (.256-in) Revelli machine-guns were to be installed. Although the prototype performed well, it never went into production, and the prototype was used for training.

1918 Wright Martin M.8 – Wingspan: 32 ft 10 in (10 m) – Length: 21 ft 6 in (6.55 m) – Maximum speed: 143 mph (230 kph) – Engine: Wright-Hispano H, 300 hp. The first two-seater monoplane fighter produced in the United States, the M.8 was powered by the Wright-Martin version of the Hispano-Suiza engine. The plane was so impressive that the US Army bought two and used them after 1918 for engine testing.

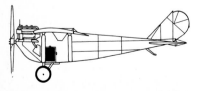

1918 Curtiss O-1 – Wingspan: 39 ft 4.5 in (12 m) – Length: 27 ft 1 in (8.26 m) – Maximum speed: 146 mph (236 kph) – Engine: Liberty 12,400 hp. The British Bristol F.2B Fighter was chosen when an already-tested plane was wanted for the installation of the new 400-hp American Liberty engine. Curtiss received an order for 2,000 machines before testing began. But the idea was dropped after a crash, and the project was scrapped.

1918 Curtiss HA – Wingspan: 36 ft (10.97 m) – Length: 30 ft 9 in (9.37 m) – Maximum speed: 132 mph (212 kph) – Engine: Liberty 12, 380 hp. This was the first fighter plane of the United States Navy. It was produced to Navy specifications issued in mid-1917. It was a two-seater biplane with a central float, armed with four machine-guns.

1918 Curtiss 18-T – Wingspan: 31 ft 10 in (9.7 m) – Length: 23 ft 4 in (7.11 m) – Maximum speed: 160 mph (258 kph) – Engine: Curtiss (Kirkham) K-12, 400 hp. One of the best Curtiss designs, this two-seater triplane was the first US Navy landplane fighter. Two were built (with four machine-guns planned).

1914-15

Germany

1915-17   1917-18   1918

When war broke out, the German air force comprised slow unarmed planes, designed exclusively for observation of and reconnaissance for the ground forces. Germany, like other countries, had first be sceptical about the military uses of the aeroplane. German military aviation was originally part of the army. The air units (*Feldfliegerabteilungen*, generally six planes each) were under the direct control of corps and army commanders. But military aviation soon became a semi-autonomous branch, and its structure and organization evolved in answer to combat requirements. Naval aviation developed in much the same way. German air power reached a high level

and played a decisive role in various phases of the conflict. Indeed the Allied victory in the air owed more to numerical superiority than to the quality of their planes and engines. Throughout the war Germany continued to produce outstanding planes, designed by such men as Fokker, Junkers, Heinkel, Platz and Thelen. The designers were supported by a large industrial complex working under full steam. German planes could hold their own against any of the Allied planes and sometimes outdid them.

A total of 24 planes was built in Germany in 1911. The number rose to 136 in 1912, 446 in 1913, and 1,348 in

245

1914. In 1915, 4,532 were built, and 8,182 in 1916. The last two years of the war saw an enormous production effort: 19,746 planes were turned out in 1917, and 14,123 were built up to November 1918. Total war production amounted to 48,537 planes of all kinds. In an attempt to improve the structure of military aviation, Germany set up a rigid classification for military planes, according to function. Letters were used as prefixes to indicate plane type: A – unarmed monoplanes; B – unarmed biplanes; C – reconnaissance biplanes, armed first with one and then with two machine-guns; CL – light reconnaissance biplanes; CLS/CL-type planes for ground attack; D – single-seater biplane fighters, with two machine-guns; J – two-seaters for ground attack and infantry support; DJ – single-seater J-type planes; E – single-seater armed monoplanes; Dr – single-seater armed triplanes; G – two-engined biplane bombers; R – multi-engined long-range bombers; S – ground attack planes. Production data show that the most widely-built classes were C and D, armed reconnaissance planes and fighters.

It was the fighter that formed the hard core of German aviation during the war. The various phases of German control of the air were conditioned by the quality of their fighters. The first fighter, the Fokker monoplane, appeared in 1915. Although the plane was originally intended for defensive service (as a reconnaissance escort), its offensive potential soon became evident. The appearance of the fighter led to a major reorganization of German aviation. In the autumn of 1916 the *Jasta* units were established, fighter squadrons made up exclusively of 'hunters'. Similar units were set up for ground attack and bombing (the *Schlachstaffeln* or *Schlastas* and the *Bombenstaffeln*). During the summer of 1917, the German high command went even further and decided to create even larger homogeneous units. These were the *Jagdgeschwaders*, each usually comprising four *Jastas*. The first to go into action was the Richthofen *Jagdgeschwader* (J.G.1) which combined Jastas 4,6,10, and 11 under the command of Manfred von Richthofen.

The custom of naming *Jastas* and then *Jagdgeschwaders* after their commanders did much for morale and contributed to the friendly rivalry between units trying to outdo one another in combat. Many German aces were given their own *Jastas*, and the *Jastas* became breeding grounds for new aces. At the end of the war, Germany boasted 366 air aces. The top ace of the entire war was Manfred von Richthofen, the 'Red Baron', who shot down 80 planes. Then, with 62, came Ernst Udet who was one of the driving forces behind the revival of German aviation on the eve of the Second World War. He was followed by Erich Loewenhardt with 53 victories. Then came 30 pilots with between 30 and 48 'kills', including Oswald Boelcke, the man who had done most to develop German air power during the war. Thirty-eight aces had scores between 20 and 30, while 96 others each shot down between 10 and 20 enemy planes.

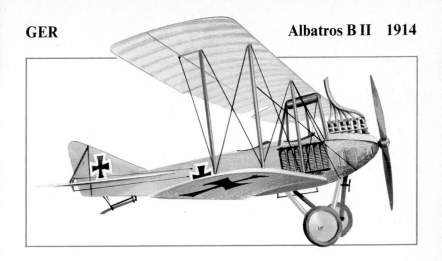

Albatros B II

The BII was designed by Ernst Heinkel and appeared before the war broke out. This plane set an altitude record of 14,764 feet (4,500 m), with Ernst von Lössl at the controls. In service the Albatros B II was a good performer. A great many examples were built, and the Albatros B II became the most widely-employed reconnaissance plane of the early war years. Various German factories manufactured it, and small numbers were also supplied to the Austro-Hungarians. These latter planes were extensively modified in two new versions (series 21 and series 22). They had more powerful engines and incorporated structural changes, and proved themselves superior to the basic German model. The Albatros B II remained in active service until 1915, when other armed two-seaters appeared. It was then reassigned to training units, where it remained in service until the end of the war.

Aircraft: **Albatros B II**
Manufacturer: **Albatros Werke G.m.b.H.**
Type: **Reconnaissance**
Year: **1914**
Engine: **Mercedes 6-cylinder liquid-cooled inline, 100 hp**
Wingspan: **42 ft (12.8 m)**
Length: **25 ft 0.5 in (7.63 m)**
Height: **10 ft 4 in (3.15 m)**
Weight: **2,356 lbs (1,071 kg)**
Maximum speed: **66 mph (105 kph) at sea level**
Ceiling: **9,840 ft (3,000 m)**
Endurance: **4 hrs**
Armament:
Crew: **2**

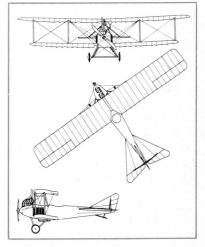

D.F.W. BI

The *Deutsche Flugzeug-Werke*, which had produced the famous *Taube* monoplane in the years just before the war, built the *D.F.W.* BI. And this plane reflected the influence of the *Taube*. It had the same wing shape and was immediately nicknamed the 'flying banana'. The pronounced curved sweep of the wings was designed to increase the plane's stability, and the *D.F.W.* BI was, indeed, extremely pleasant to handle. It was in action as soon as the war broke out, and was used by observation units on the Eastern and Western Fronts. Since it carried no armament, this biplane was soon replaced by the series C model, an armed two-seater that entered service in 1915. The BI and its successor, the BII, were reassigned to training duty. The CI version of the *D.F.W.* was essentially a reinforced type B, with a 150-hp engine and a machinegun.

Aircraft: **D.F.W. B I**
Manufacturer: **Deutsche Flugzeug-Werke G.m.b.H.**
Type: **Reconnaissance**
Year: **1914**
Engine: **Mercedes 6-cylinder, 100 hp**
Wingspan: **45 ft 11.25 in (14 m)**
Length: **27 ft 6.75 in (8.4 m)**
Height: **9 ft 10 in (3 m)**
Weight: **2,233 lbs (1,015 kg)**
Maximum speed: **75 mph (120 kph)**
Ceiling: **9,840 ft (3,000 m)**
Endurance: **4 hrs**
Armament: **none**
Crew: **2**

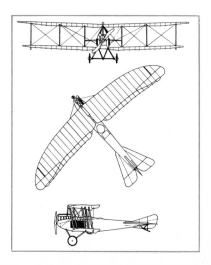

A.E.G. B II

Like the other B-category planes built early in the war, the *A.E.G.* was a transitional aircraft. It equipped air units until armed models (known collectively as type C) began coming out in 1915. The B II was built by the aviation section of the *Allgemeine Elektrizitäts Gesellschaft* of Henningsdorf (Berlin). It was an adaptation of the earlier B I, but smaller and more manoeuvrable. The structure was of wood and steel tubing, covered with canvas. The engine was housed in a metal cowling with cooling louvres. This plane did not play an important part in the war, but it did provide the basis for various type C models that appeared in 1915. The C IV was the model produced in the largest quantity. It appeared in 1916 and saw service until the end of the war. The C I was little more than a B II modified to carry a Bergmann or Parabellum flexible machine-gun.

Aircraft: **A.E.G. B II**
Manufacturer: **Allgemeine Elektrizitäts Gesellschaft**
Type: **Reconnaissance**
Year: **1914**
Engine: **Mercedes B II 6-cylinder liquid-cooled inline, 120 hp**
Wingspan: **42 ft 7 in (13 m)**
Length: **25 ft 7 in (7.8 m)**
Height: **10 ft 2 in (3.1 m)**
Weight:
Maximum speed:
Ceiling:
Armament: **none**
Crew: **2**

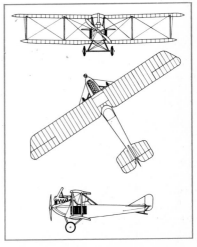

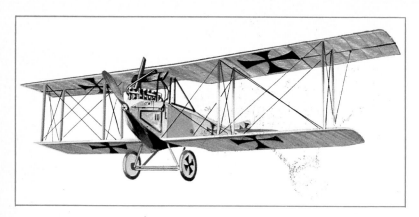

Aviatik C I

The Aviatik C I came out in 1915 and was the successor of the type B planes (B I and B II), which were built in 1914 and saw service on the Western and Eastern Fronts in the early months of the war. The plane's structure was wood covered with canvas. The biplane wings were of unequal span. The upper wing had a slight dihedral and ailerons. Tailplane and elevator were 'heart-shaped', a design feature inherited from its predecessors. The C I had the same general lines as well, together with the 'inverted' arrangement of cockpits (observer forward, pilot behind). This limited the gunner's field of fire, so the positions were changed in the C Ia version. Later models, the C II and C III series, were produced in large numbers. They had more powerful engines. Aviatik C-type planes were assigned in 1916 to reconnaissance units and to a bomber group on the Western Front.

Aircraft: **Aviatik C I**
Manufacturer: **Automobil und Aviatik A.G.**
Type: **Reconnaissance**
Year: **1915**
Engine: **Mercedes D II 6-cylinder liquid cooled inline, 160 hp**
Wingspan: **41 ft 0.25 in (12.5 m)**
Length: **26 ft (7.925 m)**
Height: **9 ft 8 in (2.95 m)**
Weight: **2,732 lbs (1,242 kg)**
Maximum speed: **89 mph (142 kph)**
Ceiling: **11,480 ft (3,500 m)**
Endurance: **3 hrs**
Armament: **1 machine-gun**
Crew: **2**

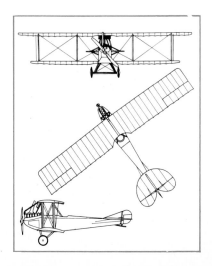

Ago C II

In the years 1915–1916 Ago developed four C-type planes. Models C I, C II, and C III were all pusher biplanes with two tail booms. The two tail booms were veritable fuselages of light wooden construction. Although this formula was considered outdated, the planes were very successful. The C II went into action at the end of 1915, and proved to be a fast and easy-to-handle plane with exceptional range. It remained in service until the end of 1916. A variant of the C II, with greater wingspan, was produced in small quantities, and a seaplane version was also planned for the German navy. The C IV, the last in the series, was a conventional biplane with a tractor propeller.

Ago also built two variants of the basic C II. First, there was a floatplane version, the C II-W, which perched on a pair of large floats; and second, there was a large-span three-bay landplane.

Aircraft: **Ago C II**
Manufacturer: **Ago Flugzeugwerke**
Type: **Reconnaissance**
Year: **1915**
Engine: **Benz Bz. IV 6-cylinder liquid-cooled inline, 220 hp**
Wingspan: **47 ft 7 in (14.5 m)**
Length: **32 ft 3.5 in (9.84 m)**
Height: **10 ft 5 in (3.175 m)**
Weight: **4,281 lbs (1,946 kg)**
Maximum speed: **86 mph (137 kph)**
Ceiling: **14,764 ft (4,500 m)**
Range: **360 miles (580 km)**
Armament: **1 machine-gun**
Crew: **2**

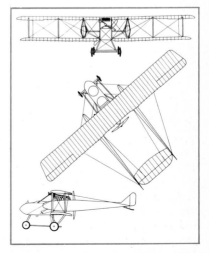

L.V.G. C II
L.V.G. C VI

The *L.V.G.* C I was the first German two-seater reconnaissance plane to be armed with a 'flexible' machine-gun in the observer's cockpit. The C I was the first of one of the most popular series of C-type reconnaissance planes in the German air force. Like most 1915 German planes, the C I was developed by the *Luft-Verkehrs Gesellschaft* from the unarmed B type reconnaissance planes that had been produced during the first year of the war.

The first four models, C I, C II, C III, and C IV, were designed by Franz Schneider. Shortly after its ap-pearance in the first half of 1915, the C I was followed by an improved model, the C II. This plane entered service at the end of the year, and large numbers were produced. The two models served in reconnaissance units until 1916. They were also assigned to light bombing missions. On November 28, 1916, a C II reached London in broad daylight and unloaded its six 22-pound (10-kg) bombs on Victoria Station.

The C III and C IV models were not produced in large quantities. In the years 1917–18, two more versions

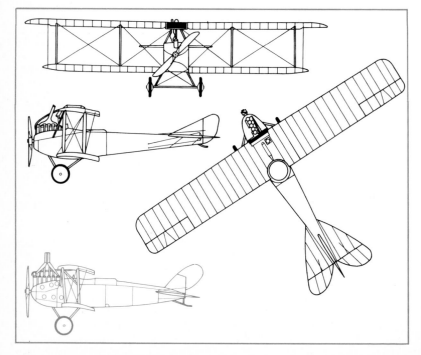

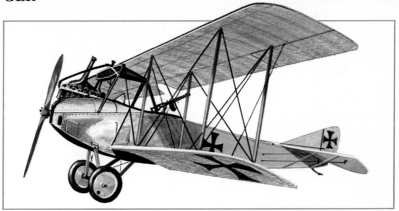

were produced, the C V and the C VI, and these were substantially different from their predecessors. Both models were designed by a former *D.F.W.* engineer who had gone to work for *L.V.G.* So it is no wonder that the C V closely resembled the comparable plane produced by *D.F.W.* The *L.V.G.* C V was an excellent plane, strong and agile despite its size; and it served on all fronts in reconnaissance, observation and light bombing roles.

The C VI appeared in 1918. It was superior to the C V in performance and armament. The fuselage was deepened, and fields of vision for both the pilot and the observer were improved by staggering the wings, reducing the wing-gap and providing large cut-outs in both wing inner trailing edges. The C V and the C VI served side by side in the last year of the war. About 1,000 examples were built. In August 1918, about 500 C Vs and C VIs were in front-line service. A later model, the C VIII, appeared in the second half of 1918. It was pow-

Aircraft: **L.V.G. C II**
Manufacturer: **Luft-Verkehrs Gesellschaft m.b.H.**
Type: **Reconnaissance**
Year: **1915**
Engine: **Mercedes D III 6-cylinder liquid-cooled inline, 160 hp**
Wingspan: **42 ft 2 in (12.85 m)**
Length: **26 ft 7 in (8.1 m)**
Height: **9 ft 7.25 in (2.93 m)**
Weight: **3,091 lbs (1,405 kg)**
Maximum speed: **81 mph (130 kph)**
Ceiling: **16,405 ft (5,000 m)**
Endurance: **4 hrs**
Armament: **1-2 machine-guns**
Crew: **2**

Aircraft: **L.V.G. C VI**
Manufacturer: **Luft-Verkehrs Gesellschaft m.b.H.**
Type: **Reconnaissance**
Year: **1918**
Engine: **Benz Bz. IV 6-cylinder liquid-cooled inline, 200 hp**
Wingspan: **42 ft 7.75 in (13 m)**
Length: **24 ft 5.25 in (7.45 m)**
Height: **9 ft 2.25 in (2.8 m)**
Weight: **3,058 lbs (1,309 kg)**
Maximum speed: **118 mph (190 kph)**
Ceiling: **21,325 ft (6,500 m)**
Endurance: **3 hrs 30 mins**
Armament: **2 machine-guns; 243 lbs (110 kg) of bombs**
Crew: **2**

ered by a 240-hp Benz engine and incorporated structural improvements, but never went beyond the prototype stage.

Rumpler C I
Rumpler C IV

The Rumpler *Flugzeug-Werke* (which manufactured *Taube* monoplanes in 1911–14) produced its own B-type unarmed biplane, the B I. This plane served on the Western Front in 1914–15. The Rumpler C I, a fine plane that remained in service until February 1918, appeared early in 1915. It was an armed two-seater biplane. A large production programme was set up, and licences were granted to the G.F.W., Rinne, M.F.W., and Bayru companies to build the plane. In October 1916, about 250 C Is were in service, and production continued until June 1917.

It was one of the longest-lived C-class planes in the German air force.

The Rumpler C I saw duty on the Eastern and Western Fronts and in Palestine and Macedonia. It was on the Palestine front, in the spring of 1917, that C Is played an important role in the battles for Gaza, as observation and liaison aircraft. The planes were ideal for photographic reconnaissance because of their stability in flight.

The second Rumpler model to see extensive service was the C IV. It appeared after the not altogether successful C III of 1916. The C IV owed

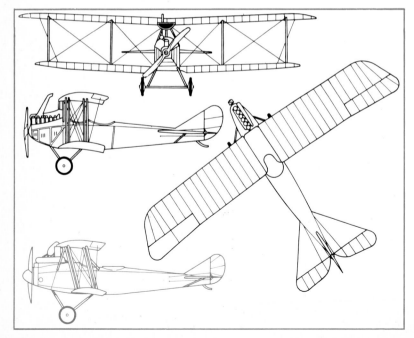

much of it success to the new 260-hp Mercedes D IV engine. The C IV model kept the very elegant lines of its predecessor, but there were changes in wing and empennage structure, and in type and placement of the ailerons.

In action, the plane proved to be an extremely fast climber and even at high altitudes it could outmanoeuvre enemy fighters. The C IV was particularly well-suited for long-range reconnaissance, a role it performed on both the Eastern and Western Fronts. It was also used for bombing and could carry about 220 pounds (100 kg) of bombs. Enemy pilots found it a hard plane to shoot down.

The next production version was the C VII. The plane was powered by a 240 hp high-compression Maybach Mb IV engine, which generated full power to an altitude of 23,950 feet (7,300 m). On these reconnaissance flights, the crew were issued heated suits and oxygen masks, absolutely vital for prolonged operations at high altitudes.

Aircraft: **Rumpler C I**
Manufacturer: **E. Rumpler Flugzeugwerk G.m.b.H.**
Type: **Reconnaissance**
Year: **1915**
Engine: **Mercedes D III 6-cylinder liquid-cooled inline 160 hp**
Wingspan: **39 ft 10.5 in (12.15 m)**
Length: **25 ft 9 in (7.85 m)**
Height: **10 ft 0.5 in (3.06 m)**
Weight (empty): **1,745 lbs (793 kg)**
Weight (loaded): **2,867 lbs (1,333 kg)**
Maximum speed: **95 mph (152 kph) at sea level**
Ceiling: **16,405 ft (5,000 m)**
Endurance: **4 hrs**
Armament: **2 machine-guns; 220 lbs (100 kg) of bombs**
Crew: **2**

Aircraft: **Rumpler C IV**
Manufacturer: **E. Rumpler Flugzeugwerk G.m.b.H.**
Type: **Reconnaissance**
Year: **1917**
Engine: **Mercedes D IV 6-cylinder liquid-cooled inline, 260 hp**
Wingspan: **41 ft 6.5 in (12.66 m)**
Length: **27 ft 7 in (8.405 m)**
Height: **10 ft 8 in (3.25 m)**
Weight (empty): **2,376 lbs (1,080 kg)**
Weight (loaded): **3,366 lbs (1,530 kg)**
Maximum speed: **107 mph (171 kph) at 1,640 ft (500 m)**
Ceiling: **21,325 ft (5,500 m)**
Endurance: **3 hrs 30 mins**
Armament: **2 machine-guns; 220 lbs (100 kg) of bombs**
Crew: **2**

Fokker E III

'The Scourge' is the epithet the English applied to the Fokker monoplane in 1915. The planes themselves were not exceptional, but their armament revolutionized air warfare and gave Germany control of the air for many months: the Fokker monoplane was the first fighting plane to have a forward-firing machine-gun synchronized with the propeller. This innovation was made when Allied planes were poorly armed at best and made the Fokker the first really modern fighter. The fixed machine-gun gave this relatively agile single-seater an enormous advantage over the Allies' clumsy two-seater aircraft. With Allied reconnaissance planes being massacred, the Royal Flying Corps decided early in 1916 to send at least three escort planes along with every reconnaissance plane on missions behind the German lines. But the

'Fokker Scourge' was finally driven back only when French and British fighters appeared with synchronized weapons.

The synchronization device that Anthony Fokker developed for his monoplane was not altogether original. Franz Schneider of *L.V.G* had patented a similar device in 1913. And the same year Raymond Saulnier had built and tested a synchronization mechanism in France. Poplavko and Symsolv-Dybovski had tried out something of the kind in Russia. There was also an element of luck in the Fokker development. A Morane-Saulnier Type L monoplane came down near Courtrai on April 19, 1915. It was piloted by the French ace Roland Garros and had a recently installed rudimentary deflector system: metal plates on the propeller deflected the occasional bullet from the unsynchronized machine-gun that would otherwise have struck the propeller. The Germans decided it was worth copying. Anthony Fokker and

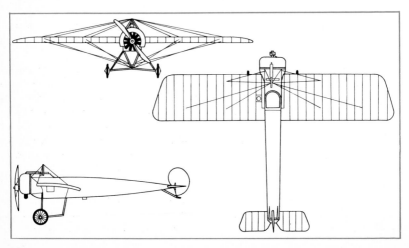

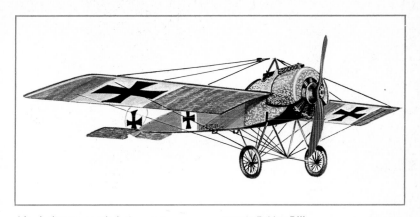

his designers carried the matter one step further and developed an actual synchronization, or rather inter-rupter, mechanism and installed it on one of his type M 5k monoplanes. It worked extremely well and the new weapon was put into large-scale pro-duction at once. (The interrupter gear worked very simply: a cam was at-tached to the crankshaft of the engine in line with each propeller blade; when the blade reached a position in which it might be struck by bullets from the machine-gun, the relevant cam ac-tuated a pushrod which, by means of a series of linkages, stopped the gun from firing. When the blade was clear, the linkages 'retracted', once again allowing the gun to fire.)

This monoplane, which was given the military designation E I, went into action right away. Two other models, the E II and the E III, differed in engine power and wing size. The Fok-ker E III appeared on the Western Front in August 1915, and served in fighter units alongside the E I and the E II. Its basic armament was an LMG

Aircraft: **Fokker E III**
Manufacturer: **Fokker Flugzeug-Werke G.m.b.H.**
Type: **Fighter**
Year: **1915**
Engine: **Oberursel U I 9-cylinder air-cooled rotary, 100 hp**
Wingspan: **30 ft 10.5 in (9.41 m)**
Length: **23 ft 11.25 in (7.3 m)**
Height: **9 ft 1.75 in (2.79 m)**
Weight: **1,342 lbs (610 kg)**
Maximum speed: **87.5 mph (140 kph) at sea level**
Ceiling: **11,483 ft (3,500 m)**
Endurance: **1 hr 30 mins**
Armament: **1-2 machine-guns**
Crew: **1**

08/15 machine-gun, but some planes carried two weapons. The two-gunned planes, however, performed less effec-tively. Max Immelmann, the famous German ace, mounted three machine-guns on a Fokker E IV but soon reverted to two guns. The Fokker monoplanes shot down French and British planes by the dozen. German aces dominated the air, and the names of pilots such as Max Immelmann (who was shot down in a Fokker on June 18, 1916), Oswald Boelcke, Kurt Wintgens, and von Gerstoff became famous. The Fokkers' supremacy in the air came to an end early in 1916.

A.E.G. G IV

The *A.E.G.* G IV went into service towards the end of 1916 and was the most widely-used of the G-type bombers that the *Allgemeine Elektrizitäts Gesellschaft* produced between 1915 and 1918. This plane combined the best qualities of its predecessors (G I, G II and G III) and was powered by more reliable engines. The G IV had a mixed structure of wood and steel tubing. The lower wing had dihedral, and the upper wing had ailerons. The G IV was a short-range, low-altitude plane and was used chiefly for tactical bombing missions. It remained in service until the end of the war. Experimental versions were also developed, including the G IVb, with a larger wingspan, and the G IVk, with a bi-plane tail, armour-protected engines, and a 20-mm cannon. The final version, the G V, came out too late to take part in the war, but was used as an airliner after the war.

Aircraft: **A.E.G. G IV**
Manufacturer: **Allgemeine Elektrizitäts Gesellschaft**
Type: **Bomber**
Year: **1916**
Engines: **Two Mercedes D IVa 6-cylinder liquid-cooled inlines, 260 hp each**
Wingspan: **60 ft 4.5 in (18.4 m)**
Length: **31 ft 10 in (9.7 m)**
Height: **12 ft 9.5 in (3.9 m)**
Weight: **7,986 lbs (3,630 kg)**
Maximum speed: **103 mph (165 kph) at sea level**
Ceiling: **14,760 ft (4,500 m)**
Endurance: **4 hrs 30 mins**
Armament: **2 machine-guns; 882 lbs (400 kg) of bombs**
Crew: **3**

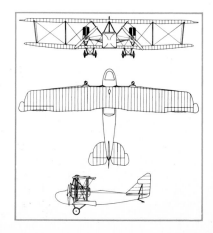

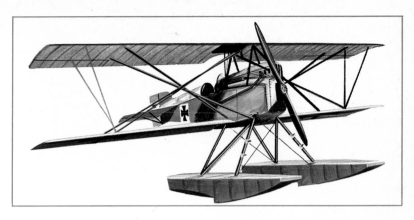

Hansa-Brandenburg *K.D.W.*

Designed by Ernst Heinkel in mid-1916, the *K.D.W.* (*Kampf Doppeldecker Wasser*, or biplane seafighter) was a two-float seaplane developed from an earlier landplane. It was designed to complement other naval fighters already in service in the defence of seaplane bases in the Adriatic and in the North Sea. The first Hansa-Brandenburgs went into combat late in 1916. Fifty-eight planes were built, in five production lots, each incorporating different structural details and different engines. Production was very slow, so that many *K.D.W.*s reached their units after newer and better aircraft had been developed and rendered the *K.D.W.* all but obsolete. The type was also licence-built for the Austro-Hungarian air services by Phönix and Ufag, both of whom later did considerable development on the 'star-strut' interplane bracing formula.

Aircraft: **Hansa-Brandenburg K.D.W.**
Manufacturer: **Hansa und Brandenburg-ische Flugzeug-Werke G.m.b.H.**
Type: **Fighter**
Year: **1916**
Engine: **Benz Bz. III 6-cylinder liquid-cooled inline, 150 hp**
Wingspan: **30 ft 4.25 in (9.25 m)**
Length: **26 ft 3 in (8 m)**
Height: **11 ft (3.35 m)**
Weight: **2,662 lbs (1,210 kg)**
Maximum speed: **106 mph (170 kph) at sea level**
Ceiling: **13,123 ft (4,000 m)**
Endurance: **3 hrs**
Armament: **1-2 machine-guns**
Crew: **1**

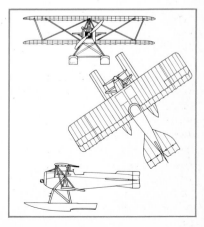

Halberstadt D II

The Fokker monoplane's domination of the air ended in late spring 1916, and Germany had to wait until the new Albatros fighter appeared the following autumn to regain control of the skies. Another fighter plane appeared in the interim. The D-type Halberstadts were inferior to the Albatros D I, but they were excellent transitional planes and saw extensive service on the Western Front until the new fighters arrived. The Halberstadt D II went into service in the summer of 1916 and was first assigned to escort duty. It was a slim and elegant plane, very strongly built. The last production model was D IV, but the D II and almost identical D III models were the most widely used, especially from late 1916 until the early months of 1917, during which time they were assigned to many of the reorganized fighter squadrons. Later they were reassigned to training duty.

Aircraft: **Halberstadt D II**
Manufacturer: **Halberstädter Flugzeug-Werke G.m.b.H.**
Type: **Fighter**
Year: **1916**
Engine: **Mercedes D II 6-cylinder liquid-cooled inline, 120 hp**
Wingspan: **28 ft 10.5 in (8.8 m)**
Length: **23 ft 11.5 in (7.3 m)**
Height: **8 ft 9 in (2.66 m)**
Weight: **1,696 lbs (771 kg)**
Maximum speed: **90 mph (145 kph)**
Ceiling: **13,123 ft (4,000 m)**
Endurance: **1 hr 30 mins**
Armament: **1 machine-gun**

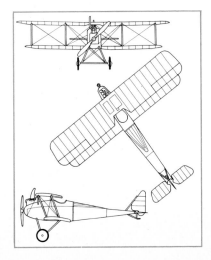

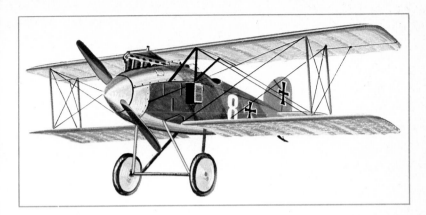

Albatros D II

The Fokker monoplane gave Germany control of the air from late 1915 until the following spring. The next German plane to dominate the skies was an elegant, high-performance biplane with excellent firepower, the Albatros. The first Albatros, the D I, was developed in August 1916 by Robert Thelen of the Albatros *Werke*. The D I was the first German fighter to have two synchronized fixed machine-guns and still maintain an excellent performance. The new plane began reaching the *Jagdstaffeln* (fighter squadrons) in early autumn. It was soon joined by an improved model, the D II. Although the combat career of the Albatros D II lasted only a few months (until the appearance of the D III) it did much to swing the balance of air power back to Germany.

The main advantage enjoyed by the D I and D II over their successors was that they were not sesquiplanes.

Aircraft: **Albatros D II**
Manufacturer: **Albatros Werke G.m.b.H.**
Type: **Fighter**
Year: **1916**
Engine: **Mercedes D III 6-cylinder liquid-cooled inline, 160 hp**
Wingspan: **27 ft 10.75 in (8.5 m)**
Length: **24 ft 3 in (7.4 m)**
Height: **8 ft 6.5 in (2.95 m)**
Weight: **1,954 lbs (888 kg)**
Maximum speed: **109 mph (175 kph)**
Ceiling: **17,060 ft (5,200 m)**
Endurance: **1 hr 30 mins**
Armament: **2 machine-guns**

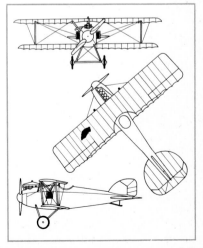

Albatros C III
Albatros C I
Albatros C V
Albatros C VII
Albatros C X
Albatros C XIII

The C-series Albatros reconnaissance planes, direct successors to the B-type two-seater unarmed biplanes, appeared in 1915, and many different models were built. Improved models continued to be developed to the end of the war, and Albatros C-class machines were some of the most widely used reconnaissance planes of the First World War.

The Albatros C I was developed early in 1915 and resembled its predecessor, the unarmed two-seater B II, designed by Ernst Heinkel in 1914. The C I kept the general structure and excellent handling qualities of the B II. Its engine was more powerful than the usual Allied engines, and its rear machine-gun made the C I a formid-able plane. The C I saw service on all fronts, and future aces Boelcke and von Richthofen began their air careers in the C I.

An improved version of the Albatros reconnaissance plane appeared at the end of 1915, in the form of the C III. The C III was based on the 1914 B III, and had the same lines and empennage. The C III was faster, stronger and more manoeuvrable than the C I, although more C Is were produced than any other C type Albatros. The C III went into action early in 1916 and remained in service till 1917. It operated on all fronts for artillery-spotting, photographic reconnaissance, and light bombing.

A few C IVs were produced before a completely new model, the C V, was designed. This 1916 design was slightly larger than the C III, and it had a more powerful engine and a more streamlined fuselage. More than 400 C Vs were built, but the model was not a great success. The Mercedes engine gave a lot of trouble, and the plane was hard to handle. The C VII was a compromise design that reutilized

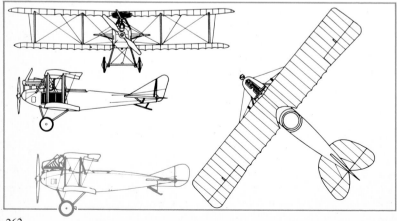

many components of the various C V models, but nevertheless turned out to be a success. Although it was not the final development of the C V type, it was produced in large numbers and remained in service until the early months of 1917.

A particularly high-performance plane was the C X model, which appeared in mid-1917. Much of its success was due to its new engine, the 260-hp Mercedes D IVa. The Albatros C X served with reconnaissance and artillery-spotting units until the middle of 1918. Experience with the C X made possible the realization of another model, the C XII, the crowning achievement of the formula that had been introduced with the C V. The C XII can be considered the finest plane in the Albatros C series. Its performance was surpassed only by later D series aircraft. The C XII had the same engine as the C X, but the newer design's fuselage was thoroughly steamlined, and it was considered the best-looking German two-seater on

Aircraft: **Albatros C I**
Manufacturer: **Albatros Werke G.m.b.H.**
Type: **Reconnaissance**
Year: **1915**
Engine: **Mercedes D III 6-cylinder liquid-cooled inline, 160 hp**
Wingspan: **42 ft 4 in (12.9 m)**
Length: **25 ft 9 in (7.85 m)**
Height: **10 ft 3.5 in (3.14 m)**
Weight: **2,618 lbs (1,190 kg)**
Maximum speed: **82 mph (132 kph) at sea level**
Ceiling: **9,840 ft (3,000 m)**
Endurance: **2 hrs 30 mins**
Armament: **1 machine-gun**
Crew: **2**

Aircraft: **Albatros C III**
Manufacturer: **Albatros Werke G.m.b.H.**
Type: **Reconnaissance**
Year: **1916**
Engine: **Mercedes D III 6-cylinder liquid-cooled inline, 160 hp**
Wingspan: **38 ft 4.25 in (11.69 m)**
Length: **26 ft 3 in (8 m)**
Height: **10 ft 2 in (3.1 m)**
Weight: **2,977 lbs (1,353 kg)**
Maximum speed: **87.5 mph (140 kph) at sea level**
Ceiling: **11,155 ft (3,400 m)**
Endurance: **4 hrs**
Armament: **1-2 machine-guns; 220 lbs (100 kg) of bombs**
Crew: **2**

the Western Front. The C XII continued to give excellent performance up to the end of the war.

263

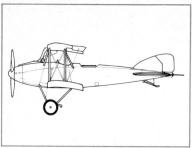

Aircraft: **Albatros C V**
Manufacturer: **Albatros Werke G.m.b.H.**
Type: **Reconnaissance**
Year: **1916**
Engine: **Mercedes D IV 8-cylinder liquid-cooled inline, 220 hp**
Wingspan: **41 ft 11.25 in (12.78 m)**
Length: **29 ft 4.5 in (8.95 m)**
Height: **11 ft 8 in (3.56 m)**
Weight: **2,387 lbs (1,585 kg)**
Maximum speed: **106 mph (170 kph)**
Ceiling: **16,405 ft (5,000 m)**
Endurance: **3 hrs 15 mins**
Armament: **2 machine-guns; 220 lbs (100 kg) of bombs**
Crew: **2**

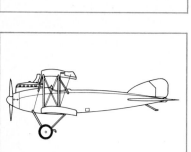

Aircraft: **Albatros C VII**
Manufacturer: **Albatros Werke G.m.b.H.**
Type: **Reconnaissance**
Year: **1916**
Engine: **Benz Bz. IV 6-cylinder liquid-cooled inline, 200 hp**
Wingspan: **41 ft 11.25 in (12.78 m)**
Length: **28 ft 6.5 in (8.7 m)**
Height: **11 ft 11.75 in (3.6 m)**
Weight: **3,410 lbs (1,550 kg)**
Maximum speed: **106 mph (170 kph)**
Ceiling: **16,405 ft (5,000 m)**
Endurance: **3 hrs 20 mins**
Armament: **2 machine-guns; small bomb load**
Crew: **2**

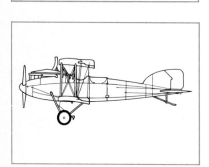

Aircraft: **Albatros C X**
Manufacturer: **Albatros Werke G.m.b.H.**
Type: **Reconnaissance**
Year: **1917**
Engine: **Mercedes D IVa 6-cylinder liquid-cooled inline, 260 hp**
Wingspan: **47 ft 1.5 in (14.36 m)**
Length: **30 ft 0.25 in (9.15 m)**
Height: **11 ft 2 in (3.4 m)**
Weight: **3,669 lbs (1,668 kg)**
Maximum speed: **109.5 mph (175 kph)**
Ceiling: **16,405 ft (5,000 m)**
Endurance: **3 hrs 25 mins**
Armament: **2 machine-guns; light bomb load**
Crew: **2**

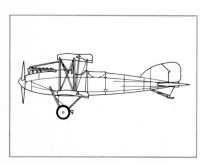

Aircraft: **Albatros C XII**
Manufacturer: **Albatros Werke G.m.b.H.**
Type: **Reconnaissance**
Year: **1918**
Engine: **Mercedes D IVa 6-cylinder liquid-cooled inline, 260 hp**
Wingspan: **47 ft 2 in (14.37 m)**
Length: **29 ft 0.5 in (8.85 m)**
Height: **10 ft 8 in (3.25 m)**
Weight: **3,606 lbs (1,639 kg)**
Maximum speed: **109 mph (175 kph)**
Ceiling: **16,405 ft (5,000 m)**
Endurance: **3 hrs 15 mins**
Armament: **2 machine-guns; small bomb load**
Crew: **2**

A.E.G. C IV

The finest C-type reconnaissance plane that *A.E.G.* built was the C IV. It was designed in 1916 and kept much of the structure and general lines of the earlier C II model. The wingspan was increased, and the housing of the 160-hp Mercedes D.III engine had an unusual, high-drag shape. The cylinder heads were exposed, and the large exhuast pipe, shaped like a rhinoceros horn, protruded above the upper wing. The C IV went into service in the spring of 1916, in reconnaissance and observation units, and served until the middle of 1918. This excellent plane was used on almost all fronts, and was also flown by Turks and Bulgarians. It was so highly rated that a night bombing version was developed late in 1916. This plane, the C IVN, could carry six 110-pound (50-kg) bombs and was considered one of the best planes of its kind. Its only drawback was an insufficiently powerful engine.

Aircraft: **A.E.G. C IV**
Manufacturer: **Allgemeine Elektrizitäts Gesellschaft**
Type: **Reconnaissance**
Year: **1916**
Engine: **Mercedes D III 6-cylinder liquid-cooled inline, 160 hp**
Wingspan: **44 ft 2 in (13.46 m)**
Length: **23 ft 5.5 in (7.15 m)**
Height: **11 ft (3.35 m)**
Weight: **2,464 lbs (1,120 kg)**
Maximum speed: **99 mph (158 kph)**
Ceiling: **16,405 ft (5,000 m)**
Endurance: **4 hrs**
Armament: **2 machine-guns; 220 lbs (100 kg) of bombs**
Crew: **2**

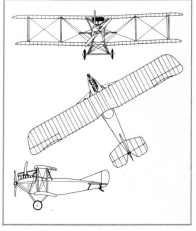

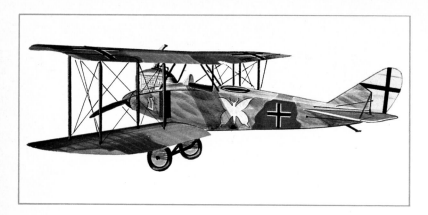

D.F.W. C V

The C V built by the *Deutsche Flugzeug-Werke* came out in the summer of 1916, and was a development of the C IV. The C V was the same size, but it had a 200-hp Benz engine, instead of the C IV's 150-hp engine. The C IV and the C V were the best C-type planes that the *D.F.W.* produced during the war, and their fine qualities made them very popular with their crews. The C V was produced in larger numbers than any other German plane during the war, and in addition to the *D.F.W.*, three other manufacturers produced the C V. The C V remained in front-line service over the Western Front from summer 1916 until early 1918. When the Armistice was signed, more than 600 *D.F.W.* C Vs were still in service. It was such a fine plane that, in the hands of expert pilots, it could outmanoeuvre most of the modern enemy fighters of the last period of the war.

Aircraft: **D.F.W. C V**
Manufacturer: **Deutsche Flugzeug-Werke**
Type: **Reconnaissance**
Year: **1916**
Engine: **Benz Bz. IV 6-cylinder liquid-cooled inline, 200 hp**
Wingspan: **43 ft 6.5 in (13.27 m)**
Length: **25 ft 10 in (7.875 m)**
Height: **10 ft 8 in (3.25 m)**
Weight: **3,146 lbs (1,430 kg)**
Maximum speed: **97 mph (155 kph) at 3,281 ft (1,000 m)**
Ceiling: **16,405 ft (5,000 m)**
Endurance: **3 hrs 30 mins**
Armament: **2 machine-guns; 220 lbs (100 kg) of bombs**
Crew: **2**

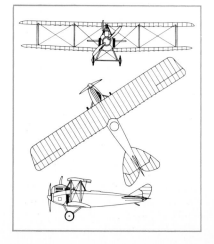

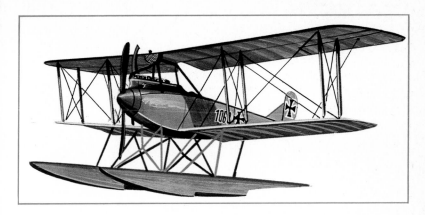

Rumpler 6B 1

The three most widely used naval fighters, the Rumpler 6B 1, the Albatros W 4, and the Brandenburg K.D.W., were all modelled after landplanes. The starting point of the Rumpler was the C I reconnaissance two-seater. Extensive structural changes were made, and the first production model, the 6B 1, appeared in the summer of 1916. Production was slow, and the last of the 38 planes produced was delivered at the end of May 1917. Most of these seaplanes saw service at North Sea bases, while others were sent to the Black Sea to defend German bases from Russian seaplanes. In autumn 1917, the 6B 2 appeared. It had a slightly greater wingspan and other structural alterations. The Rumpler 6B 2 had the same engine as the 6B 1, but performed more poorly than the earlier model. Nevertheless deliveries continued until January 1918.

Aircraft: **Rumpler 6B 1**
Manufacturer: **E. Rumpler Flugzeug-Werke G.m.b.H.**
Type: **Fighter**
Year: **1916**
Engine: **Mercedes D III 6-cylinder liquid-cooled inline, 160 hp**
Wingspan: **40 ft 0.5 in (12.2 m)**
Length: **29 ft 8.5 in (9.05 m)**
Height: **11 ft 6 in (3.5 m)**
Weight: **2,508 lbs (1,140 kg)**
Maximum speed: **95 mph (153 kph) at sea level**
Ceiling: **16,405 ft (5,000 m)**
Endurance: **4 hrs**
Armament: **1 machine-gun**
Crew: **1**

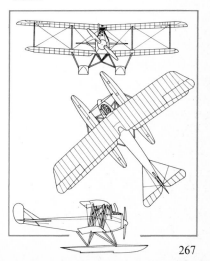

Friedrichshafen G III

Along with the Gotha and the giant Zeppelin bomber aircraft, the G-series Friendrichshafens were the most famous German heavy bombers of the last years of the war. While the Gotha and the Zeppelin were used for night bombing raids on England, the Friedrichshafens were used mainly for bombing missions on the continent.

The first G-series Friedrichshafen appeared in autumn 1914, but it remained only a prototype: its performance was disappointing and it could not carry a large payload. The plane was manufactured by a company (founded by von Zeppelin) that had

experience with seaplanes but was new to bombers. The second model, the G II, was developed two years later and was a great improvement over the first model. But it, too, had a rather small bomb capacity, about 331 pounds (150 kg). Only a few G IIs were produced, and they served in bombing units until late in 1917. The next model, the G III, was a thoroughly successful bomber. A great many were built and the type stayed in service until the end of the war.

The Friedrichshafen G III entered service in February 1917. It was larger than the earlier models, had more

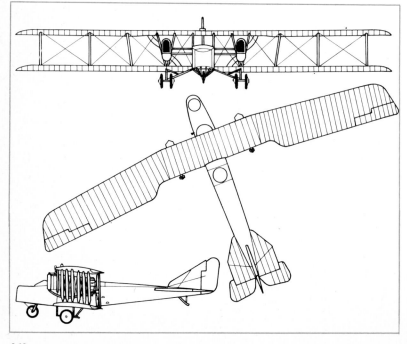

powerful engines, was a tougher plane, and had a really substantial bomb capacity. The three-man crew had two defensive gun positions at their disposal, one forward and one aft of the wings, each with one or two machine-guns. The rear installation was dangerously close to the pusher propellers, and a metal screen was provided to protect the gunner.

The Friedrichshafen equipped three German bombing groups, and operated over France and Belgium. In the summer of 1917, the Friedrichshafens of *Kagohl* 1 (*Kampfgeschwader der Obersten Heeresleitung* or High Command Battle Group) began night raids on the British base at Dunkirk and did great damage, especially in the port area. Many raids on Paris were completed in the following months.

Early in 1918, a modified version, the G IIIa, appeared. This had a bi-plane tail and other structural modifications. Production licences for both models were granted to Hansa and Daimler, who built a total of 338 planes.

Aircraft: **Friedrichshafen G III**
Manufacturer: **Flugzeugbau Friedrich-shafen G.m.b.H.**
Type: **Heavy bomber**
Engines: **Two Mercedes D IVa 6-cylinder liquid-cooled inlines, 260 hp each**
Wingspan: **77 ft 9.25 in (23.7 m)**
Length: **42 ft (12.8 m)**
Height: **12 ft (3.66 m)**
Weight: **8,646 lbs (3,930 kg)**
Maximum speed: **84.5 mph (135 kph) at 3,281 ft (1,000 m)**
Ceiling: **14,765 ft (4,500 m)**
Endurance: **5 hrs**
Armament: **2-3 machine-guns; 3,307 lbs (1,500 kg) of bombs**
Crew: **3**

The final expression of the Friedrichshafen design philosophy was reached in 1918 with the G IV, only a few of which were built before the end of the war. Based on the earlier G III and G IIIa, the G IV had a very odd appearance: the nose of the fuselage was cut off short, just in front of the leading edge of the lower wing, giving the machine a truncated appearance. A compound tail was again used. But in the G IV the designers had resort for the first time to tractor propellers. Only one gun was carried.

Gotha G V

For the British generally, and for Londoners in particular, the Gotha was synonymous with heavy bombing raids. Gotha raids began in May 1917, and a total of 27 attacks was made on the British capital over the next year, the first time in history that a single target was bombed systematically. Although the material effects were only relatively serious, the psychological effects were profound. But the Gotha was not the outstanding aeroplane that contemporary propaganda made it out to be. Highly manoeuvrable and well-armed as it was, the fuselage and landing gear were weak. Special land-

ing strips had to be prepared for the plane. And more Gothas were lost in accidents than to enemy fire. During the London raids, 36 planes were lost in accidents, and only 24 were shot down.

The first Gotha, the G I, was designed by Oskar Ursinus and by Major Friedel of the German Army for the *Gothaer Waggonfabrik A.G.*, and appeared in January 1915 as a ground attack aircraft. It saw service on both the Western and Eastern Fronts. The G II, designed by Hans Burkhard in 1916, had various structural defects. Together with the G III,

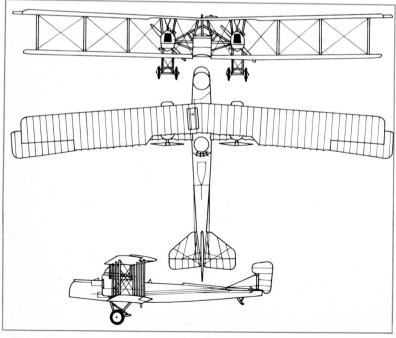

it was a transitional model to the first major production variant, the G IV. This plane, which appeared early in 1917, was earmarked for raids on Britain, and about 230 aircraft were built. Day raids on England began in May, and in September it began to be sent on night missions as well. In the meantime, the second production model, the G V, had entered service, in August 1917.

The Gotha G V had more powerful engines and incorporated structural changes. Its general performance was much higher. It was extremely manoeuvrable for its size, well-armed (three or four machine-guns), and difficult to shoot down. The bomb load varied with target distance. The plane could carry up to 1,322 pounds (600 kg) on short- and medium-range missions, but it carried about half that weight in the raids on Britain.

Two minor variants, the G Va and G Vb, were also developed. They had biplane tails, and the forward part of the fuselage was shortened. The bi-

Aircraft: **Gotha G V**
Manufacturer: **Gothaer Waggonfabrik A.G. Gotha**
Type: **Heavy bomber**
Year: **1917**
Engines: **Two Mercedes D IVa 6-cylinder liquid-cooled inlines, 260 hp each**
Wingspan: **77 ft 9.25 in (23.7 m)**
Length: **40 ft (12.2 m)**
Height: **14 ft 1.25 in (43 m)**
Weight: **8,745 lbs (3,975 kg)**
Maximum speed: **87.5 mph (140 kph) at 11,483 ft (3,500 m)**
Ceiling: **21,325 ft (6,500 m)**
Range: **520 miles (835 km)**
Armament: **2-3 machine-guns; 1,102 lbs (500 kg) of bombs**
Crew: **3**

plane tail was meant to improve the rear gunner's field of fire. The G Vb was designed to overcome one of the G V's weak points, its susceptibility to hard landings, and two extra pairs of wheels were added.

An unusual and highly successful feature of both the G IV and G V was the gunner's 'sting in the tail': he was provided with a wide ventral tunnel, this allowing him to fire downwards and towards the rear, much to the discomfiture of attackers.

271

Zeppelin (Staaken) R VI

On September 28, 1917, Londoners faced a new menace for the first time. Gothas had been bombing the city since May, but now the Zeppelin (Staaken) R VI began its strategic bombing raids. The R VI was the largest of the Zeppelin (Staaken) bombers, and a formidable instrument of war. It made 28 bombing raids on Britain, and dropped 26.75 tons (27,180 kg) of bombs. On February 16, 1918, a Zeppelin R VI dropped the first 2,205-lb (1,000 kg) bomb on the Royal Hospital in Chelsea. Twenty-one people were killed and 32 were injured.

The first Zeppelin *Riesenflugzeug* (Giant aeroplane), the V.G.O. I, was designed late in 1914 by B. G. Klein and H. Hirth. It made its first flight on April 11, 1915. The plane was powered by three Maybach Mb IV engines, of 240 hp each, two with pusher propellers and one with a tractor propeller. The plane went into service, together with the similar V.G.O. II, late in 1916, but it proved to be underpowered. The number of engines was increased to five. A six-engined version, the V.G.O. III, was then produced, with each Mercedes inline developing 160 hp. Four were installed

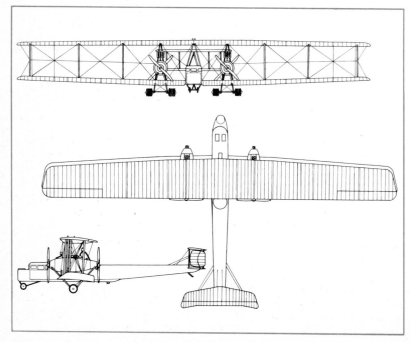

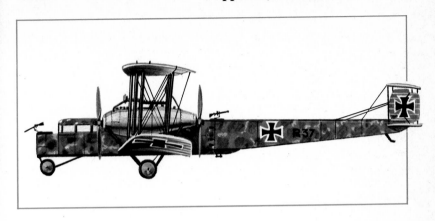

in tandem in two nacelles, and the other two were installed in the nose of the fuselage, each pair of engines driving one propeller. Other experimental models were built: the R IV, R V, and R VII. The prototypes were used operationally, but production models were never built.

The first giant Zeppelin to go into general production was the R VI. A total of 18 was built, seven by Schütte-Lanz, six by Aviatik, four by O.A.W., and one by Zeppelin (Staaken). Installing the engines in tandem in two nacelles (with two tractor and two pusher propellers) made it possible to increase forward armament and house the crew in a central cabin. The plane could carry up to 4,409 lbs (2,000 kg) of bombs, though a 2,204-lb (1,000-kg) load was the norm on longer flights. Up to 18 220-pound (100-kg) bombs could be carried internally, but the 2204-lb (1,000-kg) bomb was carried semi-externally. To increase cruising altitude and avoid anti-aircraft fire, two R VIs were equipped

Aircraft: **Zeppelin (Staaken) R VI**
Manufacturer: **Zeppelin Flugzeugwerft G.m.b.H., Staaken, Berlin**
Type: **Heavy bomber**
Year: **1917**
Engines: **Four Mercedes D IVa 6-cylinder liquid-cooled inlines, 260 hp each**
Wingspan: **138 ft 5.5 in (42.2 m)**
Length: **72 ft 6.25 in (22.1 m)**
Height: **20 ft 8 in (6.3 m)**
Weight: **25,269 lbs (11,462 kg)**
Maximum speed: **80 mph (129 kph) at sea level**
Ceiling: **12,467 ft (3,800 m)**
Endurance: **7-8 hrs**
Armament: **4-7 machine-guns; 4,409 lbs (2,000 kg) of bombs**
Crew: **7**

with an additional 120-hp engine that worked a supercharging compressor. One of these planes reached an altitude of almost 20,000 feet (6,000 m).

The *Riesenflugzeug* programme was in its entirety an odd one. Very great amounts of money were spent on research into structures, materials, superchargers and methods of gearing several engines onto one propeller, but the results were small. On the look always for improvements, the Germans never standardised a single type and mass produced it.

Albatros D III

'Bloody April' is how the British remember April 1917, when German air power reached a peak with the appearance of a new fighter plane, the Albatros D III, which served alongside the earlier D II model. The D III was undoubtedly the best Albatros fighter: it went into service in January 1917 and was supplied to all the German fighter squadrons, gradually replacing the D I and D II models. In November 1917 there were 446 D IIIs in service at the front. The plane was flown by such aces as Manfred von Richthofen, Werner Voss, Ernst Udet, Eduard von Schleich, and Bruno Loerzer.

The appearance of the French Nieuport 17 fighter spurred the Germans to improve on their own Albatros D II. Robert Thelen, the designer of the D III, kept the D II fuselage and fitted it with a more powerful engine and sesquiplane wings braced by V-shaped struts, like those of the French Nieuports. A high-compression version of the Mercedes D III was installed; this engine maintained its power output even at high altitude. The new biplane had cleaner and more elegant lines than its predecessors: it performed superbly at high altitudes and had a very fast rate of climb, surpassing the D II in both respects.

The plane was put into production immediately after it appeared, and one of the first units to receive the new plane was von Richthofen's *Jasta* 11. By spring 1917, all 37 front-line fighter squadrons had received Albatros D IIIs. It became the standard fighter, and remained so even after the arrival of the newer D V. It was the outstanding fighter of the second half of 1917, and only began to lose ground with the arrival of the Spad S.VII, the

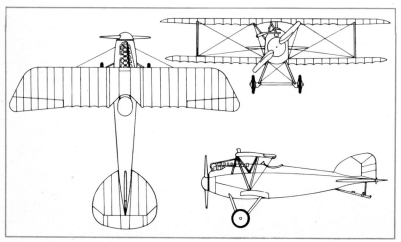

Sopwith Triplane and Camel, and the R.A.F. S.E.5a. Production of D III ended early in 1918, after more than 800 planes had been turned out.

This German fighter was also used by the Austro-Hungarian air force, for which Oeffag built the series 53, series 153, and series 253. Apart from minor details, the chief difference between these planes was engine power. The series 53 was powered by the 185-hp Austro-Daimler, the series 153 by the two 200-hp model, and the series 253 by the 225-hp model. The Austrian models needed more power because they operated at higher altitude over the Alps.

The Albatros D III also saw service in Palestine and Macedonia, and in those zones the plane was equipped with another wing radiator to keep the engine from over-heating.

Good as it was, though, the D III was not without its failures. The most important of these was the basic weakness of all sesquiplanes: at high speeds or in tight manoeuvres the

Aircraft: **Albatros D III**
Manufacturer: **Albatros Werke G.m.b.H.**
Type: **Fighter**
Year: **1917**
Engine: **Mercedes D IIIa 6-cylinder liquid-cooled inline, 175 hp**
Wingspan: **29 ft 8.25 in (9.05 m)**
Length: **24 ft 0.5 in (7.33 m)**
Height: **9 ft 9.25 in (2.98 m)**
Weight: **1,949 lbs (886 kg)**
Maximum speed: **109 mph (175 kph) at 3,281 ft (1,000 m)**
Ceiling: **18,044 ft (5,500 m)**
Endurance: **2 hrs**
Armament: **2 machine-guns**
Crew: **1**

narrow-chord lower wing, with only a single attachment point to the interplane strut on each side, tended to flutter. This could sometimes result in the lower wings breaking away, with disastrous consequences. A partial cure was found in the provision of small auxiliary struts from the lower wing leading edge to the front leg of the 'vee' strut. On later models, the radiator was offset from the upper wing centre line to avoid scalding water falling onto the pilot should the radiator be punctured.

275

Fokker Dr I

The legend of the 'Red Baron', Manfred von Richthofen, came to an end when he crashed in his Fokker Dr I triplane (*Nr.* 425/17) on April 21, 1918. He came down in no-man's land in the Somme valley near Sailly-le-Sec. But the legend of this fine plane continued. The success of the triplane Reinhold Platz designed in 1917 was closely bound to the epic of von Richthofen and his *Jagdgeschwader Nr.* 1, the unit that went down in history as the 'Flying Circus'.

Anthony Fokker's company produced this triplane fighter in answer to the Sopwith triplane. But Reinhold Platz's plane was not a carbon copy of the fighter Herbert Smith designed for Sopwith. The only things the two planes had in common were the triplane formula and the rotary-type engine. After test flights, the Fokker prototype (the V 3) had wing struts

added to stop vibration in its cantilever wings, and two fixed and synchronized 'Spandau' machineguns (with 1,000 rounds) installed forward. This variant was the V4. Two more prototypes were ordered, and then 318 production models were built. Two of the four pre-production models were assigned to Manfred von Richthofen's *Jagdgeschwader Nr.* 1, and they were an immediate success. The third prototype was given to Werner Voss on August 28, 1917. It shot down its first plane two days later, and 20 more followed in little more than three weeks of operations. On September 23, Voss was shot down by an S.E.5a of No. 56 Squadron, R.F.C.

A couple of weeks later, delivery of the production triplane, the Dr I, began. But there was a structural defect in the upper wing, and the plane was

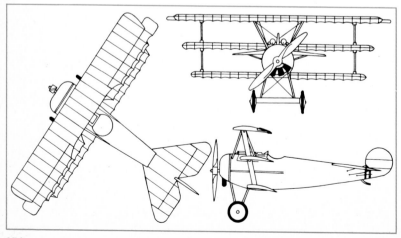

not put into active service for some time. All the triplanes already built were grounded, and Fokker stopped production until the defect was corrected. The Dr I was declared combat-ready at the end of November.

The triplane proved to be an excellent fighter in skilled hands, and was outstanding in manoeuvrability. Many front-line units were supplied with the Dr I. By May 1918 there were 171 planes in service. Production came to an end at this time, and the Dr I was gradually replaced by the Fokker D VII biplane, 19 of which were already in action by May 1. A few triplanes remained in home defence units until the end of the war, but most of them were reassigned to training duty.

Various modifications were made on the Dr I during production. A variant model appeared on October 30, 1917, with a 160-hp Goebel Goe.III engine. This plane was superior to the standard fighter, but not many were manufactured. Later

Aircraft: **Fokker Dr I**
Manufacturer: **Fokker Flugzeug-Werke G.m.b.H.**
Type: **Fighter**
Year: **1917**
Engine: **Thulin-built Le Rhône 9J 9-cylinder air-cooled rotary, 110 hp**
Wingspan: **23 ft 7.5 in (7.19 m)**
Length: **18 ft 11 in (5.77 m)**
Height: **9 ft 8 in (2.95 m)**
Weight: **1,289 lbs (586 kg)**
Maximum speed: **103 mph (165 kph) at 13,123 ft (4,000 m)**
Ceiling: **19,685 ft (6,000 m)**
Endurance: **1 hr 30 mins**
Armament: **2 machine-guns**
Crew: **1**

models were powered by the 178-hp Goe.IIIa engine, and with the 160-hp Siemens-Halske Sh.III rotary engine. This last variant of the Dr I had a phenomenal rate of climb and a very high ceiling. But its excessive torque reaction made the plane hard to handle.

Despite the fact that it was obsolescent by the time of its introduction, the Dr I was a superb defensive weapon in the hands of an expert with cool nerves and a steady hand. To a novice the machine could be fatal.

Halberstadt CL II

The first plane built after the CL class of armed two-seaters was established in early 1917 was the Halberstadt CL II, one of the best and most widely used ground attack fighters of the war. This new category had been created chiefly to provide air support for ground troops. CL planes, therefore, were generally smaller and lighter than C-class planes. The CL II began reaching units in summer 1917 and quickly proved its worth as a fighting plane. With two or three machine-guns and five 22-pound (10-kg) anti-personnel bombs, the plane was well suited to its purpose. By early 1918, all the *Schlachtstaffeln* (Battle Squadrons) had been equipped with the Halberstadt. Early in 1918 an improved version, the CL IV, was developed, with aerodynamic improvements to make the machine easier to handle.

Aircraft: **Halberstadt CL II**
Manufacturer: **Halberstädter Flugzeug Werke G.m.b.H.**
Type: **Ground attack**
Year: **1917**
Engine: **Mercedes D III, 160 hp**
Wingspan: **35 ft 4 in (10.77 m)**
Length: **23 ft 11.5 in (7.3 m)**
Height: **9 ft 0.25 in (2.75 m)**
Weight: **2,493 lbs (1,133 kg)**
Maximum speed: **103 mph (165 kph) at 16,405 ft (5,000 m)**
Ceiling: **16,700 ft (5,090 m)**
Endurance: **3 hrs**
Armament: **2-3 machine-guns; 110 lbs (50 kg) of bombs**
Crew: **2**

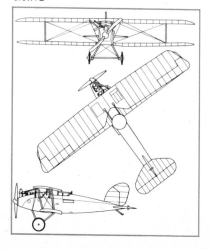

Hansa-Brandenburg W 12

The Hansa-Brandenburg W 12 was designed by Ernst Heinkel late in 1916, and made its first flight in January 1917. It was designed for the German navy as a two-seater biplane naval fighter with rear defence. The observer in the rear cockpit had a machine-gun with a wide field of fire. A total of 145 planes was built between April 1917 and March 1918. It was assigned to German naval and seaplane bases and was highly respected for the enemy for its fighting qualities. Towards the end of 1917, the W 12 was joined in operations by an improved model, the W 19. The two versions remained in service until the end of the war.

W 19s and W 12s often acted in co-operation in the early part of 1918: the W 19, a reconnaissance machine, would find a target for the W 12 fighter to dispatch with its heavy machine-gun armament.

Aircraft: **Hansa-Brandenburg W 12**
Manufacturer: **Hansa und Brandenburg-ische Flugzeug-Werke G.m.b.H.**
Type: **Fighter**
Year: **1917**
Engine: **Benz Bz. III 6-cylinder liquid-cooled inline, 150 hp**
Wingspan: **36 ft 9 in (11.2 m)**
Length: **31 ft 6 in (9.6 m)**
Height: **10 ft 10 in (3.3 m)**
Weight: **3,199 lbs (1,454 kg)**
Maximum speed: **100 mph (161 kph) at sea level**
Ceiling: **16,405 ft (5,000 m)**
Endurance: **3 hrs 30 mins**
Armament: **2-3 machine-guns**
Crew: **2**

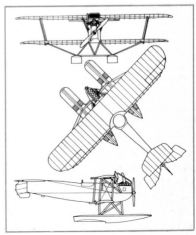

Pfalz D III

After building Roland fighters under licence, the Pfalz *Flugzeug-Werke* designed and produced a plane of their own, the D III. This aircraft, the creation of Rudolf Gehringer, appeared in spring 1917, and betrayed the influence of the Roland models. It was, however, a better-built and stronger plane, and more streamlined than its predecessors. After test flights the prototype was accepted by the military. The plane quickly went into production, and delivery to fighter squadrons began in August 1917. But the Pfalz D III was not as fine a performer as the Albatros D Va and Fokker D VII. An improved model, the D IIIa, was also produced, and the two Pfalz fighters made an important contribution to the German war effort. About 1,000 of both models were built, and by April 1918, 433 D IIIas were serving with front-line units.

Aircraft: **Pfalz D III**
Manufacturer: **Pfalz Flugzeug-Werke G.m.b.H.**
Type: **Fighter**
Year: **1917**
Engine: **Mercedes D III 6-cylinder liquid-cooled inline, 160 hp**
Wingspan: **30 ft 10 in (9.4 m)**
Length: **22 ft 9.75 in (6.95 m)**
Height: **8 ft 9 in (2.67 m)**
Weight: **2,056 lbs (933 kg)**
Maximum speed: **102.5 mph (165 kph) at 9,842 ft (3,000 m)**
Ceiling: **16,995 ft (5,180 m)**
Endurance: **2 hrs 30 mins**
Armament: **2 machine-guns**
Crew: **1**

Albatros D Va

After the great success of their D III, the Albatros *Werke* developed an improved version of the fighter, one that could match the new French and British fighters. The D V appeared about the middle of 1917, almost simultaneously with a structurally reinforced model, the D Va. The plane was modelled directly on the D III type, but was more advanced aerodynamically and had generally cleaner lines. Although the planes had a more powerful Mercedes engine, the D V and D Va were little better overall than the D III in performance. The first planes began reaching combat units in July (D V) and November (D Va) 1917. In November there were 526 D Vs at the front, while the D Va reached its service peak in May 1918, when 928 planes were in service.

The D V and D Va suffered from the same structural problems with the wings and the D III.

Aircraft: **Albatros D Va**
Manufacturer: **Albatros Werke G.m.b.H.**
Type: **Fighter**
Year: **1917**
Engine: **Mercedes D IIIa 6-cylinder liquid-cooled inline, 180 hp**
Wingspan: **29 ft 8.25 in (9.05 m)**
Length: **24 ft 0.5 in (7.33 m)**
Height: **8 ft 10.25 in (2.7 m)**
Weight: **2,061 lbs (937 kg)**
Maximum speed: **116 mph (187 kph) at 3,281 ft (1,000 m)**
Ceiling: **18,700 ft (5,700 m)**
Endurance: **2 hrs**
Armament: **2 machine-guns**
Crew: **1**

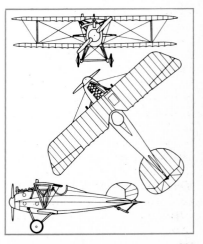

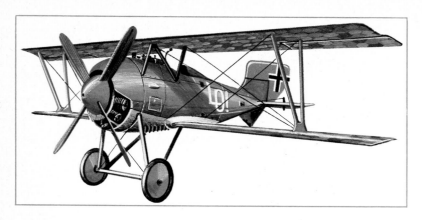

Siemens-Schuckert D III

The D III fighter turned out in late 1917 by the Siemens-Schuckert *Werke* was designed around the new Siemens-Halske Sh.III 160-hp rotary engine, which was produced by another division of the company. It was very manoeuvrable and possessed an excellent rate of climb. The designer was Harald Wolff, who tested three prototypes in June 1917: the D II, D IIa, and D IIb. Further development of the design led to the production version, the D III. A first order for 20 planes was placed in December 1917. A total of 80 D IIIs was built. They saw service with eight fighter squadrons and some home defence units, as well as a couple of flying schools. The best features of this plane were its manoeuvrability and rate of climb, and the D III was a success in combat. The improved D IV version came out in August 1918, and was even faster and more manoeuvrable than the earlier model.

Aircraft: **Siemens-Schuckert D III**
Manufacturer: **Siemens-Schuckert Werke**
Type: **Fighter**
Year: **1918**
Engine: **Siemens-Halske Sh.III 11-cylinder air-cooled rotary, 160 hp**
Wingspan: **27 ft 8 in (8.43 m)**
Length: **18 ft 8.5 in (5.7 m)**
Height: **9 ft 2.25 in (2.8 m)**
Weight: **1,595 lbs (725 kg)**
Maximum speed: **112 mph (180 kph)**
Ceiling: **26,246 ft (8,000 m)**
Endurance: **2 hrs**
Armament: **2 machine-guns**
Crew: **1**

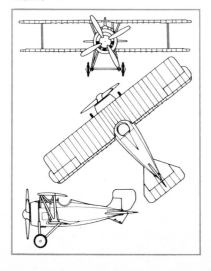

L.F.G. Roland D VIb

The first competition to choose a D-type fighter plane was held at Aldershot in January and February 1918. The best plane present was the Fokker that came to be designated D VII. The other excellent aircraft present in the competition were no match for the D VII. One of these was the *L.F.G.* Roland D VIb. Limited production of the D VIb was begun in case there were delays in the delivery of the Fokker D VII. The D VIb was a fine plane, with a good rate of climb and fine flight performance. In some ways, indeed, it was superior to the Fokker. Its most distinctive feature was its wooden-planked fuselage, like that of a boat, giving the D VIb's fuselage great rigidity at a reasonable weight. The D VIb saw limited front-line service.

The D VIa differed from the D VIb only in being powered by the 160-or 180-hp Mercedes D III.

Aircraft: **L.F.G. Roland D VIb**
Manufacturer: **Luftfahrzeug G.m.b.H.**
Type: **Fighter**
Year: **1918**
Engine: **Benz Bz. IIIa 6-cylinder liquid-cooled inline, 200 hp**
Wingspan: **30 ft 10 in (9.4 m)**
Length: **20 ft 8.75 in (6.322 m)**
Height: **9 ft 2.25 in (2.8 m)**
Weight: **1,892 lbs (860 kg)**
Maximum speed: **114 mph (182 kph)**
Ceiling: **19,685 ft (6,000 m)**
Endurance: **2 hrs**
Armament: **2 machine-guns**
Crew: **1**

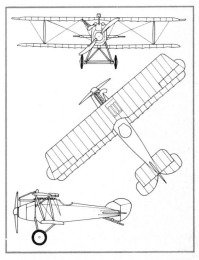

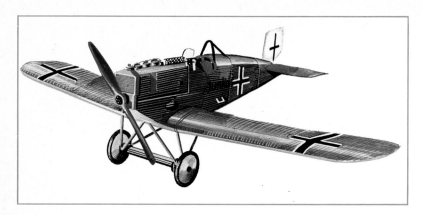

Junkers D I

The world's first all-metal plane appeared at the end of 1915. This was the
J 1, designed by Hugo Junkers. Various models were developed. The J 9
model appeared in March 1918 and
was given the military designation D I.
This plane was a development of the
J 7, which had appeared during the
previous October, but it was larger and
had a more powerful engine. The
structure was the same: a steel tube
framework covered with corrugated
metal skinning. The D I used both the
185-hp B.M.W. and the 180-hp
Mercedes engines and was both fast
and easy to handle. Construction
difficulties limited production to a
total of 41, which were assigned to
front-line units. The D I type was also
developed into the CL I two-seater
version, larger, more manoeuvrable,
and better-armed. A roll-bar over the
cockpit protected the pilot if the plane
should turn over.

Aircraft: **Junkers D I**
Manufacturer: **Junkers Flugzeug-Werke A.G.**
Type: **Fighter**
Year: **1918**
Engine: **B.M.W. IIIa 6-cylinder liquid-cooled inline, 185 hp**
Wingspan: **29 ft 6.5 in (9 m)**
Length: **23 ft 9.5 in (7.25 m)**
Height: **7 ft 4.5 in (2.25 m)**
Weight: **1,835 lbs (834 kg)**
Maximum speed: **119 mph (185 kph)**
Ceiling: **19,685 ft (6,000 m)**
Endurance: **1 hr 30 mins**
Armament: **2 machine-guns**
Crew: **1**

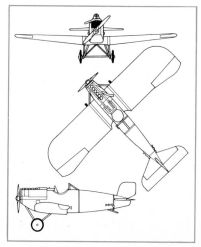

Halberstadt C V

Together with the Rumpler C VII, the Halberstadt C V was the German photographic reconnaissance plane that saw most service in the last year of the war. The C V was developed from the C III by Karl Theiss late in 1917. Although it resembled the earlier plane, it performed much better at high altitude thanks to the installation of the high-compression 220-hp Benz Bz. IV engine. The cameras were set in the floor of the observer's cockpit, photographing through an opening in the bottom of the fuselage. The prototype of the C V appeared early in 1918, and the plane went into service in the summer, remaining in service until the end of the war. The plane was manufactured by Aviatik, *B.F.W.*, and *D.F.W.*, and other models were developed. The most interesting of these was the C VIII, which could reach an altitude of 29,527 feet (9,000 m).

Aircraft: **Halberstadt C V**
Manufacturer: **Halberstädter Flugzeug-Werke G.m.b.H.**
Type: **Photographic reconnaissance**
Year: **1918**
Engine: **Benz Bz.IV 6-cylinder liquid-cooled inline, 220 hp**
Wingspan: **44 ft 8.75 in (13.62 m)**
Length: **22 ft 8.5 in (6.92 m)**
Height: **11 ft 0.25 in (3.36 m)**
Weight: **2,730 lbs (1,365 kg)**
Maximum speed: **106 mph (170 kph)**
Ceiling: **16,405 ft (5,000 m)**
Endurance: **3 hrs 30 mins**
Armament: **2 machine-guns**
Crew: **2**

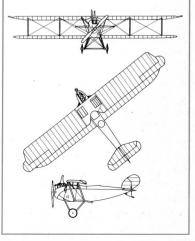

Fokker D VII

The great importance of the Fokker D VII as a fighting plane is indirectly revealed by one of the clauses of the Armistice agreement. In Article IV, all Fokker D VIIs were mentioned as part of the war material that the defeated Germans had to hand over the Allies, for the D VII was unanimously considered the finest German fighter of the war. It was the last effort of the German war industry to control the air. Although it was slower than the best French and British fighters, the D VII was generally superior to the Spad S.XIII, the S.E.5a, and the Sopwith Camel. And the F version of the D.VII had very good rate of climb and gave excellent performance at high altitudes.

Reinhold Platz designed the D VII

late in 1917. The prototype was given the factory designation of Fokker V 11. It was presented at the German D-type competition at Adlershof in January and February 1918. The plane proved far superior to the other contestants (about 30 of them) and the pilots who tested it were very enthusiastic. One of these pilots was Manfred von Richthofen, who recommended some minor changes before the plane went into production. A first order was placed for 400 planes to be manufactured by Fokker. Other sizeable orders were given to Albatros and O.A.W. Total orders were placed for 2,000 planes, but only about 1,000 were built before the end of the war.

The first D VIIs entered service in April 1918, and the first consignment

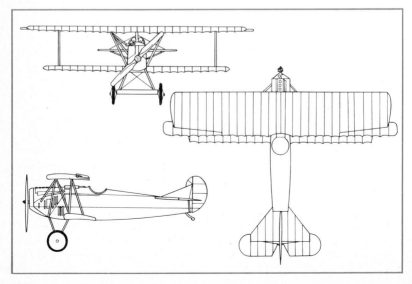

went to Manfred von Richthofen's famous *Jagdgeschwader Nr.* 1. It was customary at the time to supply the best squadrons first, giving preference to the squadron's most experienced pilots. The various Albatros and Pfalz fighters were slowly replaced by the Fokker D VII, and many units had to wait several weeks for the new fighter. A month before the Armistice about 800 Fokkers were in front-line service, and most squadrons had at least a few of them.

The Fokker D VII was strong, fast, manoeuvrable and, above all, superb at high altitudes. And performance was improved with the F variant (which came out in August) which was powered by a 185-hp B.M.W. IIIa engine. The F version was comparable with the original in speed and manoeuvrability, but its B.M.W. could maintain a high power output up to 19,685 feet (6,000 m). Rate of climb was also improved. The D VIIF took 14 minutes to reach an altitude of 16,405 feet (5,000 m), while the D VII

Aircraft: **Fokker D VII**
Manufacturer: **Fokker Flugzeug-Werke G.m.b.H.**
Type: **Fighter**
Year: **1918**
Engine: **Mercedes D III 6-cylinder liquid-cooled inline, 160 hp**
Wingspan: **29 ft 3.5 in (8.9 m)**
Length: **22 ft 11.5 in (7 m)**
Height: **9 ft 2.25 in (2.75 m)**
Weight: **1,870 lbs (850 kg)**
Maximum speed: **124 mph (200 kph) at sea level**
Ceiling: **19,685 ft (6,000 m)**
Endurance: **1 hr 30 mins**
Armament: **2 machine-guns**
Crew: **1**

with its Mercedes engine took 38 minutes.

When the war ended, Fokker fighters continued to be manufactured in Holland, where Anthony Fokker clandestinely transferred 400 engines and the dismantled parts of 120 C I and D VII planes. The fighter's career continued for some years, and the D VII served in the Dutch air force both at home and in the colonies. Some planes, spoils of war, were converted into two-seaters by the Belgian air force and saw training duty until 1926.

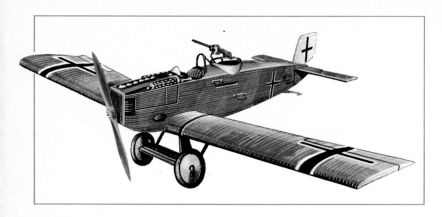

Junkers CL I

The Junkers CL I was developed from
the D I monoplane fighter, and kept
the basic structure of steel tube covered with corrugated metal skinning.
It was designed by Hugo Junkers and
flew for the first time on May 4, 1918.
Production began that summer, and a
total of 47 planes was built. The CL I
was strong, agile, and quite fast. And
it was well-armed: machine-guns, and
bomb-racks on the sides of the fuselage. The plane carried anti-
personnel bombs for use on ground
attack missions. The CL I turned out
to be the best German ground attack
plane of the war, but only a few
aircraft got to the front before the war
ended. A seaplane version of the CL I
was developed in 1918. Although it
was faster than the original (112 mph,
or 180 kph), the seaplane did not get
beyond the prototype stage. The
gunner's field of fire from his raised
cockpit was excellent.

Aircraft: **Junkers CL I**
Manufacturer: **Junkers Flugzeug-Werke A.G.**
Type: **Ground attack**
Year: **1918**
Engine: **Mercedes D IIIa 6-cylinder liquid-cooled inline, 180 hp**
Wingspan: **39 ft 6 in (12.04 m)**
Length: **25 ft 11 in (7.9 m)**
Height: **7 ft 8.5 in (2.65 m)**
Weight: **2,310 lbs (1,050 kg)**
Maximum speed: **100 mph (161 kph)**
Ceiling: **19,685 ft (6,000 m)**
Endurance: **2 hrs**
Armament: **3 machine-guns; few bombs**
Crew: **2**

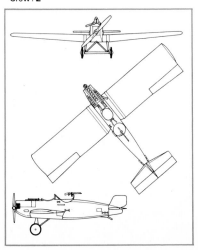

Pfalz D XII

Like other excellent German planes
that appeared during the last year of
the war, the Pfalz D XII was not quite
up to the level of the Fokker D VII.
The plane was evaluated at Aldershof
in the second D-type competition,
between May 27 and June 21, 1918,
and the version powered by a Mercedes engine was put into production.
About 800 D XIIs were built and
delivered to fighter units, where the
Fokker D VII was already in service.
Unfortunately, the direct comparison
of the two planes reduced pilots' confidence in the Pfalz's capabilities. The
Pfalz was not as much an all-round
performer as the D VII, but it was still
a very strong, fast and manoeuvrable
aircraft. And it stood up well in combat. Some variant models of the D XII
came out before the Armistice.
Among them was the D XV, tested
during the very last days of the war,
with a 185-hp B.M.W IIIa engine.

Aircraft: **Pfalz D XII**
Manufacturer: **Pfalz Flugzeug-Werke**
Type: **Fighter**
Year: **1918**
Engine: **Mercedes D IIIa 6-cylinder liquid-
cooled inline, 180 hp**
Wingspan: **29 ft 6.5 in (9 m)**
Length: **20 ft 10 in (6.35 m)**
Height: **8 ft 10.25 in (2.7 m)**
Weight: **1,989 lbs (902 kg)**
Maximum speed: **106 mph (170 kph) at
9,842 ft (3,000 m)**
Ceiling: **18,537 ft (5,650 m)**
Endurance: **2 hrs 30 mins**
Armament: **2 machine-guns**
Crew: **1**

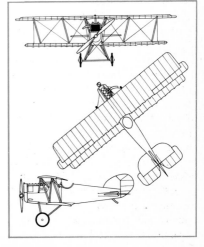

Fokker E V/D VIII

The Fokker V 26/28 reached an altitude of 19,685 feet (6,000 m) in 16 minutes. It was a record performance, but rate of climb was only one of the excellent features that made the Fokker V 26/28 the best plane to take part in the second fighter plane competition at Aldershof. The E V type, one of the last First World War Fokker fighters, lived up to the reputation of its illustrious predecessors: it was fast, easy to handle, and formidable in combat, even though it was powered by a rotary engine, which was considered outdated at the time.

The E V project was developed by the same Reinhold Platz who had created other almost legendary planes. In his search for simplicity and efficiency, Platz turned out several monoplanes with parasol wings and various types of engines, but all marked by an extremely functional structure. The fuselage had a steel tube framework, and the cantilever wing was made of wood and joined to the fuselage by a simple pyramidal arrangement of steel struts. The three prototypes presented at Aldershof in the summer of 1918 were powered by different engines: the 110-hp Oberursel UR II rotary (V 26), the 145-hp Oberursel UR III rotary, and the 160-hp Goebel Goe.III rotary (in two V 28s), and a 'stationary' 195-hp Benz (V 27). The armament of all three consisted of two fixed and synchronized LMG 08/15 machine-guns.

The winning version was put into production with a first order for 400 planes. The aircraft was to have been equipped with the 145-hp Oberursel

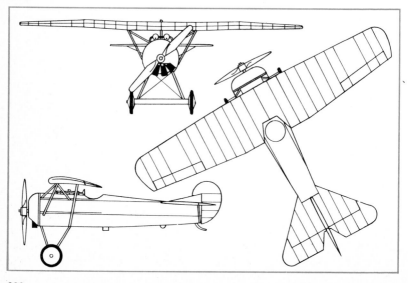

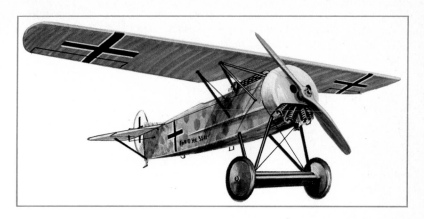

rotary engine or the 200-hp Goebel Goe.III, but there was a delay in the final production of both engines. So the 110-hp Thulin-built Le Rhône and the 110-hp Oberursel UR II engines were both used. The first planes, which had been given the military designation E V, were delivered at the end of July and became operational with *Jagdstaffel* 6 one week later. But the plane had a series of bad accidents. Three planes crashed within two weeks, all three because the wings broke off. The E V was grounded, and production halted, while the inquiry board got to work. Like the Dr I triplane before it, the E V was found to be free from design and structural defects. The accidents were caused by unsuitable materials or errors in assembly. When production was resumed, the plane was redesignated D VIII. The board of inquiry demanded no changes in the plane.

Delivery had been delayed, of course, and the planes reached the front late in October. The first planes

Aircraft: **Fokker E V/D VIII**
Manufacturer: **Fokker Flugzeug-Werke G.m.b.H.**
Type: **Fighter**
Year: **1918**
Engine: **Oberursel UR II 9-cylinder air-cooled rotary, 110 hp**
Wingspan: **27 ft 6.75 in (8.4 m)**
Length: **19 ft 4 in (5.865 m)**
Height: **9 ft 3 in (2.82 m)**
Weight: **1,238 lbs (562 kg)**
Maximum speed: **115 mph (185 kph) at sea level**
Ceiling: **20,670 ft (6,300 m)**
Endurance: **1 hr 30 mins**
Armament: **2 machine-guns**
Crew: **1**

went into action on October 24. By November 1, 1918, 85 planes were in service with seven *Jagdstaffeln*. In barely three weeks of combat, and despite the low power of its Le Rhône and Oberursel engines, the D VIII proved its mettle in battle. While not as agile as the Dr I triplane, it was much easier to handle than the D VII. It was generally considered a fine fighting plane, for although it was slower than the latest types, it had superb altitude performance and was very agile.

Minor types

1914 Otto B – Wingspan: 49 ft (14.94 m) – Length: 35 ft 4.75 in (10.79 m) – Maximum speed: 68 mph (109 kph) – Engine: Mercedes, 100 hp. Developed from the pusher biplanes of prewar days, it was used until early 1915 as a bomber and reconnaissance plane. Slow but sure and reliable, the Otto B was part of a special unit set up for bombing Great Britain. It played a minor part in the first night raid over Dunkirk in January 1915.

1914 Etrich Taube (Albatros) – Wingspan: 50 ft (15.24 m) – Length: 34 ft (10.36 m) – Maximum speed: 64 mph (103 kph) – Engine: Mercedes, 100 hp. The monoplane designed by the Austrian Igo Etrich in 1910 was the first of a whole series of planes similar in concept and form, but different in size and performance, produced by about 10 different companies. At the outbreak of war the planes were already outdated.

1915 Siemens-Schuckert R I. – Wingspan: 91 ft 10.5 in (28 m) – Length: 57 ft 5 in (17.5 m) – Maximum speed: 69 mph (110 kph) – Engines: Three Benz, 150 hp each. Designed by Franz and Bruno Steffen, the 'R' giant Siemens-Schuckerts turned out in 1915 were among the first German heavy bombers. The concept behind them was quite original: the three engines were inside the fuselage but drove propellers set between the wings.

1915 L.F.G. Roland C II – Wingspan: 33 ft 9.5 in (10.3 m) – Length: 25 ft 3.25 in (7.7 m) – Maximum speed: 103 mph (165 kph) – Engine: Mercedes, 160 hp. Nicknamed *Walfisch* (Whale) because of the shape of the fuselage, the C II model was produced by Roland in October 1915, and had a great influence on later German designs. It started its career as a reconnaissance plane and ended up as a two-seater fighter.

1916 Albatros W 4 – Wingspan: 31 ft 2 in (9.5 m) – Length: 27 ft 10.75 in (8.5 m) – Maximum speed: 100 mph (161 kph) – Engine: Mercedes, 160 hp. The Albatros W 4 floatplane fighter was based on the landplane D I and D II, and deliveries began in September 1916. The following year it served at German seaplane bases and proved to be fast and efficient. It remained in combat until the arrival of the two-seater Hansa-Brandenburg W 12, which was better protected against attack from above.

1916 Albatros G II – Wingspan: 55 ft 9.75 in (17.01 m) – Length: 39 ft 1 in (11.91 m) – Maximum speed: — Engines: Two Benz, 150 hp each. This attempt to build a multi-engined bomber was a smaller version of the 1916 prototype G I, which had four engines. The G II did not come up to par, and another version followed, the G III.

1916 Siemens-Schuckert DI – Wingspan: 24 ft 7.5 in (7.5 m) – Length: 19 ft 8.25 in (6 m) – Maximum speed: 97 mph (155 kph) – Engine: Siemens-Halske rotary, 110 hp. When the Fokker monoplanes were outmatched in summer 1916, the Germans were so impressed by the new French Nieuport fighters that they decided to copy them. The DI was an almost exact copy of the Nieuport 17, except for the engine and the nose.

1916 Sablatnig SF 2 – Wingspan: 60 ft 9.5 in (18.53 m) – Length: 31 ft 3 in (9.525 m) – Maximum speed: 81 mph (130 kph) – Engine: Mercedes, 160 hp. Designed by Joseph Sablatnig, the SF 2 was derived from the SF 1 of 1915. Twenty-six were built, and delivered between June 1916 and May 1917 as training seaplanes for navy pilots. A two-seater biplane with twin floats, the SF 2 never made a really good combat plane (even in later variants).

1917 Pfalz Dr I – Wingspan: 28 ft 0.5 in (8.55 m) – Length: 18 ft 0.5 in (5.5 m) – Maximum speed: 103 mph (165 kph) – Engine: Siemens-Halske rotary, 160 hp. The appearance and success of the Sopwith Triplane led German makers to copy the formula in an attempt to develop a plane to match the English fighter. There were numerous attempts, and the Pfalz triplane was fairly successful. But it was not on a level with the Fokker Dr I.

1917 Sablatnig N I – Wingspan: 52 ft 6 in (16 m) – Length: 28 ft 6.5 in (8.7 m) – Maximum speed: 78 mph (125 kph) – Engine: Benz, 200 hp. Better known for its seaplanes, the Sablatnig firm also built landplanes. The N I was the night bombing version of the C I, developed in 1917. This large two-seater biplane was completely equipped for night flight.

1917 Albatros J I – Wingspan: 46 ft 4.75 in (14.14 m) – Length: 28 ft 11.75 in (8.83 m) – Maximum speed: 87.5 mph (140 kph) – Engine: Benz, 200 hp. Designed as a close support plane, this was very much like the C XII, especially in the wings and empennage. The front part of the fuselage, with the fuel tanks and cockpits, was armour-plated. Although the engine turned out to be highly vulnerable in combat, the plane was employed up to the end of the war and was very popular.

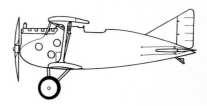

1917 Rumpler D I – Wingspan: 27 ft 7.5 in (8.42 m) – Length: 18 ft 10.5 in (5.75 m) – Maximum speed: 113 mph (180 kph) – Engine: Mercedes, 160 hp. After its successful series of reconnaissance planes, the E. Rumpler *Flugzeug-Werke* tried to develop a single-seater biplane fighter. The project began in 1917 and went through various types. The final version was the D I, which proved unsuitable for combat.

Minor types

1917 L.F.G. Roland D II – Wingspan: 29 ft 4 in (8.94 m) – Length: 22 ft 9 in (6.93 m)– Maximum speed: 112.5 mph (180 kph) – Engine: Mercedes, 160 hp. From the successful C II a single-seater version was later developed. This plane, the D II, went into action at the start of 1917. It was a good fighter, but it could not compete with the various Albatros models, then at the height of their fame. As a result, it was used chiefly on the Eastern Front and in Macedonia.

1918 Hansa-Brandenburg W 29 – Wingspan: 44 ft 3.5 in (13.5 m) – Length: 30 ft 8.5 in (9.36 m) – Maximum speed: 109 mph (175 kph) – Engine: Benz, 150 hp. Ernst Heinkel developed a completely new type of seaplane towards the end of 1917: a two-seater low-wing monoplane. It was a great success, thanks to its excellent performance and fire power. Allied planes operating in the North Sea sector considered it a formidable adversary.

1918 Hannover CL III – Wingspan: 38 ft 4.75 in (11.7 m) – Length: 24 ft 10.5 in (7.58 m) – Maximum speed: 103 mph (165 kph) – Engine: Argus, 180 hp. One of the final versions of a successful biplane developed by the *Hannoversche Waggonfabrik*. It was designed in 1917, and 357 CL IIIs were subsequently built. They were widely used during the summer and autumn of 1918. The plane was very easy to handle.

1918 Dornier D I– Wingspan: 25 ft 7 in (7.8 m) – Length: 20 ft 11 in (6.37 m) – Maximum speed: 125 mph (201 kph) – Engine: B.M.W., 185 hp. This biplane fighter was of very advanced design. The wings required no struts, thanks to their metal structure and partial Duralumin covering. But the top wing broke away during test flights at Adlershof, and the plane did not go into general production.

1918 Albatros D XI – Wingspan: 26 ft 3 in (8 m) – Length: 18 ft 3.75 in (5.58 m) – Maximum speed: 119 mph (190 kph) – Engine: Siemens-Halske rotary, 160 hp. This plane appeared early in 1918 and marked a change in the Albatros tradition of inline engines. The D XI had a Siemens-Halske rotary engine. Two prototypes were built, the second of which was tested at Aldershof in April 1918. The D XI was inferior to the other designs.

1918 Junkers J I – Wingspan: 52 ft 6 in (16 m) – Length: 29 ft 10.5 in (9.1 m) – Maximum speed: 97 mph (155 kph) – Engine: Benz, 200 hp. Designed by Hugo Junkers as a close support plane for ground troops, this was the best German armoured aircraft of the First World War. The front section, housing engine, crew, and fuel tank, was a single shell 5-mm (.2-in) thick. The rest was covered with corrugated metal skinning.

Austria-Hungary

Thirty-six aircraft, a dirigible, and 10 balloons made up the fighting power of the Austro-Hungarian air force at the start of the First World War. The planes were chiefly the *Taube* type, with a few Lohner biplanes. Austrian military leaders had not been particularly interested in developing air power, but the war set them to reorganizing and strengthening their forces. Austria-Hungary had some excellent domestically-manufactured engines, including the Daimler and the Hiero, and engines of these types powered most of the new planes.

And Austria-Hungary soon put fairly good planes of her own into action, including Lohners, Brandenburgs, and Lloyds, along with German planes built under licence. The Oeffag company manufactured about 20 Albatros D IIs, an outstanding plane. Austrian air power increased the following year, with the appearance of such fighters as the Aviatik D I designed by von Berg, Oeffag's Albatros D III, and the Gotha G IV.

The first two were the most successful fighters. In 1917, there was a radical reorganization of the Austro-Hungarian air forces, and three squadron types were established: *Aufklärungskompagnien* (reconnaissance companies), for reconnaissance and artillery-spotting, equipped with eight or ten C-class two-seaters and three or four escort fighters; *Jagdkompagnien* (fighter companies), with 16 to 20 fighter planes; and *Geschwader* or *Fliegerkompagnien-G* (bomber companies), with 10 bombers and four escort fighters. During the last year of the war, five new nationally-built planes appeared: the Phönix C I, the Ufag C I, and the Phönix D I, D II, and D III. Fighter units were increased to 13. Unlike the army air units, navy units always suffered from a lack of war material; only 13 seaplanes were turned out in 1914, 75 in 1915, 102 in 1916, 231 in 1917, and 170 in 1918. In the bitter fighting on the Italian front, the top Austrian ace was Godwin Brumowski, with 40 kills.

Lloyd C II

The C-class reconnaissance planes built by *Ungarische* Lloyd *Flugzeug* were already in service before war broke out. They remained in service during the first 30 months of hostilities, especially on the Italian and Romanian fronts. The first version (C I) set a world altitude record in the summer of 1914, carrying one passenger and pilot Heinrich Bier to an altitude of more than 20,240 feet (6,170 m). The C II version, of which about 100 were built, appeared in 1915. It had a different engine, incorporated structural changes and had a greater wingspan, and was the first Lloyd variant to be armed: the observer had a Schwarzlose machine-gun. This plane was followed by other production models, the C III, C IV, and C V, which kept the main features of the basic model. They had more powerful engines and some minor changes in structure. The Lloyd C-class were not very adequate aircraft.

296

Aircraft: **Lloyd C II**
Manufacturer: **Ungarische Lloyd Flugzeug und Motorenfabrik A.G.**
Type: **Reconnaissance**
Year: **1915**
Engine: **Hiero 6-cylinder liquid-cooled in-line, 145 hp**
Wingspan: **45 ft 11 in (14 m)**
Length: **29 ft 6 in (9 m)**
Height: **11 ft 2 in (3.4 m)**
Weight: **2,976 lbs (1,350 kg)**
Maximum speed: **79.5 mph (128 kph)**
Ceiling: **9,842 ft (3,000 m)**
Endurance: **2 hrs 30 mins**
Armament: **1 machine-gun**
Crew: **2**

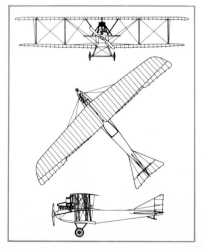

Aviatik B II

The Germans and Austro-Hungarians made good use of this reconnaissance plane until 1916. It was built by the *Oesterreichische-Ungarische Flugzeugfabrik* of Vienna and was a variant of the B I two-seater produced between 1914 and 1915 by the German *Automobil und Aviatik* company in Leipzig. The main difference between the two planes was the shape of the rudder and elevators, as well as the engine. A small series of the Austrian Aviatik B II was turned out in 1915. The B III version was the first to provide armament for the observer, and the overall structure of the plane was improved. Flight performance was lower, however; and the B III was nicknamed 'the gondola' for its tendency to rock at the slightest disturbance. The B II and B III were not outstanding planes, but they served at the front until early 1916, when they were reassigned to training duty.

Aircraft: **Aviatik B II**
Manufacturer: **Oesterreichische-Ungarische Flugzeugfabrik Aviatik**
Type: **Reconnaissance**
Year: **1915**
Engine: **Austro-Daimler 6-cylinder liquid-cooled inline, 120 hp**
Wingspan: **46 ft (14.02 m)**
Length: **26 ft 3 in (8 m)**
Height: **10 ft 6 in (3.2 m)**
Weight: **1,918 lbs (870 kg)**
Maximum speed: **68 mph (109 kph)**
Ceiling: **8,202 ft (2,500 m)**
Endurance: **4 hrs**
Armament: **44 lbs (20 kg) of bombs**
Crew: **2**

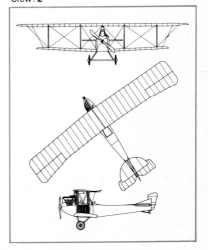

Hansa-Brandenburg C I

The Hansa-Brandenburg C I was designed by Ernst Heinkel and built in Austria by Phönix and Ufag, which turned out a total of 18 series of the plane. Apart from slight changes, the main difference between variants involved the type and power of their engines. These ranged from the 160-hp Austro-Daimler of series 23 and 26, to the 230-hp Hiero of series 429, the 160-hp Mercedes of series 63, and the 300-hp Hiero of series 69. The Hansa-Brandenburg C I entered service in spring 1916 and was used for reconnaissance, artillery-spotting, and light bombing until the war ended. Crews liked it for its easy handling, and its flight performance steadily improved as more powerful engines were installed. The plane was also used on night bombing missions, an operational task in which the C I's good air field performance was useful.

Aircraft: **Hansa-Brandenburg C I**
Manufacturer: **Phönix Flugzenug-Werke A.G. & Ungarische Flugzeugfabrik A.G.**
Type: **Reconnaissance**
Year: **1916**
Engine: **Austro-Daimler 6-cylinder liquid-cooled inline 160 hp**
Wingspan: **40 ft 2.23 in (12.25 m)**
Length: **27 ft 8.75 in (8.45 m)**
Height: **10 ft 11 in (3.32 m)**
Weight: **2,888 lbs (1,310 kg)**
Maximum speed: **87 mph (140 kph)**
Ceiling: **19,028 ft (5,800 m)**
Endurance: **3 hrs**
Armament: **2 machine-guns; 132 lbs (60 kg) of bombs**
Crew: **2**

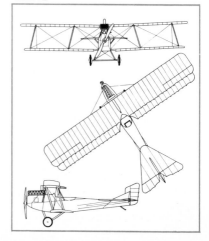

Lohner C I

The Lohner C I was the last model of a series of planes built by the Jacob Lohner company of Vienna, which was well-known for its seaplanes. The first variant (model B) was designed in 1913. When war broke out, the B I appeared, an unarmed two-seater that saw service in the early months of the war. Armament was installed on the B IV, which came out in 1915 as the successor to the mediocre B II. The B IV, with its 100-hp Mercedes engine, lost much of its power when it rose above 6,561 feet (2,000 m). The next two versions, the B VI and B VII, were better. The last model to be produced, the C I, reached reconnaissance units early in 1916. This plane kept the structural variations of the later models, but the sweep of the wings was reduced, the struts were simplified, and other general improvements were made. The plane remained in service for one year.

Aircraft: **Lohner C I**
Manufacturer: **Jakob Lohner A.G.**
Type: **Reconnaissance**
Year: **1916**
Engine: **Austro-Daimler 6-cylinder liquid-cooled inline, 160 hp**
Wingspan: **44 ft 1.5 in (13.46 m)**
Length: **30 ft 3 in (9.22 m)**
Height: **10 ft 8 in (3.25m)**
Weight: **2,998 lbs (1,360 kg)**
Maximum speed: **85 mph (137 kph) at sea level**
Ceiling: **11,482 ft (3,500 m)**
Endurance: **3 hrs**
Armament: **1 machine-gun**
Crew: **2**

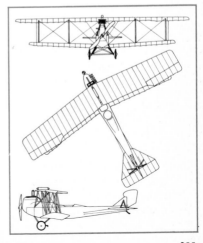

Hansa-Brandenburg D I

Although the Hansa-Brandenburg D I was not a very satisfactory combat plane, it remained in service until the middle of 1917. The fighter was not one of Ernst Heinkel's best designs. The plane was unstable, and the pilot's visibility was limited. After several accidents had occurred in autumn 1916, when the plane went into service, the D I came to be known as the 'Coffin'. A construction licence for the D I was given to the Austrian Phönix and Ufag companies. The two companies each produced about 100 planes in two models that differed in engine type and power. The structure of the small biplane was traditional (wood covered with canvas and plywood). The wing struts were wood-covered steel tubes joined together at the centre in a star shape. For this reason the plane was given a new, and less gruesome nickname: *Spinne*, or Spider.

Aircraft: **Hansa-Brandenburg D I**
Manufacturer: **Phönix Flugzeug-Werke A.G. & Ungarische Flugzeugfabrick A.G.**
Type: **Fighter**
Year: **1916**
Engine: **Austro-Daimler 6-cylinder liquid-cooled inline, 160 hp**
Wingspan: **27 ft 10.75 in (8.51 m)**
Length: **20 ft 10 in (6.35 m)**
Height: **9 ft 2.25 in (2.79 m)**
Weight: **2,024 lbs (917 kg)**
Maximum speed: **116 mph (187 kph)**
Ceiling: **16,405 ft (5,000 m)**
Endurance: **2 hrs 30 mins**
Armament: **1 machine-gun**

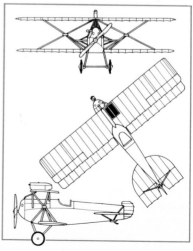

Hansa–Brandenburg CC

Designed by Ernst Heinkel early in 1916, the Hansa-Brandenburg CC seaplane was used chiefly by the Austro-Hungarian navy. The planes were built under licence by Phönix and went into service late in 1916. They had a central hull with two floats at the tips of the lower wings. The engine, which drove a pusher propeller, was set on a steel-tube mounting below the upper wing. The wings were similar to those of the D I single-seater and had the same star-shaped struts as Heinkel's other design. The cockpit was in the forward part of the hull, and the pilot had a Schwarzlose machine-gun. The Austro-Hungarian navy designated this seaplane 'Class A', and a great many were used in defence of Adriatic ports. The CC was a match for its main adversary, the Italian Nieuport 11. The initials CC stood for Camillo Castiglione, owner of the Hansa-Brandenburg company.

Aircraft: **Hansa-Brandenburg CC**
Manufacturer: **Phönix Flugzeug-Werke A.G.**
Type: **Fighter**
Year: **1916**
Engine: **Benz Bz.III 6-cylinder liquid-cooled inline, 150 hp**
Wingspan: **30 ft 6 in (9.3 m)**
Length: **25 ft 1 in (7.65 m)**
Height: **10 ft 6 in (3.2 m)**
Weight: **2,989 lbs (1,356 kg)**
Maximum Speed: **108.75 mph (175 kph)**
Ceiling: —
Endurance: **3 hrs 30 mins**
Armament: **1 machine-gun**
Crew: **1**

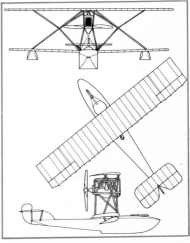

Aviatik D I

This plane was designed by Julius von Berg and was the first, and finest, all-Austrian fighter of the war. The prototype appeared early in 1917. A total of 1,200 planes were ordered, but only about 700 were built. The Aviatik D I replaced the unsatisfactory Hansa-Brandenburg D I. Various models were built, and different engines were installed. Other improvements were continually made. The machine-gun mounted on the upper wing was replaced by two synchronized weapons set over the instrument panel. But the various D Is never eliminated the plane's one defect, continual overheating problems with the Austro-Daimler engine.

The early problems with structural weaknesses were soon overcome, and the D I soon showed that its high rate of climb and good turn of speed made it a more than adequate fighter. The D II was just too late for the war.

Aircraft: **Aviatik D I**
Manufacturer: **Osterreichische-Ungarische Flugzeugfabrik Aviatik**
Type: **Fighter**
Year: **1917**
Engine: **Austro-Daimler 6-cylinder liquid-cooled inline, 200 hp**
Wingspan: **26 ft 3 in (8 m)**
Length: **22 ft 9.5 in (9.65 m)**
Height: **8 ft 2 in (2.48 m)**
Weight: **1,878 lbs (852 kg)**
Maximum speed: **115 mph (185 kph)**
Ceiling: **20,177 ft (6,150 m)**
Endurance: **2 hrs 30 mins**
Armament: **2 machine-guns**
Crew: **1**

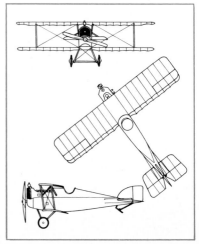

Phönix C I

The Phönix C I was derived from the Hansa-Brandenburg C II, designed in Germany by Ernst Heinkel in 1916. In Austria, the plane was manufactured by the Phönix *Flugzeug-Werke*, which built about 100 examples. This reconnaissance aircraft had a long and narrow fuselage that gave the pilot excellent visibility and the observer a wide field of fire. In addition its standard defensive armament (two machine-guns, one fixed and synchronized), the plane could carry up to 110 pounds (50 kg) of bombs. The Phönix C I went into active service in spring 1918 and remained in service up to the end of the war. After the war it was built in Sweden under licence. The Swedish Army's construction department built 30 planes powered by 220-hp Benz inline engines. The Swedish C Is were used as first-line reconnaissance aircraft right up until the late 1920s.

Aircraft: **Phönix C I**
Manufacturer: **Phönix Flugzeug-Werke**
Type: **Reconnaissance**
Year: **1918**
Engine: **Hiero 6-cylinder liquid-cooled in-line, 230 hp**
Wingspan: **36 ft 1 in (10.99 m)**
Length: **24 ft 8 in (7.52 m)**
Height: **9 ft 8 in (2.95 m)**
Weight: **2,436 lbs (1,105 kg)**
Maximum speed: **110 mph (177 kph) at sea level**
Ceiling: **17,715 ft (5,400 m)**
Endurance: **3 hrs 30 mins**
Armament: **2 machine-guns; 110 lbs (50 kg) of bombs**

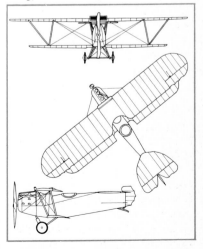

Ufag C I

Like the Phönix C I, the Ufag C I was also derived from Ernst Heinkel's Hansa-Brandenburg C II. The Ufag C I was manufactured in Austria by the *Ungarische Flugzeugfabrik*. Although the C Is of Phönix and Ufag sprang from the same origin, they were developed in complete independence of each other. In comparative tests carried out in 1917, they demonstrated very different qualities. For example, the Ufag C I was inferior to the Phönix in take-off, climb, and high altitude flight, but the Ufag model was far more manoeuvrable and much faster than its rival. As a result, both designs were put into production, and the two planes were assigned to different duties. The Phönix C I carried out high-altitude reconnaissance missions, while the Ufag C I was employed on reconnaissance missions at relatively low altitudes and in artillery-spotting.

Aircraft: **Ufag C I**
Manufacturer: **Ungarische Flugzeugfabrik**
Type: **Reconnaissance**
Year: **1918**
Engine: **Hiero 6-cylinder liquid-cooled in-line, 230 hp**
Wingspan: **35 ft 2 in (10.69 m)**
Length: **23 ft 7.5 in (7.2 m)**
Height: **9 ft 7 in (2.92 m)**
Weight: **2.315 lbs (1,050 kg)**
Maximum speed: **118 mpg (190 kph)**
Ceiling: **16,075 ft (4,900 m)**
Endurance: **3 hrs**
Armament: **2-3 machine-guns**
Crew: **2**

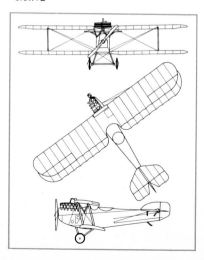

Phönix D I

Efforts by the Phönix company to improve the Hansa-Brandenburg D I led to the construction of a new prototype about the middle of 1917. The new plane differed in structure and wing form, and it had a more powerful engine. During testing, this Phönix fighter proved to be extremely fast. It was a good climber but rather hard to handle. Three series of 50 planes each were ordered. The new fighter entered action in February 1918. The D I served alongside the Albatros D III and the Aviatik D I in several *Jagdkompagnien* and proved itself a match for Italian Hanriots and Spads. In June the plane was also adopted by the navy, which assigned it to maritime patrol duty and naval defence in the northern Adriatic. The D II had balanced ailerons on the upper wings and the D III, which appeared in 1918, had ailerons on both the upper and the lower wings.

Aircraft: **Phönix D I**
Manufacturer: **Phönix Flugzeug-Werke**
Type: **Fighter**
Year: **1918**
Engine: **Hiero 6-cylinder liquid-cooled in-line, 200 hp**
Wingspan: **32 ft (9.75 m)**
Length: **21 ft 7.5 in (6.62 m)**
Height: **9 ft 2 in (2.79 m)**
Weight: **1,775 lbs (805 kg)**
Maximum speed: **112.5 mph (180 kph)**
Ceiling: **19,685 ft (6,000 m)**
Endurance: **2 hrs**
Armament: **2 machine-guns**
Crew: **1**

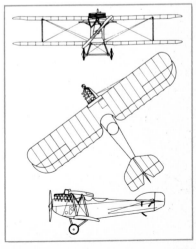

Engines

Fifteen years of aircraft development, between 1903 and 1918, led to rapid developments in engine-building and design techniques. The Wright brothers' first flight was powered by a low-powered home-made engine. The last years of the First World War produced highly sophisticated and very powerful aero engines.

But between the first engine and these last ones, there were various engines that marked important steps forward in that development. The eight types illustrated here all made decisive contributions to the history of aviation. They represent technological advances, and some of them were involved in famous flights. Suffice it to mention the important role that the Antoinette V-8 played in the very early years of aviation, and what it meant to the men and their machines. When it appeared on the scene, it solved a host of problems that had been plaguing designers and pilots. Yet Louis Blériot's exploits in 1909 were made possible in large part by a 3-cylinder engine that was not altogether reliable, the 25-hp Anzani.

The appearance of the rotary engine marked another phase. Despite its technical limitations, this engine made possible an important advance in the evolution of the aeroplane. The return of stationary engines – inline, inline V, radial – represented a return to traditional technology, and stationary engines were to characterize aviation until the 1940s when again war stimulated the design of new engines.

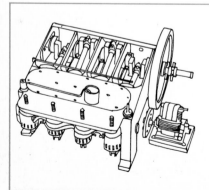

Wright – 1903 (USA)

The first engine to be installed successfully in an aeroplane. It was designed by the Wright brothers and powered their 1903 Flyer I. With four inline cylinders, this water-cooled engine generated 12 hp at 1,090 rpm; it had a dry weight of about 179 lbs (81.2 kg). It incorporated some new technical features: it had five main bearings and a fixed and pre-adjustable fuel-injection system.

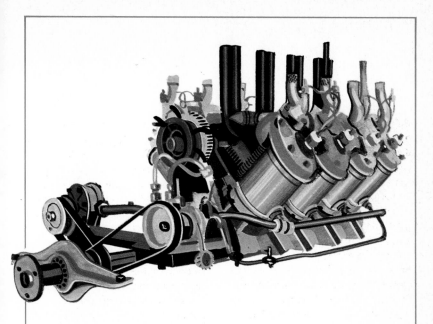

Antoinette – 1906 (F)

Designed and built in France by Léon Levavasseur, this became Europe's most widely-used engine until 1909-10. An 8-cylinder, 90° V with evaporation cooling and direct fuel-injection, highly advanced technical characteristics made the Antoinette safe, strong and fairly powerful, generating 50 hp at 1,100 rpm.

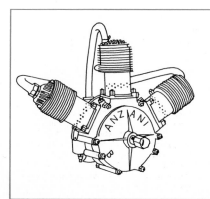

Anzani – 1909 (F)

This was the engine that powered Louis Blériot's monoplane on its crossing of the English Channel in 1909. It was a 3-cylinder, air-cooled, semi-radial engine, developing 25 hp at 1,600 rpm. Its power was relatively low for such a long flight. The engine had automatic inlet valves and mechanically operated exhaust valves, with auxiliary exhaust ports in the cylinders.

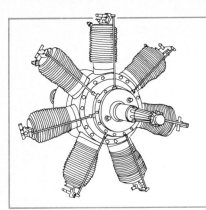

Gnome 50 hp – 1909 (F)

This engine revolutionized aviation.
Designed in France by the Seguin brothers,
it was the first of a long line of ever more
powerful engines that were produced
throughout the First World War. It was a
typical rotary engine : the crankshaft was
fixed, while the cylinders and crankcase
rotated, carrying the propeller with them.
This principle had been introduced by the
Australian Lawrence Hargrave in 1887.

Le Rhône 80 hp – 1913 (F)

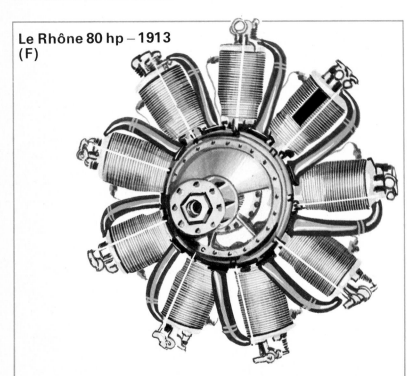

One of the war's most popular engines,
thanks to its power and reliability. Many
Allied fighters had this rotary engine. The
torque reaction and the gyroscopic effect of
the cylinders made planes powered by it
extremely easy to handle.

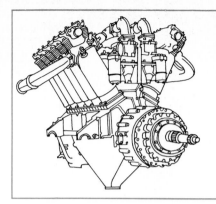

Rolls-Royce Eagle – 1915 (GB)

This liquid-cooled V-12 was developed in 1915 by Rolls-Royce; with its 'younger brother' the Falcon, it marked the beginning of a famous line of aviation engines that produced the immortal Merlins and Griffons of the Second World War. Developed in several versions, it culminated with the 375-hp Mark VII of 1917. It powered the Vimy that Alcock and Brown flew across the Atlantic in June 1919.

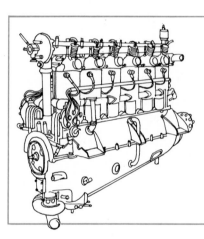

Mercedes 180 hp – 1917 (G)

This famous engine powered some of the best-known German fighter planes in the last two years of the war (Albatros D V, Fokker D VII, and Pfalz D XII). It was a class-III engine, the German designation of engines between 130 and 195 hp. This engine generated 180 hp at 1,400 rpm. It was a classic of the 6-cylinder liquid-cooled inline formula developed by Mercedes at the very start of the war.

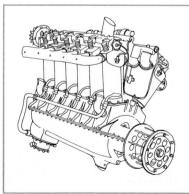

Liberty 400 hp – 1917 (USA)

This V-12 was one of the war's most powerful engines. Thousands were built. It powered the 1918 Packard Le Père-Lusac 11. The Liberty was liquid-cooled and generated 400 hp at 1,750 rpm.

Summary of Aviation History from the Origins – 1918

1783   **June 4** – The first public demonstration of a lighter-than-air machine. At Annonay, France, the Montgolfier brothers send up an unmanned hot-air balloon.

September 19 – Versailles, the Montgolfiers 'fly' animals in a hot-air balloon.

November 21 – In Paris, Pilâtre de Rozier and François d'Arlandes make the first balloon flight, almost two miles (3 km) in 25 minutes.

1785   **January 7** – Blanchard and Jeffries are the first men to fly a balloon across the English Channel.

June 15 – The first victims of a lighter-than-air machine: Romain and de Rozier die when their hydrogen and hot air balloon catches fire.

1868   **June** – The first aeronautical exposition. Designs and models are displayed at the Crystal Palace in London. Among them is a model of Stringfellow's steam triplane.

1896   **August 9** – The great German aviation pioneer Otto Lilienthal crashes in one of his gliders and dies.

1903   **October 7** – Samuel Pierpont Langley's Aerodrome fails to get off the 'ground' and ends up in the Potomac River.

December 8 – Langley's Aerodrome crashes for the second time during take-off.

December 17 – The first engine-powered aero-plane flight. The Wright Flyer I, designed and built by Orville and Wilbur Wright, takes off, flies and lands successfully at Kill Devil Hills, near Kitty Hawk, North Carolina.

1904   **September 20** – Wilbur Wright flies the first complete circle in his Flyer II, at the Huffman Prairie. Two weeks earlier, on September 7, the Wright brothers had inaugurated the derrick and weight-assisted take-off system.

1905   **June 6** – The first glider take-off from water: Gabriel Voisin's glider is towed by a motorboat and lifts off from the Seine.

October 5 – The first endurance record: at the Huffman Prairie, Orville Wright keeps the Flyer III in the air for 38 minutes 3 seconds.

1906   **September 13** – The first engine-powered flight is made in Europe, at Bagatelle, France. Brazilian aviation pioneer Alberto Santos-Dumont gets his Santos-Dumont 14-*bis* off the ground for a short hop.

October 23 – At Bagatelle, Santos-Dumont flies his plane almost 200 feet (60 m) It is the first flight in Europe of more than 25 metres (about 80 feet).

November 12 – Alberto Santos-Dumont's 14-*bis* flies 722 feet or 220 m (its best performance) in 21.2 seconds. It is the first flight in Europe of more than 100 metres (about 328 feet).

1907   **November 10** – The first European flight to last more than a minute: Henri Farman in a Voisin biplane at Issy.

1908 The British Army buys its first plane, a Cody Biplane.

January 13 – The first complete circle of more than one kilometre (about 5/8 mile) is flown in Europe by Henri Farman, in a modified Voisin, at Issy.

May 14 – First flight with a passenger as well as the pilot: Wilbur Wright and C. Furnas at Kill Devil Hills.

May 30 – The first passenger flight in Europe: Henri Farman carries Ernest Archdeacon.

June 28 – The first engine-powered flight in Germany. Ellehammer makes an 11-second hop in his Ellehammer IV.

July 4 – The first American flight of more than one kilometre. The plane is the June Bug. The builder and pilot, Glenn Curtiss, wins the Scientific American prize.

September 17 – The first victim of engine-powered flight. Lieutenant Selfridge, of the United States Army, is killed in an accident on board a Wright Model A, piloted by Orville Wright, at Fort Myer.

October 30 – The first 'cross-country' flight in Europe. Henri Farman flies 17 miles (27 km) from Bouy to Reims.

1909 The United States Army buys its first plane, a Wright Model A.

January 13 – First flight of a plane designed and built in Italy: Aristide Faccioli's triplane, at Turin. The plane crashes.

February 23 – First flight in the Commonwealth outside Great Britain. It is made by McCurdy in the Silver Dart, in Canada.

March 6 – The first lightplane flight: Alberto Santos-Dumont's *Demoiselle* 20.

July 23 – The first flight in Britain of a British-built aeroplane powered by a British engine: Alliott Verdon Roe in the Roe Triplane.

July 25 – The first aeroplane crossing of the English Channel: Louis Blériot flies his Blériot XI from Calais to Dover.

1910 The first experimental naval bombardment: Glenn Curtiss in his Golden Flyer.
The first ground-to-air radio link: Glenn Curtiss in the Golden Flyer.

March 11 – The world's first flying wing plane takes to the air: the Dunne D.5, designed and piloted in Great Britain by John William Dunne.

March 28 – The first flight of an engine-powered seaplane. Henri Fabre flies his *Hydravion* at La Mède, France.

October – The world's first jet plane is presented at the *Salon de l'Aéronautique* in Paris: Henri Coanda's Coanda.

November 14 – The first carrier take-off. At Hampton Roads, Virginia, Eugene Ely takes off in his Curtiss Golden Flyer from the deck of the cruiser *Birmingham*.

1911 **January 18** – The first deck-landing on a ship. Eugene Ely lands the Curtiss Golden Flyer on the deck of the cruiser *Pennsylvania*, anchored in San Francisco Bay.

July: The United States Navy buys its first plane, a Curtiss Golden Flyer derivative.

September 17 – Rodgers takes off on his transcontinental flight in a Wright Baby, from Long Island, N.Y., to Long Beach, California (about 3,000 miles or 4,830 km).

October 22 – The first wartime flight. Italian Captain Piazza, in a Blériot XI, makes a reconnaissance flight over enemy lines near Benghazi.

1912

February – The first plane flies more than 100 mph (161 kph). It is a Deperdussin monoplane, piloted by Vedrines.

May 1 – The first plane with an enclosed cockpit, Alliott Verdon Roe's Avro F, takes to the air in Britain.

1913

April – The first Schneider Trophy race for seaplanes. It is won by Prévost in a Deperdussin.

May 13 – The world's first four-engined plane, designed and built in Russia by Igor Sikorsky, takes to the air.

1914

The world's first regular air mail flight is flown by a Benoist XIV seaplane in Tampa, Florida.

August 13 – The first British plane to land in France after the outbreak of war is an R.A.F. B.E.2a of No. 2 Squadron.

October 5 – The first enemy plane is shot down by an Allied aircraft. A French Voisin 3 shoots down an Aviatik near Reims. The Voisin 3 is also the world's first plane to be armed with a cannon (a 37- or 47-mm Hotchkiss).

December 21 – The first night bombing raid of the war: a Maurice Farman M.F.11 of the R.N.A.S. over Ostend.

1915

The first fixed machine-gun to fire from a plane in flight, on a Morane-Saulnier L.

April 26 – The first Victoria Cross for bravery in the air, is awarded to Lieutenant W. B. Rhodes-Moorhouse of No. 2 Squadron.

The first plane with a fixed and synchronized forward machine-gun: the German Fokker E1.

The first all-metal plane to fly: the German Junkers J 1.

August 2 – The first ship is sunk by a plane-launched torpedo: Commander C. H. K. Edmonds in a Short 184 in the Dardanelles.

1916

The first all-Russian reconnaissance plane is built, the Lebed' 12.

May 17 – For the first time a plane is launched from another plane in flight: a Bristol Scout D takes off from a Porte Baby seaplane in flight.

November – The first plane designed for heavy night bombing goes into action, the Handley Page O/100.

1917

May – The first strategic bombing of a single objective: German Gotha G V bombers over London.

The first all-Austrian fighter plane is built, the Aviatik D I.

1918

The first strategic bomber is built in Great Britain: the Handley Page V/1500, the largest British plane to take part in the First World War.

Index

317

Bibliography

Books

C. Dollfus — H. Bouche, *Histoire de l'aéronautique*, Paris, L'illustration, 1932.

Luigi Mancini, *Grande enciclopedia aeronautica*, Milan, Edizioni Aeronautica, 1936.

Raymond Saladin, *Les temps héroïques de l'aviation*, Paris, Editions Arcadiennes, 1949.

I primi voli di guerra nel mondo, Rome, Ufficio Storico dell'Aeronautica Militare, 1951.

Lloyd Morris – Kendall Smith, *Ceiling Unlimited: The Story of American Aviation from Kitty Hawk to Supersonics,* New York, Macmillan & Co., 1953.

J. Hébrard, *L'aviation des origines à nos jours,* Paris, Robert Laffont, 1954.

Bruce Robertson, *Aircraft Camouflage and Markings 1907–1954,* Letchworth, Herts, Harleyford Publications Ltd., 1956.

Henrique Dumont Villaves, *Foto história de Santos Dumont 1898–1910,* Sâo Paulo, Comp. Melhoramentos de Sâo Paulo, 1956.

Charles H. Gibbs-Smith, *The Aeroplane: An Historical Survey,* London, Science Museum, Her Majesty's Stationery Office, 1960.

W. M. Lamberton, *Fighter Aircraft of the 1914–1918 War,* Letchworth, Herts, Harleyford Publications Ltd., 1960.

Fokker – The Man and the Aircraft, Letchworth, Herts, Harleyford Publications Ltd., 1961.

United States Army and Air Force Fighters 1916–1961, Letchworth, Herts, Harleyford Publications Ltd., 1961.

W. M. Lamberton, *Reconnaissance & Bomber Aircraft of the 1914–1918 War,* Letchworth, Herts, Harleyford Publications Ltd., 1962.

G. Bignozzi – B. Catalanotto, *Storia degli aerei d'Italia,* Rome, Editrice Cielo, 1962.

Charles H. Gibbs-Smith, *Aviation, an historical survey from its origins to the end of World War II,* London, Science Museum, Her Majesty's Stationery Office, 1970.

Peter Gray – Owen Thetford, *German Aircraft of the First World War,* London, Putnam & Co. Ltd., 1962.

A. J. Jackson, *De Havilland Aircraft,* London, Putnam & Co. Ltd., 1962.

Peter Lewis, *British Aircraft 1909–14,* London, Putnam & Co. Ltd., 1962.

Paul R. Matt, *U.S. Navy & Marine Corps Fighters 1918–62,* Letchworth, Herts, Harleyford Publications Ltd., 1962.

Owen Thetford, *Aircraft of the Royal Air Force since 1918,* London, Putnam & Co. Ltd., 3rd edition, 1962.

Owen Thetford, *British Naval Aircraft since 1912,* London, Putnam & Co. Ltd., 1962.

The American Heritage History of Flight, New York, American Heritage Publ. Co. Inc., 1962.

Charles H. Gibbs-Smith, *The Wright Brothers,* London, Science Museum, Her Majesty's Stationery Office, 1963.

Gordon Swanborough – Peter M. Bowers, *United States Military Aircraft since 1909,* London, Putnam & Co. Ltd., 1963.

Douglas H. Robinson, *LZ 129 Hindenburg,* Dallas Morgan Aviation Books, 1964.

J. M. Bruce, *War Planes of the First World War: Fighters,* Vols. I–III, London, Macdonald & Janes Ltd., 1965–69.

Charles H. Gibbs-Smith, *The World's First Aeroplane Flights,* London, Science Museum, Her Majesty's Stationery Office, 1965.

William Green – Gerald Pollinger, *The Aircraft of the World,* London, Macdonald & Janes Ltd., 3rd edition, 1965.

A. J. Jackson, *Avro Aircraft since 1908,* London, Putnam & Co. Ltd., 1965.

Peter M. Bowers, *Boeing Aircraft since 1916,* London, Putnam & Co. Ltd., 1966.

G. R. Duval, *British Flying-Boats and Amphibians 1909–1952,* London, Putnam & Co. Ltd., 1966.

Charles H. Gibbs-Smith, *The Invention of the Aeroplane 1799–1909,* London, Faber & Faber Ltd., 1966.

Philip J. R. Moyes, *Bomber Squadrons of the R.A.F.,* London, Macdonald & Janes Ltd., 1966.

Kenneth Munson, *Bombers, Patrol and Transport Aircraft,* London, Blandford Press Ltd., 1966.

Kenneth Munson, *Fighters, Attack and Training Aircraft,* London, Blandford Press Ltd., 1966.

John Stroud, *European Transport Aircraft since 1910,* London, Putnam & Co. Ltd., 1966.

C. H. Barnes, *Shorts Aircraft since 1900,* London, Putnam & Co. Ltd., 1967.

Alberto Borgiotti, *I Caccia della prima guerra mondiale,* Parma, Ermanno Albertelli editore, 1970.

John Killen, *The Luftwaffe, A History,* London, Frederick Muller Ltd., 1967.

Kenneth Munson, *Civil Aircraft of Yesteryear,* London, Ian Allan Ltd., 1967.

Edmond Petit, *Histoire mondiale de l'aviation,* Paris, Libraire Hachette, 1967.

Harald Penrose, *British Aviation: The*

Pioneer Years, London, Putnam & Co. Ltd., 1967.

Bruce Robertson, *Aircraft Markings of the World 1912–1967,* Letchworth, Herts, Harleyford Publications Ltd., 1967.

Heimer Emde – Carlo Demand, *Conquerors of the Air,* Lausanne, Edita S.A., 1968.

A. J. Jackson, *Blackburn Aircraft since 1909,* London, Putnam & Co. Ltd., 1968.

Kenneth Munson, *Aircraft of World War I,* London, Ian Allan Ltd., 1968.

Kenneth Munson, *Bombers, Patrol and Reconnaissance Aircraft, 1914–1919,* London, Blandford Press Ltd., 1968.

Kenneth Munson, *Fighters, Attack and Training Aircraft, 1914–1919,* London Blandford Press Ltd., 1968.

Gordon Swanborough – Peter M. Bowers, *United States Navy Aircraft since 1911,* London, Putnam & Co. Ltd., 1963.

Aircam "Specials" Series, Vols. I–VII, Canterbury, Osprey Publications Ltd. 1969–71.

Aircam Aviation Series, Vols. I–XVIII, Canterbury, Osprey Publications Ltd., 1967–71.

Jane's 1909–1969: 100 Significant Aircraft, London. Macdonald & Janes Ltd., 1969.

C. F. Andrews, *Vickers Aircraft since 1908,* London, Putnam & Co. Ltd., 1969.

Kenneth Munson, *Pioneer Aircraft 1903–1914,* London, Blandford Press Ltd., 1969.

Rodolfo Gentile, *Storia dell'Aeronautica,* Rome, Editrice Ali, 1958.

The Lore of Flight, Gothenburg, Tre Tryckare Cagner & Co., 1970.

Derek N. James, *Gloster Aircraft since 1917,* London, Putnam & Co. Ltd., 1971.

Periodicals

Air Classic, Canoga Park, Challenge Publications, Inc.

Aircraft Illustrated, Shepperton, Ian Allan Ltd.

Air Pictorial, London, Air League.

Air Progress, New York, Condé Nast Publication, Inc.

Aviation Magazine International, Paris, Union de Presse Européenne.

Aviation Week & Space Technology, New York, McGraw-Hill.

Aviazione di Linea Aeronautica e Spazio, Rome.

Flight International, London, IPC Business Press Ltd.

Flug Revue – Flugwelt, Stuttgart, Vereinigte Motor-Verlage GmbH.

Flying Review International, London, Haymarket Press Ltd.

Icare Revue de l'Aviation Française, Orly.

Interconair Aviazione Marina, Genova, Interconair S.A.

I primi cinquant'anni dell'aviazione italia. Rome, Rivista Aeronautica.

l'Album du Fanatique de l'Aviation, Paris, Editions Larivière.

Profile, Windsor, Profile Publications Ltd.

The Aeroplane, London.

Annuals

Jane's All the World's Aircraft, London, Macdonald & Janes.